THE
BALLAD
MATRIX

———————————

THE

PERSONALITY, MILIEU,

BALLAD

AND THE

MATRIX

ORAL TRADITION

William Bernard McCarthy

INDIANA UNIVERSITY PRESS
BLOOMINGTON & INDIANAPOLIS

The paper used in this publication meets the minimum requirements of American National
Standard for Information Sciences—Permanence of Paper for Printed Library Materials,
ANSI Z39.48-1984.

TM

Manufactured in the United States of America

Library of Congress Cataloging-in-Publication Data
McCarthy, William Bernard.
The ballad matrix : personality, milieu, and the oral tradition /
William Bernard McCarthy.
p.   cm.
Includes bibliographical references.
ISBN 0-253-33718-6 (alk. paper)
1. Ballads, English—Scotland—History and criticism.
2. Lyle, Agnes.   I. Title.
ML3655.M35   1990

782.4'3—dc20

89-46012
CIP
MN

1 2 3 4 5   94 93 92 91 90

For Eileen, Edward, and Edson
Three in three distant ages

To clarify the problem of the aesthetic relation of folklore to reality, one must know the laws of folk practice. The science of folklore should discover and describe these laws.

—Vladimir Propp

CONTENTS

Preface

Agnes Lyle's heroes and heroines have been a source of strength and courage. I am grateful to them, to her, and to her Adam Scrivener (as he called himself), William Motherwell. The staff of the Paisley Public Library, the School of Scottish Studies, the University of Glasgow Library, the Indiana University Library, and the Houghton Library of Harvard University were generous with time, books, documents, and permissions. Hamish Henderson and Sheilah Douglas introduced me to contemporary Scots ballad singers. The National Endowment for the Humanities and John Miles Foley provided a summer of reading, talking, and fellowship. And many others along the way provided a needed bit of information or a needed bit of encouragement. To all, thanks.

Some readers will be unfamiliar with oral-formulaic theory. Although fuller explanations are contained in the introduction, a word on that subject is in order here.

What is now called oral-formulaic theory was first formulated by the classicist Milman Parry and subsequently developed and refined by his student Albert Lord. Seeking to understand how an epic poet can keep a long poem or series of poems in his head, Parry was elated to discover that the art of epic poetry was still being practiced in Yugoslavia in the years before World War II. The element which gives the theory its name is the idea that oral epic poets, whether in ancient Greece or in modern Yugoslavia, use not words but metrical phrases (the oral formulas) to compose the lines of their songs. Since meter is built into these phrases and phrase patterns in a way analogous to the way grammar is built into the ordinary vocabulary of conversation and storytelling, the poet has a special metrical vocabulary of epic song. Hence it is no more strange for the epic poet to speak in meter—whether the Homeric hexameter or the South Slavic decasyllable—than it is for the storyteller to speak in sentences. Just as moulding words (or morphemes) into sentences involves a higher order of linguistic organization than moulding sounds (or phonemes) into words, so moulding metrical phrases into hexameters involves a still higher level of linguistic organization but not an unnatural level. Lord's most significant addition to the theory was the suggestion that conceptual narrative elements called "themes" form plots in a way analogous to the way the linguistic metrical elements called formulas form lines. These "themes," which are the building blocks of plot, include such typical actions and scenes as summoning an assembly, quarreling, arming the hero, fighting hand-to-hand, lamenting, and burying the dead. Because the poet has this stock of formulas and "themes," this epic vocabulary on both the metrical and narrative levels, he does not need to memorize a poem blindly. Once he knows how a poem is put together he can recreate it himself, at greater or lesser length, by drawing on his own metrical and narrative resources, much as a storyteller does not memorize a story but recreates it afresh each time he tells it.

I see the oral-formulaic theory as an important contribution to charting the mechanism of oral composition and performance. Having now completed this survey, I not only accept the essential Parry-Lord insight, I affirm that what epic singers do, ballad singers also do, *mutatis mutandis. Mutanda, autem, valde mutata.* This survey of the ballad, an oral genre so different from epic, offers the opportunity to articulate connections between the Parry-Lord insight and the insights of a number of other oral scholars both before and (especially) since. Of course, of articulating these relationships this work is barely a beginning. I have passed over important and pertinent contributors to the study of orality and poetry (Dennis Tedlock is only one obvious example). But, since we're already speaking Latin, *non possumus omnes omnia.* On the other hand, however, as a distinguished Latinist of an earlier century put it: "Tomorrow to fresh woods and pastures new."

DuBois, Pennsylvania
October 10, 1989

Introduction

Oral Theory and the Ballad

Many scholars remember the excitement of their first encounter with Albert B. Lord's *The Singer of Tales* (1960). Albert B. Friedman (1983) recaptured those heady days, albeit somewhat sarcastically, when he wrote:

> Perhaps no book in the last fifty years has so fluttered the dovecotes of philology. . . . Shortly after putting the book down, Marshall McLuhan lit the fuses to his pyrotechnic displays on media and culture, while less sensational scholars began busily tabulating the density of formulas in every likely text from Hittite epics to chivalric romances by way of establishing their aboriginal orality. (215)

Unlike Friedman, a naysayer from the first,[1] many of us found the insights of Lord and his mentor Parry so enlightening and compelling that we began to look at our own fields of particular interest because it was obvious to us that what these two had discovered about epic was in some way true about a far wider range of oral traditions.[2] At the time I was an undergraduate, callow and sophomoric. My first romantic reaction was to steep myself still deeper in ballads—by reading them, of course—so that I too could become an oral-formulaic balladeer, able to recreate the classic songs and even create new ballads of my own. Others had equally immature first reactions. James H. Jones (1961), for instance, rushed into print with a hasty statement of the ill-digested obvious. And made it even more obvious that how singers of tales recreate, even in a seemingly simple genre like the ballad, is considerably more complex than we had realized after our first imperfect reading of Lord's wise book.

By 1961, when Jones published his statement and Friedman a counter-statement, the ballad wars of the early twentieth century had almost petered out (Wilgus 1959, 3-122). In *The Critics and the Ballad*, for instance, published in that very year, Leach and Coffin could describe the theories of Gummere, a chief contender in the ballad wars, as "generally discredited today," though admitting that "there are still scholars who believe one of his main tenets, that folk groups can compose narrative material spontaneously" (vii–viii). Unfortunately the oral-formulaic approach to ballad studies has revived the ballad wars, with realigned forces, on a fresh battleground. The present study is an irenic investigation, under a white flag, of that battleground. It asks: "What is the relevance of the oral-formulaic approach to an understanding of the English and Scottish popular ballad?" But it can not possibly survey this battleground without at least considering adjacent fields where ballad battles have been fought, and in some cases won, fields such as structural analysis, text-tune relationships, repertoire studies, contextualism, oral poetics, indeed, the entire lay of the land in contemporary ballad studies. Obviously, the purpose of such an investigation is to bring overlooked data to the surface and to bring all data into a fresh perspective. The reference point for this survey will be a large and hitherto neglected repertoire of oral ballads collected from Agnes Lyle of Kilbarchan in 1825. Exploring and analyzing this repertoire can reveal much about the singing of ballads.

1. CONTEMPORARY BALLAD CRITICISM

Any consideration of ballad criticism must start with Francis James Child's *The English and Scottish Popular Ballads*, published in five two-part volumes between 1882 and 1898. Child considered balladry a "closed account"; that is, he considered that the art was for all practical purposes defunct, and significant collecting was no longer possible. He therefore felt in a position to gather "every valuable copy of every known ballad," organize and edit those copies, and publish a definitive edition on the model of Svend Grundtvig's edition of the Danish ballads, then underway. Child did not live to write the introduction which would have explained his criteria of selection. And his work has been roundly criticized since, notably in the well-known essay by Thelma James (1933). Nonetheless, Child was a careful editor, sinning on the side of generosity rather than strictness, and he found practically everything then available. In *The English and Scottish Popular Ballads* he produced a convenient and trustworthy compendium of the ballads collected before about 1880. While he may have admitted some dubious items, he overlooked very little of value.[5]

One of the first results of the publication of this definitive statement of a closed account was a reopening of the account. Ballad collecting flourished. Early on, Campbell and Sharp discovered the Appalachian tradition, and Greig had already rediscovered the Northeast Scottish tradition. The work of these collectors and later ones such as MacColl (1965) and Kennedy (1975) in Britain, and the State and Province collectors in America, such as MacKenzie (1928), Barry et al. (1929), Davis (1929; 1960), Randolph (1946-1950), Brown (1952-1964), and Peacock (1965), climaxed in Hamish Henderson's rediscovery in the 1950s of the Traveller tradition in Scotland (see Henderson and Collinson 1965). Coffin's great bibliography-index provides the entree to the North American collections, but no similar work exists for English and Scottish collections. So vast is the number of ballad versions that have been collected in the last hundred years that a complete Child supplement, giving every version of every known ballad collected in this period, would be an unmanageable task. In the case of the more popular ballads, such as "Barbara Allen" (Child 84), "The Gypsy Laddie" (Child 200), or "Our Goodman" (Child 274), the number of available versions would run into the hundreds and the many hundreds, enough to fill a volume for each ballad. Even the number of tunes that have been collected would seem daunting. But the dauntless Bertrand Harris Bronson, between 1959 and 1972, managed to bring out a four-volume compendium of all known tunes of Child ballads, most accompanied by text. Bronson's collection, supplemented by selected other collections strong in texts though weak in tunes, such as the first Davis Virginia collection, provides a good cross section of balladry since Child. For access to narrative folksongs not in Child the two Laws bibliography-indexes are indispensable. Child, Bronson, Coffin, and Laws have hitherto consti-tuted the most basic reference works for ballad studies. To these a fifth name will probably have to be added, that of Edson Richmond, whose annotated index of all things balladic is appearing at approximately the same time as the present work. This index provides complete access to texts, articles, and books, however obscure, that relate in any direct way to the Anglo-Scottish ballad tradition and its offshoots.

Ballad collecting has continued in recent years, but serious scholars have usually subordinated collecting to some other concern. Roger Abrahams (1970b), for example, studies the interaction of personality and repertoire, in his work with Almeida Riddle, the great Ozark singer. Roger deV. Renwick (1980) shows how the mores of the larger social context have found expres-sion in the signifying structures of Yorkshire folk song and verse. James Por-ter (1976) seeks to uncover all that a singer brings to the song and derives from the song, in his study of Jeannie Robertson and "Son Davie." Leonard Roberts (1974) documents an entire family's traditions in various classic genres, in his study of the Couch family. And Wilgus and Long (e.g., 1985) expand our conception of balladry in their work on blues ballads. Contem-porary collectors, since their concerns are not narrowly "balladic," fre-quently gather other kinds of songs, and indeed other kinds of traditions as well. They seek, through recordings and films (or videos) as well as through books and articles, to document as fully as possible the whole environment of traditional song.

In general, folklorists today tend to disparage "Child and other" publica-tions, which segregate the Child ballads in a kind of first class compartment at the front of the book. In reaction to ballad romanticists they tend to stress that all data is informative, and decline to make—or deliberately reject—aesthetic value judgments. But value judgments will not go away. As Roger Abrahams (1970a) puts it:

> The problem, then, is not whether non-sophisticated peoples have arts, but whether the perspectives we have developed to understand sophisticated art make any sense in bringing about insights into folk art. The very conception of artistry in our sophisticated system carries with it an expectation of creativity. And being creative, by our usual definition, means to invest with a sense of newness in form or substance—to have the qualities of the new as opposed to the imitative. Can we discuss as creative, therefore, a performance tradition, even a highly stylized one, in which imitation and fidelity to the past are the

norm? The answer is that whether we can or not, we *want* to. (5; italics in original)

For many of us the aesthetic value of ballads was what first attracted us to folklore. We want—and I think rightly want—to approach questions of aesthetic value. But we are coming to realize that we must handle aesthetic questions with tools fashioned for the expressive modes characteristic of orality, rather than cobble out criticism of folksong with aesthetic criteria fashioned for literary modes of expression. We have found that, like amateur craftsmen, when we use the wrong instruments we dull those instruments, deface our materials, and sometimes injure ourselves.

2. THE ORAL-FORMULAIC APPROACH TO BALLADRY

Though published in 1960 and largely written even earlier, in the late 1940s, Albert Lord's *The Singer of Tales* remains the one essential statement of the oral-formulaic approach to oral traditions and the texts engendered by them. The book has aged well and dated little. Careful rereading often reveals that what at first seemed exaggerated or hasty claims are in fact carefully qualified and moderated generalizations.

Though Lord's explicit topic is the South Slavic oral epic, and his principal applications are to Homeric and medieval epic, many of his comments seem to bear on balladry as well. Lord's book, for example, is usually seen as an explanation of how an oral-formulaic system can generate verbally unique extended texts of traditional poems, that is, texts which duplicate the diction and wording neither of previous performances by the singer in question nor of any other singer or writer. But Lord is also at pains to explain that this same oral-formulaic system can generate texts of moderate length which are remarkably stable, both in repeated performances of an individual singer and in the wider tradition of a community or region over a substantial period of time, texts analogous in many ways to ballad texts. Both the longer variable and the shorter stable South Slavic texts are products of the same oral-formulaic system (125).

It is clear that the ballad tradition is a moderately stable tradition. Since objections to applying oral-formulaic theory often hinge on this point, it might be well to look more closely at what Lord says about stability in *The Singer of Tales*, to see if his ideas on this subject are in any way applicable to the ballad. Since he finds stability on all levels of oral-formulaic expression, from formula through complete song, it seems appropriate to begin at the simplest level.

Lord restricts the word *formula* to expressions of a half-line or a line, though he admits that for singers who sing in couplets instead of lines the term should be extended to cover formulaic couplets as well (57). Some formulas are remembered from previous singings or from other singers, while

some are created anew "by analogy with other phrases," at the time of singing (43). Though he seems to conceive formulas on a substitutionary model
(35–36), there is nothing in his presentation which would rule out the deep-
structure generative models which have been developed since by Nagler,
Kiparsky, and Andersen, among others.[4] I will be assuming that formula formation is sometimes generative, sometimes substitutionary.[5] Formulaic stability comes about because a formula is particularly useful, or particularly
pleasing. In South Slavic epic the most useful and most stable formulas are
names, usually modified by an epithet, title, or patronymic; verbs for common actions, which may fill out a formula alone, or may require set modifi-
ers; and terms for time and place (34–35). But other lines and half lines may
stabilize if they exhibit particularly pleasing sound patterns, especially assonance, alliteration, and internal rhyme (55–56). And, "just as formulaic lines
with internal rhyme or with a striking chiastic arrangement have a long life,
so couplets with clearly marked patterns persist with little if any change"
(57). If stable couplets emerge in the stichic South Slavic tradition, it does not
seem surprising that stable quatrains should emerge in the strophic Anglo-
Scottish tradition.[6]

Lord goes on to speak of longer passages or runs, which tend to stabilize,
sometimes word for word, because the singer uses them often. These runs
can approach the length of a ballad. But a short example will have to suffice,
the following description of a horse, his trappings, and his rider, which Lord
found the same, word for word, in two distinct epics from the singer
Ugljanin:

> Na kulaša sedla ni samara,
> Sem na kula drvenica gola.
> S jedne strane topuz od čeljika;
> On ga tiče, on mu se spotiče.
> A na Tala od jarca ćakšire,
> Dlake spolja; sva koljena gola.

> On the mouse-grey horse was neither saddle nor pack-carrier,
> But only a bare wooden frame on the mouse-gray.
> From one side (hung) a steel mace;
> It struck the horse and caused him to stumble.
> Tale was wearing goatskin trousers,
> The hairy side out; his whole knee was bare. (1960, 60)

Significantly, Lord does not see such passages as an argument against the
oral-formulaic nature of a text. Indeed, he calls the presence of such passages "one of the characteristic signs of oral style."

The next larger unit in Lord's analysis of South Slavic epic is the
"theme."[7] A "theme" is like a ballad in significant ways. First, it is often of
approximately the length of a typical ballad. Second, a "theme" often exhibits remarkable structural stability of the sort that Buchan ascribes to the ballads of Mrs. Brown. Although significant verbal stability is not part of Lord's

definition of "theme" in *The Singer of Tales*, the stable set of elements of which a "theme" is composed often includes verbally stable runs such as have just been discussed. Moreover, the first example that Lord alleges from the *Iliad*, the arming of the hero, while expanded or contracted as the arming is more or less important, exhibits word-for-word stability in the shared lines which structure the "theme." Indeed, for Lord, though not for all later oral theorists, some such verbal correspondence eventually comes to be considered a defining characteristic of the "theme" (e.g., 1974, 20; cf. Foley 1988, 49, 53, 68–69, 72–74). Third, although a "theme," according to Lord, "does not have a single 'pure' form either for the individual singer or for the tradition as a whole," the singer's "latest rendering of it will naturally be freshest in his mind" (94). Finally, "themes," like ballads, have "a semi-independent life of their own." Wilgus and Long's analysis (1986) of ballads into thematic and narrative units that also have "a semi-independent life of their own" and may on occasion circulate independently as ballads in their own right, strengthens the analogy here drawn between "theme" and ballad.

On the next level, that of the whole epic, stability does occur among oral-formulaic poets, not only in structure but also in wording, provided the epic is short enough. But such stability does not guarantee word-for-word correspondence all the way through, nor does it mean that a singer can't, on occasion, vary a run, "theme," or epic which he habitually sings in a stable form (125).[8]

Beyond utility and acoustic attractiveness, the chief additional factor promoting stability on the level of run, "theme," and epic, is habit:

> If one takes two texts of the same song, as we have above, and underlines the verses that are common to both, one discovers a characteristic picture. There will be a series of lines unmarked [indicating no verbal or formulaic repetition] followed by a series of underlined verses with occasional small breaks perhaps, followed in turn by another "clear" spot. If a singer sings a song many times the underlinings, as in Zogić's case, will be many, but this will not be the case with a song infrequently sung. One obtains thus a photograph of the individual singer's reliance on habitual associations of lines and of the degree to which habit has tended to stabilize, without fixing or petrifying, passages of varying length. (60)

As the above comments would indicate, singers vary in degree of reliance on stability as opposed to spontaneous creativity. The South Slavic practice of the oral-formulaic system, in this respect as in all respects, is not monolithic. As Lord puts it: "All singers use traditional material in a traditional way, but no two singers use exactly the same material in the same way. The tradition is not all of one mold. We can differentiate individual styles" (63).

This variation in stability and style, however, does not imply variation in degree of "formulicity," to use Lord's term (44). What he says in this regard about epics also seems to apply to ballads. Formulas are not mere decorations or optional devices; they are "all pervasive" and essential: "There is nothing in the poem that is not formulaic" (47).

If, then, one were to plot out the characteristics of formulas, couplets, runs, "themes," and short epics in a stichic oral-formulaic tradition, and extrapolate from that to a hypothetical oral tradition specializing in rather shorter strophic songs (ranging from the length of the longer runs to the length of the very shortest epics), one would arrive at something suspiciously like the ballad. Songs would be as different in structure, wording, formulaic usage, and "feel" as Mrs. Brown's and Agnes Lyle's respective versions of "Johnie Scot" (Child 99), on the one hand, and as similar in structure, wording, formulaic usage, and "feel" as Agnes Lyle's and the Campbell Manuscript's respective version of "Johnie Scot," on the other. Formulas and formulaic clusters would have what Lord (65–66), speaking of epic formulas, calls overtones, and what Andersen (1985, 34), speaking of commonplace stanzas, calls supra-narrative functions. The "apprentice" singer would acquire, simply by listening, the sense of meter, of special poetic syntax, of "linking of phrases by parallelism, balancing and opposition of word order" and the "instinctive grasp of alliterations and assonances . . . [such that] one word begins to suggest another by its very sound; one phrase suggests another not only by reason of idea or by a special ordering of ideas, but also by acoustic value" (Lord 1960, 32–33). By listening, too, the singer would acquire a stock of fixed lines and strophes, and an even more crucial stock of patterns within which to create new lines and even strophes (42–45).

In applying insights of the oral-formulaic school to balladry, one must be careful of terminology. Implicit in Lord's description of the oral-formulaic technique is a distinction between stable and fixed texts and a corresponding distinction between remembering and memorizing.[9] The singer of tales:

> does not "memorize" formulas, any more than we as children "memorize" language. He learns them by hearing them in other singers' songs, and then by habitual usage, makes them part of his singing as well. Memorization is a conscious act of making one's own, and repeating, something that one regards as fixed and not one's own. The learning of an oral poetic language follows the same principles as the learning of language itself, not by the conscious schematization of elementary grammars but by the natural oral method. (36)

Much of the confusion in the oral-formulaic ballad war centers on failure to recognize this fundamental double distinction between stable and fixed, remembered and memorized. Memory obviously plays an important role in oral creation, and sometimes leads to stable songs. But remembering and recreating are not the same process as memorizing a fixed text.

A common term for recreation or oral composition is *improvisation*. But such usage is certainly open to misinterpretation. Lord cautions that oral-formulaic composition is improvisation only in a particular restricted sense:

> If we equate it [i.e., oral composition] with improvisation in a broad sense, we are again in error. Improvisation is not a bad term for the process, but it too must be modified by the restrictions of the particular style. The exact way in which

oral composition differs from free improvisation will, I hope, emerge from the following chapters. (5)

In a later publication, he shies away even from that usage, calling "true improvisation, as distinct from composition by formula and theme, . . . indeed, *sui generis*, and of considerable interest in its own right" (Lord 1986b, 470). An understanding of oral "improvisation" as more or less free improvisation, rather than as improvisation within the limits of the formulaic linguistic system—and within the limits of the individual tradition of community and particular ballad—is one of the bases for misunderstanding between proponents and opponents of the application of oral-formulaic terminology to balladry. Misunderstanding of terms, whether *improvisation* or *memory* or *textual stability*, has occurred in all camps. But Eleanor Long is not far from the kingdom of heaven when she writes that "the process of ballad-making is one that falls between the two extremes of rigid memorization of fixed texts and totally free improvisation" (1986, 208). In any case, improvisation is not the essence of the oral-formulaic theory. Oral composition and the consequent aesthetic are.

After the Jones-Friedman duel of 1961, no major champion appeared, pen in hand, to defend Parry and Lord until David Buchan entered the ballad battlefield in 1972. Reading between the lines of publications of that era, however, one gets the impression that skirmishes were being fought, appropriately enough, in the oral arena. Eleanor Long, for instance, in an article published in 1973 but written in 1971, says that "it should be clearly understood that [certain methods of singing ballads] may quite accurately be called 'oral-formulaic' " (236). Her comment is clearly polemical, but to whom the polemic is directed cannot be clearly understood from the literature on the ballad that precedes this comment. Doubtless she is directing it to disputants in the oral arena. (Thus, paradoxically, though her comment is a written one, the context of the comment is purely oral.)

David Buchan's *The Ballad and the Folk* synthesizes much that is best in the two not always contiguous academic fields of folklore and oral tradition. The book is oral-formulaic in its understanding of the ballad of the classic period, and has excellent things to say about the sound patterns of formulas, their "connotative reverberations" (171), freedom in using formulas, and multiformity.

But two other aspects of the book are at least as significant. The title is a clear indication of one of these aspects. Buchan examines ballads in relation to the folk who produce them, both the community, in all its political and social complexity, and the individual singers, in all their individuality of inspiration, talent, and life experience. He confines his investigation to the ballads of the Northeast of Scotland, a region comprising Aberdeenshire, Banffshire, and Northern Kincardinshire. His thesis is that Northeastern balladry, originally an oral genre in the meaning of the term *oral* formulated in *The Singer of Tales*, underwent a profound change in the period from the mid-eighteenth to the mid-nineteenth century, a change conditioned by and reflective of the agricultural, industrial, and social revolutions of 1750–1830, as well as the transition from non-literacy to literacy. Dividing balladry into three periods, he presents Mrs. Brown of Falkland as representative of the pre-literate oral period, James Nicol of Strichen as representative of the transitional, loosely recreative period, and Bell Robertson of Aden as representative of the literate memorial period.

The other especially significant contribution of the book is the structuralist methodology, based on Whitman's work with the Homeric Poems (1958), which Buchan perfected. This methodology analyzes the annular, binary, and trinary patterns of organization of an oral composition to confirm that it is indeed oral, to clarify how the oral mind works, and to highlight stylistic individuality of a given singer. In later work Buchan has concentrated on ballad roles (e.g., hero, heroine, villain), analogous to the tale roles in Propp, emphasizing their utility in defining ballad sub-genres and in understanding otherwise unclear ballads. He has also produced a useful essay (1983) on "Hugh Spenser's Feats in France" (Child 158) that stresses the political climate out of which ballads come.

As might have been expected, Buchan's cogently argued presentation of the literate Mrs. Brown of Falkland as a classic oral-formulaic ballad singer did not go unchallenged. Holger Nygard's essay, appearing in 1978, suggests that the differences in different redactions of Mrs. Brown's ballads are not as great as Buchan, as well as Bronson, had previously represented. His most significant piece of evidence is the E text of "The Lass of Roch Royal" (Child 76). As a ballad with two notably different redactions, the Child D and E texts, "The Lass of Roch Royal" served as something of a centerpiece in the argument for oral recreation. But Nygard sees D as nothing more than an imperfectly remembered version of E, and E itself as a remembered, not a recreated text. Otherwise, how explain the extraordinary closeness between E and the text Mrs. Gillespie gave Gavin Greig, more than a hundred years later? The first fourteen stanzas of the E text and the Gillespie text correspond line for line, as do most of the remaining stanzas. Nygard concludes that the Gillespie and Brown versions are essentially the same version, a version that antedates Mrs. Brown. He concludes that "Mrs. Brown, like other tradition-bearers in balladry, recalled an oral text," and she would have trouble recognizing herself in Buchan's portrait of a singer who learns a method of singing instead of fixed texts. Instead, "the variants she has left us would suggest that she was a transmitter of ballad texts with words not of her invention, but of the impersonal language of the tradition that she bore" (84).

The case of Mrs. Gillespie is a bit of a mystery, wherever and however she learned her version. While it is almost certain that she could not have read a copy of Mrs. Brown's text, it is still possible to posit some sort of oral connection between the two texts. But even in memorial traditions such as those that existed in Aberdeen after Mrs. Brown's day, textual closeness of this sort is rare for a classical ballad, though not for a broadside song. Whatever the status of these two texts, Nygard's comments do not touch the issue

of the particularly oral structuring and phraseology of oral texts like those of
Mrs. Brown. But cataloging and accounting for such distinctively oral qualities is the most important item on the agenda of oral-formulaic studies. The
success of that agenda does not rest on the shoulders of a minister's wife
from Aberdeen, however strong those shoulders eventually prove to be.

At approximately the same time Nygard was composing his paper, Flemming G. Andersen and Thomas Pettitt were preparing the essay that opened
the 1979 volume of the *Journal of American Folklore*, an essay that surveys
some of the same ground and reaches some of the same conclusions.[10] Like
Nygard, they concede that Mrs. Brown's ballads, as Andersen put it later,
"reflect a genuine oral, popular tradition" (1985, 301), but they do not concede that the tradition can properly be called "oral-formulaic." Like the present writer they are puzzled by the case of "The Lass of Roch Royal" and
have only the same explanations to offer, though they seem more satisfied
than he with the explanation that either a previous fixed-text oral tradition
lies behind both the Brown and Gillespie renditions or that the Gillespie
rendition is directly and orally dependent on the Brown rendition (or rather,
on a distinct but virtually identical *oral* rendition by Mrs. Brown). Against
this piece of evidence they balance the other two Brown ballads extant in
independent versions, "Child Waters" (Child 63) and "Bonnie Baby Livingston" (Child 222), each put down like "The Lass of Roch Royal," on two
occasions separated by an appreciable time interval and each showing appreciable differences in the two versions. For these two ballads they find the
evidence for oral recreation ambiguous. There are some differences that
might be attributed to "improvisation," and there are many more similarities
that they would like to attribute to memorization. Referring to Mrs. Brown's
"high degree of textual stability," they assert that "this implies, surely, memorial transmission" (1979, 18). On the contrary, for Lord stability over the
short haul (and most ballads manage to tell their story over the short haul) is
equally characteristic of oral-formulaic transmission (see above).

Though rejecting formulaic improvisation as they understand it, Andersen and Pettitt are sensible of the oral characteristics of Mrs. Brown's ballads. They conclude their essay on this note:

> There can be no doubt that ballads, in Scotland and elsewhere, show the formu-
> laic and structural features that Buchan has so carefully analyzed. It is equally
> certain that these features have something to do with the ballad's transmission,
> and extremely likely that they are involved in the transmission by word of
> mouth. But precisely how they function is still an open question. (24)

Shortly before the end of their essay, Andersen and Pettitt promise "an
alternative hypothesis" on "a later occasion" (23). That occasion was the
publication in 1985 of Andersen's book *Commonplace and Creativity*. Here
Andersen asserts that formulas exist in the ballad on the level of commonplace, but on no other level. He singles out some thirty commonplaces, a few
linear, but most stanzaic, as meeting his definition of *formula*, which includes

unity of idea on the deep level, multiformity of expression on the surface or narrative level, and unity again, of affect, on the connotative or "supra-narrative" level. Affects cluster around the motifs of love and death, sometimes polarizing within a single commonplace so that a stanza that in one context evokes associations of love, in another context evokes associations of death.[11] These "supra-narrative" affects are functional, either characterizing the actors of the ballad drama or presaging the outcome. On the narrative level, meanwhile, the commonplaces are functioning to articulate the structural development of the ballad story.

Andersen is a brilliantly perceptive reader of ballads. He seems quite correct in his analysis of the narrative and supra-narrative function of a privileged group of commonplaces in Anglo-Scottish balladry. In his discussion of how the ballad is built around the commonplace he is reminiscent of Lord on the role of "theme," both denotative and connotative, in the epic—though he would probably not appreciate the comparison. But, in accounting for the role of commonplaces, he does not account for all that comes between and around them. He does admit the term *formulaic* for ballad language generally but reserves the term *formula* itself for the commonplaces, because only they have a fixed supra-narrative function, a necessary requirement in his definition. His rejection of the term *oral-formulaic* seems more political than conceptual, since he admits a recreative role for the singer, and describes balladry as an oral art built around the formula, albeit a more restricted kind of formula than Lord posits.

Perhaps the time has come to drop the term *oral-formulaic* as too restrictive to describe a field that, despite infighting, is a single field: the study of oral *poesis* in its oral particularity. Indeed, Foley, in his recent survey of the field (1988), though he occasionally uses the term *oral-formulaic theory*, favors by his usage the simpler term *oral theory*. The qualifier *formulaic*, while accurate enough, accounts for but a single aspect of the material. In fact, a focus on single aspects of single genres within single traditions has been characteristic of the landmark publications in oral poetics in the twentieth century. One thinks of Propp on the Russian folk tales, Lévi-Strauss on South American myth, and Lord on southeast European epic. Their disciples are now starting to talk to each other and learn from each other. Scholars like Buchan are synthesizing elements from various approaches to oral tradition, in his case Proppian tale roles, Whitmanian annular structures, Olrikian binary and trinary structures, and folkloristic performance and context. Such an approach is not eclectic but properly integrative, an exercise in oral theory properly so called.

3. THE PRESENT STUDY

One of the principal difficulties in applying oral theory to balladry has been the limited nature of the collected material. Hitherto, scholars have centered their remarks on the ballads of Mrs. Brown of Falkland because no other comparably large repertoire was known. But partially concealed in the pages of Child and in one of the manuscripts upon which Child drew is a repertoire of 22 full-length ballad texts, and fragments or titles for another 10, giving a total of 32 items in all, as compared to 33 full texts and titles of 5 more for a total of 38 items in Mrs. Brown's extant repertoire. This repertoire constitutes a major hitherto unrecognized set of folkloric and balladic data. Although the extant repertoire surely represents only a small percent of the actual song repertoire of this singer, even that small percent is remarkably extensive for the period.

The singer in question, Agnes Lyle, daughter of a Renfrewshire weaver, comes from the opposite end of Scotland, socially as well as geographically, from that inhabited by Mrs. Brown. Her repertoire has special value because it appears to be very typical for a singer of the period. One would naturally expect, for example, that a singer would know not just ballads but many other kinds of songs as well. Hitherto, however, there has been no readily available evidence that such was the case. Agnes Lyle's repertoire finally provides documentation for what common sense would suggest.[12] Of course, since Motherwell was interested in collecting ballads, the repertoire as collected contains a preponderance of ballads. Most of these seem to be fully oral pieces, but displaying varying degrees of control. Some the singer seems to have known very well, others she seems to have been barely able to complete. But at least two of the full-length pieces are fixed-text songs, not oral ballads. Most of the fragments are broadside texts filtered through tradition. One of the three items in the repertoire known by title only is a weaving song. Agnes Lyle knew most of the kinds of songs then current in the West. Since some of the pieces seem to be oral-formulaic and some seem to be fixed-text, she must have been capable of "switching codes" to fit the kind of song she was singing at the moment. If such a heterogeneous repertoire was typical, and it seems likely that it was, then code-switching devices may need to be built into the model of Scottish oral-formulaic technique. In her case the mechanism may have been metrical. Certainly her technique seems to rely heavily on the standard ballad quatrain, for the set of her ballads with structural difficulties or other kinds of anomalies is exactly congruent with the set of her ballads in other meters than the standard ballad quatrain. Consideration of these anomalous texts can bring into sharper focus the distinctive technique of her regular oral-formulaic texts. Understanding her oral-recreative technique can in turn deepen appreciation for her aesthetic achievement, whether in the ballads in which she has worked within the limitations of her technique or in the ballads in which she has transcended those limitations.

One aim of this study is to make clear the value of an orderly and complete analysis of a single singer's entire repertoire, insofar as it is known. Traditionally ballad scholars, following Child, have concentrated on comparative studies of variant texts of the same ballad. While variant texts can cast much light on a ballad, much can also be learned by comparing a singer's text with other texts in the repertoire. In the present study the repertoire approach has been particularly helpful in bringing out the degree to which the singer influences the form her ballads take on her lips. The great unity exhibited in this diverse repertoire reflects the shaping force of a strong creative talent. The songs present a single set of political and social attitudes, personal prejudices, ethical values, and aesthetic standards, an axiological complex influencing even the character development and plot structure of this singer's versions. The proposed substantiation of this axiological unity in the repertoire relies to some extent on the techniques and even the very analyses perfected by Roger deV. Renwick in *English Folk Poetry* (1980). It further relies on Andersen's analysis of the supra-narrative function of commonplaces in his *Commonplace and Creativity* (1985). But it also utilizes standard literary-critical analysis of leitmotifs. And finally it incorporates historical reconstruction of the context of the singing.

In addition to demonstrating the axiological unity of this repertoire, it is also necessary to demonstrate its orality. The term *orality* refers not so much to derivation from a word-of-mouth performance as to vocal composition out of an oral as opposed to a literate mind-set. Lord sets up three criteria for determining orality: (1) pervasive formulicity or, as he was later to term it, formulaic density; (2) nonperiodic enjambment; and (3) composition by "theme." Andersen, speaking of ballads, takes the second criterion for granted— as, generally speaking, I will too, in this study—substitutes commonplace for "theme" in the third criterion, defines formula as commonplace, and thus effectively combines the first and third criteria. While not going so far, I am convinced by his analysis that for the ballad the third criterion must be re-expressed as composition by commonplace and "theme." To these I would add a fourth, following Buchan: (4) composition according to annular, binary, and trinary principles on the relevant levels of structure. Application of these criteria, if successful, will function simultaneously as exposition of Agnes Lyle's oral-recreative technique.

Because application of the fourth criterion is in some ways the most complex and time-consuming, it may be well to take time here to explain the terms and structures involved. Applying this methodology to a tradition rather different from that of the Scottish Northeast should provide an opportunity to reassess it in terms of validity and practicality, and to confirm its significance as a contribution to ballad studies and to the theory of oral tradition.

For Buchan, an essential characteristic of oral poetry is that the singer "recreates . . . by moulding the story in the shaping dies, verbal and architectonic, of his tradition" (1972, 58). These shaping dies are the annular, binary, and trinary patterns found in the stanzaic, narrative, and character structures of the ballad.

There are, in fact, three major synchronic structurings: the stanzaic structure, which involves the arrangements in scenes of a unified group of stanzas; the character structure, which involves the deployment of the actors; and the narrative structure, which involves the arrangement of the units of action. At times these three structures correspond exactly; at others, particularly in the longer ballads, they co-exist in a kind of structural counterpoint. (88)

The stanzaic structure, then, is the arrangement of stanzas, the character structure is the arrangement of characters in the order in which they appear in the ballad, and the narrative structure is the plotting or arrangement of events. It should be noted that these are all surface structures. Buchan also identifies a fourth, less important surface structure, which he calls tonal because it "regulates the tone and emotional temperature of the ballad" (132). Drawing on Plato's distinction between "imitation" and "simple narration," he defines this fourth kind of structure in terms of the difference between those parts of the ballad in which the story is told through speech and dialogue and those in which it is told through narration. Unlike the first three structures, this fourth does not seem an important element in Agnes Lyle's technique. It figures prominently in only a few ballads, usually in idiosyncratic patterns.

Typically, the stanzaic, character, and narrative structures are permeated by annular, binary, and trinary patternings. Trinary patterning, the "rule of three" in folk narrative, is well known, and obvious examples from balladry come instantly to mind: there are three sisters, for instance, in "Babylon," and in "Mary Hamilton" word is (1) to the kitchen, and word is (2) to the hall, and word is (3) up to Madame the Queen. In Agnes Lyle's ballads, as in those analyzed by Buchan, this "rule of three" is operative throughout the ballad, on all levels of structure.

Binary patterning is the result of "the habit of thinking in balances, antitheses, oppositions and parallelisms [which] is intrinsic to the oral mind. It manifests itself both conceptually, in the arrangement of the narrative 'ideas,' and verbally, in the arrangement of the line and stanza word groups" (88). This patterning in diads and balances is likewise operative throughout these ballads on all levels.

Repetition is the most obvious way of achieving binary and trinary structures. Andersen (1985, 72–78) has achieved an elegant typology of ballad repetition, static and dynamic. His five types, emphatic, causative, narrative, recurrent, and progressive, have proved most apt for analyzing the diads and triads of Agnes Lyle's repertoire. (See especially chapter 3, below.)

Binary and trinary structures are immediately apparent aids to creativity. Annular or ring structure is more difficult to explain.[15] The image is a spatial one. The idea is that a narrative is conceived as a series of concentric rings, with some central point in the structure as the focus or pivot of these rings. To get through the narrative, one must start at the outermost ring and work through all the rings to the center, and then on to the other side, passing out from each ring at a point opposite to the point at which it was entered. Annular patterning is a valuable device to help narrators keep their stories clearly in mind. If they become lost in the first part of the story they do not have to figure out the whole rest of the story; they need only recall the pivot point and then figure out how to get there from where they are. This process of narrating the first half of the story will impress the structure of the second half on their minds. If then, narrators get lost in the second half, they need only recall the first half, already successfully negotiated. The successive points which got them into the heart of the story can act as a road map or series of milestones to guide them out of the story again. They simply work back out through the same rings to an exit point on the opposite side of the outermost ring.

Annular patterning is exactly opposite from typical literary structure. A narrator passing out of the story passes elements in reverse order from the order in which they were passed in entering the story. Literary style, on the other hand, arranges elements of a composition in parallel structure, that is, in the same order every time they occur. Oral, annular structure arranges elements thus:

$$A B \ldots N \ldots B A$$

Literary, parallel structure, as every student in freshman composition knows, arranges elements thus:

I.
    A.
    B.
    C.
II.
    A.
    B.
    C.

The simplest form of annular structure is one ring around the center (or focus, or pivot):

This pattern may also be diagrammed thus:

A
B
A

The two A's may then be spoken of as framing B. This way of speaking involves a change of metaphor, of course, but has the advantage of providing a convenient term, the *frame*. More complex annular or framing structures may then be analyzed as frames within frames. Chiasmus, a common device in oral narrative, is a special type of annular structure in which there are framing elements but no central focal element; e.g.:

A B B A

Annular patterns, like binary and trinary patterns, are found on all levels of structure. Moreover, structural units themselves group into larger structural units according to these same patterns. One can, for example, have diads of diads, triads of diads, or framed diads. Looking at the way these patterns structure the elements of a short sample ballad from the repertoire of Agnes Lyle will help clarify how they work.

"Lord Derwentwater" (Child 208A)

1. Our king has wrote a lang letter,
   And sealed it owre with gold;
   He sent it to my lord Dunwaters,
   To read it if he could.

2. He has not sent it with a boy, with a boy,
   Nor with anie Scotch lord;
   But he's sent it with the noblest knight
   Eer Scotland could afford.

3. The very first line that my lord did read,
   He gave a smirkling smile;
   Before he had the half o't read,
   The tears from his eyes did fall.

4. "Come saddle to me my horse," he said,
   "Come saddle to me with speed;
   For I must away to fair London town,
   For me was neer more need."

5. Out and spoke his lady gay,
   In child-bed where she lay:
   "I would have you make your will, my lord Dunwaters,
   Before you go away."

6. "I leave to you, my eldest son,
   My houses and my land;
   I leave to you, my second son,
   Ten thousand pounds in hand.

7. "I leave to you, my lady gay—
   You are my wedded wife—
   I leave to you, the third of my estate;
   That'll keep you in a lady's life."

8. They had not rode a mile but one,
   Till his horse fell owre a stane:
   "It's warning gude eneuch," my lord Dunwaters said,
   "Alive I'll neer come hame."

9. When they came into fair London town,
    Into the courtiers' hall,
    The lords and knichts in fair London town
    Did him a traitor call.

10. "A traitor! a traitor!" says my lord,
    "A traitor! how can that be,
    An it was na for the keeping of five thousand men
    To fight for King Jamie?

11. "O all you lords and knichts in fair London town,
    Come out and see me die;
    O all you lords and knichts into fair London town,
    Be kind to my ladie.

12. "There's fifty pounds in my richt pocket,
    Divide it to the poor;
    There's other fifty pounds in my left pocket,
    Divide it from door to door."

"Lord Derwentwater" is a short, perfectly constructed ballad. The events of the ballad seem based on the career of James Ratcliffe, Earl of Derwentwater (in this version called Lord Dunwaters), who participated in the rising in the north of England in support of the Old Pretender ("King Jamie," in this version identified with the king of England). He was executed on February 24, 1716. Only twenty-seven at the time, he had already won a reputation for unusual generosity and liberality with his friends, his tenants, and the poor of the country. While some details of this story come through in the Lyle rendition, the basic plot has undergone a sea change. Stanza 2 implies that Dunwaters is a Scots lord, not an English. In stanza 4 Dunwaters goes to succor the king in London because, as he believes, "For me was neer more need." In stanza 10 Dunwaters is shocked to be called a traitor. Has he not raised troops in the king's support?

Interpreted in this way, the ballad represents a simpler relationship between England and Scotland than prevailed in the days of the Earl of Derwentwater, a relationship, rather, very like that which prevailed in the days of Agnes Lyle. And interpreted in this way the ballad offers an unparalleled story of perfidy: Lord Dunwaters has raised five thousand men to fight for his king. When the war is over he returns to his home in Scotland. But back at court enemies conspire against him, finally convincing the king that he is a traitor. In order to get the young lord back to London the king writes an impassioned plea, urging his need of Dunwaters in some new crisis. Loyal Dunwaters does not hesitate. But his young wife has a more suspicious nature. She urges her husband to make a will before he goes. Once underway, Dunwaters himself receives a sign that danger lies ahead. Even so, when he reaches London he is stunned to find that he has been tricked and trapped. His past service counts for nothing. And yet he manages to retain his generosity and nobility to the end.

In this rendition of the story, the stanzaic structure falls into three groups of four stanzas, which, as separate "acts" of the story, might be entitled "Summons," "Premonitions," and "Betrayal" (see Diagram 1). In the first act the two stanzas describing the king's letter and Dunwaters's response to it frame the two central stanzas describing the sending and reading of the letter. These two central stanzas, paired and adjoining, constitute a *balance*. In the second act the two stanzas describing Lady Dunwaters's premonition and Lord Dunwaters's subsequent premonition frame the balance containing the nuncupative will. This balance in turn contains within itself a trinary structure, the three-part will. The third act contains two balances, the first describing the accusation and denial, and the second describing the execution.

DIAGRAM 1
Stanzaic and Tonal Structures in "Lord Derwentwater"

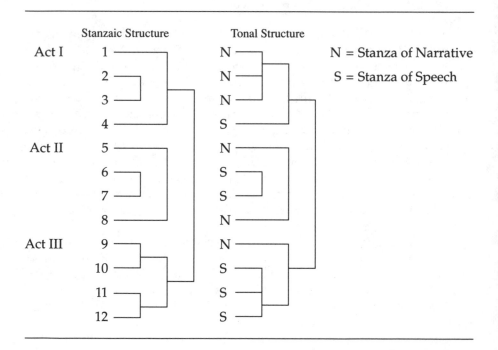

The ballad, then, exhibits trinary structure in the three act divisions and in the tripartite nuncupative will. Each act is organized around binary structures. And two of the acts frame binary structures with an annular structure. The whole ballad, too, exhibits annular structure, with the nuncupative will as the focal point.

While all three kinds of patterns prevail in the stanzaic structure of the Lyle ballads, annular patterns predominate in the character and narrative structures (Diagram 2). In this ballad, for instance, the character and narrative structures are typically annular, though they exhibit some binary and trinary patterning as well. In the character structure, the diad of king and lords and the diad of hero and lords frames the central triad in which Dunwaters is shown first alone, then with his wife, then alone again.[14] But these diads and triads are weak, and the character structure might be diagrammed almost as aptly as a series of frames within frames within frames, with the perfidious English king of the opening opposed to the noble Scot of the closing. Like the character structure, the narrative structure admits of analysis into frames, diads, and triads. But the overall annular force is very strong. Action involving the king and his lords, and Dunwaters and these same lords frames action involving Dunwaters and his wife. The singer enters the song through rings describing the king's treachery, Dunwaters's loyalty, and the wife's premonition, to the central symbolic act of making a will. From there she moves back out through the opposite sides of the same rings, singing of Dunwaters's own premonition confirming his wife's premonition, the false accusation against the loyal Dunwaters, and the noble acceptance of the fate the king has wrought.

In "Lord Derwentwater" the stanzaic, character, and narrative structures

DIAGRAM 2

Character and Narrative Structures in "Lord Derwentwater"

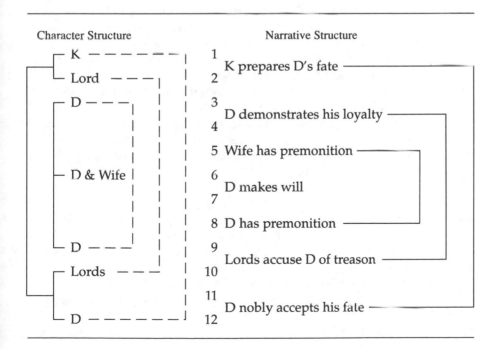

counterpoint or complement each other rather than reinforcing each other as they sometimes do elsewhere in the repertoire. The tonal structure, on the other hand, usually rather attenuated in pieces in this repertoire, is remarkably clear in this ballad and reinforces the three-act division of the stanzaic structure (see Diagram 1). The first act, presented in three stanzas of narrative followed by one of speech, balances the third act, presented in three stanzas of speech preceded by one of narrative. The middle act consists of a diad of speech, the nuncupative will, set in a frame of stanzas combining narrative and speech. Thus, though the structural texture is generally polyphonic, all the structures come together, like a great chord, to emphasize the nuncupative will at the heart of the ballad, a will that anticipates the nuncupative will with which Dunwaters concludes his gallows speech.

A good deal of emphasis has been put on annular, binary, and trinary structures as aids to composition within the restrictions of metrical performance. And indeed, they are probably very helpful to the performer in getting through the piece. But their greater significance is aesthetic (cf. Lord 1986a, 54–55). They help the performer end up with a *beautiful* piece. These structures provide solutions, within the oral folk aesthetic, to what are probably the three most significant aesthetic problems in any art, on any level, namely the problems of unity, organization, and sufficiency. Annular forces unify the whole ballad. On the narrative level, for instance, the ballad is usually annular from first to last. On the stanzaic level the ballad is often framed by a prologue and epilogue, as in "Mary Hamilton" (Child 173), and individual acts are often framed as well, as in the final act of "Mary Hamilton." Binary forces organize the ballad on a finer level, especially in the stanzaic structure. In "Lord Derwentwater," for instance, each act is either a balance of balances or a framed balance. Trinary forces give a sense of sufficiency. Three acts, for instance, makes a complete story. The interaction often involves three primary characters. And if an act needs to be long and full, as in the case of Act I and Act III of "Mary Hamilton," three balances or diads will give that sense of fullness.

The presence of these patterns, and of the other criteria mentioned above, does not in itself prove that the immediate singer from whom a ballad comes is an orally recreative singer. If, however, the entire repertoire of a singer presents a consistent pattern of formulicity and consequent enjambment, of composition by commonplace and "theme," and of annular, binary, and trinary structuring, especially if complemented by an axiological unity stemming from consistent and distinctive treatment of key ideas, all suggesting that the songs are the work of a single artist with a single vision, then it is fair to assert that the immediate and ultimate source of the versions is a single singer, an orally recreative "singer of tales."

Such a singer of tales was Agnes Lyle of Kilbarchan. The following study, after providing background on the singer, her times, and the manuscript in which her songs are preserved, will apply criteria of orality to her songs. The resulting close examination will disclose not only her traditional mastery of a traditional ballad technique and corpus but also a more personal set of attitudes toward family and class structures, expressed especially in leitmotifs that run through the entire corpus. The final pages of the study will compare the technique of this singer with that of Mrs. Brown and conclude by moving from consideration of particular cases to generalizations about ballad formulas, ballad technique, and oral theory.

PART ONE

The Ballads of Agnes Lyle
Background

The Radical and the Tory

Time: 1825
Place: A village in Scotland
Characters: Agnes Lyle, daughter of a weaver
William Motherwell, Sheriff-Clerk Depute

The town and parish of Kilbarchan, situated at the center of Renfrewshire, had a population, according to the 1821 census, of 4213 souls. The two main roads that served Renfrew in the 1820s ran just north and just south of the town. Paisley, the principal market town, stood as it stands today, five and one-half miles east. The walk or ride to Paisley was not difficult but those who preferred could cross to Johnstone, one and one-half miles east, and take the canal boat that ran several times a day. Coaches to Glasgow passed a mile south of the village.

The climate, although humid, was remarkably healthy, and people often lived to extreme age. *The New Statistical Account* mentions one woman of 108 years (1845, 7: 356–357). This good health was doubly remarkable considering the damp working conditions imposed on weavers and their families by the practice of keeping the warp moist while weaving. The statistical minister does admit that "something morbid in the lower extremities" was common. The parish had at least one spinning mill, but the principal industry was weaving. Scarcely a cottage in the area stood without its loom and "our operatives have, it is believed, deservedly the reputation of rather superior skill and experience" (*The New Statistical Account*, 1845, 7: 372).

Kilbarchan, and indeed all of Renfrewshire, was blessed not only with weavers but also with ballad singers "of rather superior skill and experience." William Motherwell, in little more than a year of collecting, gathered approximately two hundred texts in the county, more than forty of these from singers in Kilbarchan. A Mrs. Thomson sang nine, Agnes Laird sang six, a Mrs. King sang five, Edward King and Janet Holmes each sang a single item, and the rest came from one Agnes Lyle, who had learned ballads from her father, a weaver. Kilbarchan thus stood at the center of a rich ballad region, but Renfrewshire, its ballads, and its ballad singers do not fit the stereotypes which have grown up in the popular imagination and, to a lesser extent, in the scholarly literature.

Ever since Walter Scott, at least, enthusiasts have sought to associate bal-

lads with one particular type of community. This community is often seen as
a border community, and the term *border ballad* sometimes replaces the simpler term *ballad*. Amerigo Paredes, for instance, gives *With His Pistol in His
Hand* the subtitle: *A Border Ballad and Its Hero*. Paredes is at pains to show
how the particular conflicts of a border region contribute to the creation of
balladry. And David Buchan, in his magnificent *The Ballad and the Folk*, after
demonstrating that Scottish collectors have found more ballads in the Northeast than on the English Border, spends a chapter exploring the significance
of the fact that the Northeast itself, a Lowland Scots region, borders on the
Gaelic Highlands (1972, ch. 4). But no one would call Kilbarchan a border
region. It sits squarely in the center of Renfrew, a county entirely surrounded
by counties similar in economics and culture. And yet Kilbarchan, right at
the center of things, was part of a great ballad community still flourishing in
the 1820s.

Such ballad communities are often conceived of as agricultural, isolated,
and illiterate. Yet the West of Scotland, the Strathclyde district, with its min-
ing, manufacturing, ship-building, and shipping, still today something of an
industrial center, was probably the single most heavily industrialized region in
the world during the 1820s. The Clyde River, running down from Glasgow,
was Scotland's gateway to the world. The constant traffic of merchants, mer-
chandise, emigrants, and returning colonists made isolation impossible. Not
agriculture but the textile industry dominated the economy, both urban and
rural.[1] Indeed, because of dependence on water power to run mills, the textile
industry began as a largely rural industry and "all but the most sparsely popu-
lated districts participated in this process of mechanization" (Shaw 312).
Though the mills often employed children, they did not leave them illiterate.
It was customary to include schooling in the child laborer's day. The Presbyterian emphasis on literacy would not countenance anything else. For non-
laboring children there were parochial schools.[2] Girls as well as boys attended
these schools. Indeed, William Motherwell's poem "Jeanie Morrison" is a description of a fellow student. Thus girls as well as boys had opportunity to
develop a great love of books, as Dorothy Wordsworth discovered while tour-
ing this part of Scotland with Samuel Taylor Coleridge and her brother William in 1803. In her account of the journey she describes giving a young girl a
tip and then asking what she planned to do with the money. Buy books, the
girl said, to Dorothy's delight. On the same trip the chambermaid at an inn
impressed Dorothy with the shelf of books she kept in her room (Wordsworth
1874, 22, 34). For boys, however, the opportunities were better. As Brock
points out in *Scotus Americanus:* "Scotland had an unusually effective educa-
tional system," with high schools and academies beyond the parochial school,
bursaries to support the poor even at university level, some university education for non-professional people, and a "high standard of literacy [of which]
the overall impression is clarity, precision, and workmanlike use of language"
(1982, 19). Contrary to stereotype, then, this ballad community was more industrial than agricultural, far from isolated, and far from illiterate.

It has long been customary to speak of ballads as medieval, or at least as echoing a medieval world order. Such an approach has its roots in the late nineteenth-century view of folklore as a survival of older times and older ways of life. But the ballads considered in this book reflect the time and place where they were collected, southwest Scotland in the 1820s, with its peculiar social and political conflicts and in particular its attitudes toward the monarchy and the class system. External details from an older order of things do sometimes "survive" in these songs, of course, but in essence the ballads are nineteenth-century, not medieval. The social and political spirit of the songs is the social and political spirit of the Strathclyde weavers.

What sort of people were these weavers from whom Agnes Lyle, the Kilbarchan singer, sprang? David Gilmour, in *Reminiscences of the Pen Folk*, answers the question this way: "But when the century was in her teens what a band they were of single-minded, energetic, knowledgeable men" (1879, 9). Brenda Gaskin, in an Edinburgh Ph.D. dissertation, expands a bit on Gilmour's succinct comment:

> In the fifty years preceding 1815 there had been no more prosperous trade in Scotland than hand-loom weaving, nor a trade that employed a more enlightened and knowledgeable body of men. In education and understanding, in zest for reading and argument, and in intelligence and skill in their own trade they had no equals. (1955, 109)

Wages were high, and one needed to work only four or five days a week—this in an era when the six-day, sixty-hour week was considered light. Thus the weaver had "both leisure and income to satisfy his taste for reading and argument. Chat and argument went on for hours on every conceivable subject, but more particularly on literature, morals, and politics" (Gaskin 1955, 110).

After 1815, in the wake of the Napoleonic Wars, the handloom industry almost sank. Gaskin considers oversupply of labor to be the principal cause of the decline. Unlike most trades, weaving had no protective unions or guilds to keep out the inexperienced or untrained. Young men from the Highlands, no longer needed in the army, poured into the weaving trade, along with Irish immigrants, women and children, and all who wanted a craft that was easily learned.

Despite its central location, Kilbarchan itself, perhaps because it had no weaving factories, seems to have been relatively untouched by this flood of immigrants sweeping into the Southwest. The population showed steady growth, with no sudden spurts, over some seven decades:

A.D. 1755: 1485 people
1774: 2305
1791: 2506
1821: 4213[3]

Nor does the 1838 survey for the *New Statistical Account* provide any evidence of a large influx of Highlanders or Irish. Both groups were predominantly Catholic, but the survey turned up only six Catholics in Kilbarchan. Sheltered from the over-supply of labor, the village may have been touched a little less roughly by the hard times which afflicted the weavers of the Southwest after the Napoleonic Wars.

Nothing could protect the Kilbarchan weavers, however, from the effects of under-demand for their product. Weavers associated this under-demand with the Corn Laws of 1815, which, in addition to making grain prohibitively expensive, destroyed much of the foreign market for textiles. Countries which could not export grain to Britain refused to import textiles from Britain.

Shaw points to yet another factor in the decline of the textile industry in general in rural areas. Between 1760 and 1790 the artisans themselves had controlled the industry. But between 1790 and 1820 the merchant manufacturers gradually took over, introducing new and costly technology, especially the substitution of steam for water power:

> By the 1820s conditions were right for a move to urban locations. The textile industry was controlled by merchant manufacturers with no vested interest in maintaining rural employment; energy requirements were growing beyond the capabilities of most streams; and improvements in communications and technology were reducing the cost of steam-power. Thus urban centres which had access to raw materials by sea, to coal by canal or sea also, which had good access to markets, and which could house a highly centralised labour force began to develop, and during the 1820s the urban textile industry grew at a remarkable rate. The water-powered textile industry [and the concomitant handloom industry] was essentially rural and dispersed. The steam-powered industry was centralised and urban. The decline of the rural industry was inevitable. (314)

The general depression of the hand-loom industry found dramatic expression in a shocking decline of wages between 1816 and 1826. Skilled Paisley-shawl weavers, the highest paid of all, earned 26 shillings and 6 pence per week in 1816. In 1825 they still earned 25/9, but by 1826 they were down to 16/9. The wage for dress stuffs dropped from 15/- per week in 1816 to 12/8 in 1825 and 7/1 in 1826. Even these figures may be somewhat inflated and fail to reflect what weavers actually earned (Gaskin 1955, 77, quoting data from *Reports of Assistant Hand-Loom Weavers' Commissioners*, 1839). Motherwell was collecting ballads in this region, then, at a time when the handloom industry was experiencing a serious economic depression.

Besides economic set-backs, the weavers suffered serious political set-backs, especially in the so-called "Radical War" of 1820. This tense series of events typifies the political and social context of Agnes Lyle's ballads. The year 1819 had been one of especially bad trade. Thousands were out of work and Scotland, unlike England, had no parish relief system. Discontent was rampant, especially among the weavers of the Southwest, a large and formidable body of workers who were not only educated and articulate but also stocky, strong, and desperate. Cockburn, in his famous *Memorials*, captures the spirit of the times, discontent on the part of the under-employed and a corresponding fear and disdain on the part of the gentry:

> The year 1819 closed, and the new one opened, amidst the popular disturbances called, gravely by some and jocularly by others, "The Radical War." The whole island was suffering under great agricultural and manufacturing distress. This was taken the usual advantage of by demagogues: and consequently there was considerable political excitement . . . Some people . . . were clear that a great blow would be struck by the Radical army—an army talked of but never seen, on the last night of the year. The perfect facility with which a party of forty or fifty thousand weavers could march from Glasgow and seize upon the banks and castles of Edinburgh, without ever being heard of till they appeared, was demonstrated. (1974, 242–243)

The expected invasion of Edinburgh by fifty thousand weavers did not occur, nor was anything of the sort likely to occur. Such was not the precise temper of the Radical movement, nor could the Radicals muster an army large enough to take on the British empire. And yet, on Sunday, 2 April 1820, the people of Glasgow and all the major centers of Lanark, Stirling, Renfrew, Dumbarton, and even as far away as Ayr, woke to find their towns plastered with a strange handbill, a declaration, signed by a "Provisional Government," calling to arms and strike, and dated April 1. In the event, the date, April Fools' Day, was appropriate, for the document was spurious, a colossal piece of entrapment designed to draw revolutionaries out of the woodwork.

> What the Radical forces, preparing to answer the call of their "Provisional Government," did not know was that the twenty-eight man Provisional Government were in Glasgow Jail and, in fact, had been there since March 21 [!] when they had all been arrested at a meeting in the Gallowgate: that the proclamation calling for the rising was the work of Government agents who, having infiltrated the Scottish Radical organization and knowing its weakness as an armed force, were precipitating the rising in order that superior Government forces could quell the insurrection and that the Radicals could be brought to heel by a lesson underlined with military defeat, trials for high treason and execution. (Ellis and Mac a' Ghobhainn 1970, 34–35)

Radical response to the proclamation amounted to no more than strikes and scattered raids on arms depots or private homes thought to hold weapons.[4] No great uprising broke out, for none had been planned. But the "revolution," such as it was, was put down with unprecedented severity. Huge quantities of ammunition were requisitioned from England. All available military forces were mobilized: hussars, rifle brigades, regiments of sharpshooters, armed associations, yeomanry squadrons, artillery, and cavalry. Even the village of Kilbarchan was divided by the conflict. On the very Sunday morning when the first proclamation appeared, John Fraser, a Radical schoolmaster, carried a copy to Kilbarchan for the benefit of fellow Radicals there, while on Monday the Kilbarchan Armed Association, eighty strong, mustered to defend the Crown. Although strikes raged over the ensuing few weeks, only occasional military encounters with raiding parties took place. But soon the military defeat of the Radicals was proclaimed, with trials for high treason and executions following in due course.

As symbolic statements these trials and executions were even more important than the show of military muscle that preceded them. And more infuriating. Nothing infuriates an angry person more than cold rationality does. The weavers of the region were already angry, and a trial is a cold and rational process.

From 21 June until 9 August a special commission made the rounds of the five counties involved, conducting a series of grand-jury hearings, arraignments, and trials, in a flagrant display of English power, a flagrant violation of English and Scottish law, and a flagrant affront to the dignity of the Scottish nation. Because the treason trials of 1817, in connection with the Paisley riots, had proved disastrous, Lord Sidmouth, the home secretary, did not trust the Scottish courts to conduct treason trials again. So he sent a prominent London barrister, John Hullack, to conduct the prosecution, despite the fact that no barrister may practice in a Scottish Court without a Scottish law degree.

The defendants were prosecuted under English, not Scottish law. The Treaty of Union of 1707 had guaranteed Scottish law for Scotland, but an Act of Queen Anne had abrogated that part of the treaty with respect to laws of treason, providing that in such cases English law was to be followed. This provision meant, for instance, that only one witness, not two, was required for conviction. Since the Scottish judges would not be familiar with English procedure, Sidmouth appointed Sir Samuel Shepherd, the lord chief baron, to the commission, giving him the impertinent job of instructing the judges in pertinent English law.

The commission, English baron and all, opened grand-jury hearings in Stirling on 23 June 1820. True bills for high treason were found against thirty-eight men. The commission then moved to Glasgow, Dumbarton, Paisley, and Ayr, where more "true bills" followed in due course. A second progress of the five counties followed, to arraign the prisoners and hear the pleas. Then yet a third time, to conduct the trials, the commission made a progress through the five counties.

Nothing more calculated to incense and incite can be imagined than this triple progress of the special commission, representing English law, seating an English judge, listening to an English prosecutor (who finally went home in disgust with the whole proceedings), and presuming to judge Scotsmen, in a region where Radicalism was rife and republican and democratic sentiments attracted progressive thinkers. And the Crown, in whose name this commission sentenced twenty-two stout sons of Presbyterians, was the libertine George IV, successor to the demented George III. Understandably enough, during the months of June, July, and August all was not quiet. The military was fired upon by concealed gunmen, and the military in turn fired upon unarmed crowds. Strikes and even an assassination attempt added to the unrest.

Yet this display of English power had the full support of the landed and business interests of Scotland, more nearly a single class than in England and Tory to the core. All true Scottish gentlemen responded with disdain and terror to the hordes of weavers roaming the countryside, pilfering potatoes, and sleeping in barns. Like safe people everywhere, in all times, they panicked in the face of a threat to family and income. To those bankers, lawyers, merchants, mill operators, and members of the Scottish peerage, English power meant security.

Though nineteen of the twenty-two sentences were later commuted to transportation for life, three men had to face the barbarism that English law provided for treason: hanging, decapitation, and public exposure of the dead body for half an hour, followed by quartering of the torso. The first victim was James Wilson, a sixty-three-year-old weaver. His offense: removing a fowling piece from a farmhouse, a piece which he later returned (Gaskin 1955, 185). The jury which convicted him had dismissed every other charge, and recommended mercy. But all attempts to obtain that mercy failed. Doubtless the Crown felt it necessary to have at least one weaver among those hanged. Hanged he was, on 30 August 1820. Andrew Hardie and John Baird followed on 8 September. This triumph of Tory force found its laureate in Paisley versifier John Goldie, who was later to communicate two ballads to his Tory friend William Motherwell.[5]

John Goldie had his poems about the execution of the Radicals printed up for posterity, but another more important Motherwell informant left posterity no explicit record of her reaction to these proceedings. In fact she left very little record of herself at all, except the ballads. The only certain biographical data is contained in occasional field notes by Motherwell, and in the headings he affixed to fair copies of some of her songs. Motherwell's comments suggest that Agnes Lyle was born about 1775, and that her father, first name unknown, was born about 1731. The Kilbarchan Parish register does indicate the birth of an Agnes Lyle in 1775, a girl apparently named after an older sister who died in infancy. If Agnes was born in Kilbarchan, and if her family subscribed to the established church rather than to one of the dissenting persuasions, this could be the singer. Not necessarily, however. In Kilbarchan a limited stock of surnames and Christian names served a large portion of the population. In 1768, for example, two girls named Janet Lyle were born in the village; their fathers' names: John Lyle and John Lyle. Baptismal records alone, then, are not enough to identify the singer.

At the time Motherwell visited Agnes Lyle she seems to have been living in Kilbarchan itself, but her father had been a weaver in one of the outlying hamlets of the parish. Like most Lowland Scots of her day, Agnes Lyle probably attended school and learned to read and write. In her adult years she retained the family name of Lyle, suggesting that she never married. But again it is impossible to be sure, for in Scotland, as in Ireland, a woman might be known by her maiden name all her life, even after she became a wife or widow.[6] Motherwell does once refer to his woman informants as "certain aged virgins" (1827, xxvii). Though not all the women who gave him songs were aged, and not all were virgins, this reference may include Agnes Lyle.

Daughter of a weaver in a village of weavers, Agnes Lyle belonged to a politically articulate group which saw itself discriminated against by Parliament and betrayed by business and landed interests. Drawing inspiration from the American and French revolutions and its own Presbyterian heritage, and perceiving the Crown as both a moral and a political affront, this group formed the basis of the Radical and Republican movements in Scotland. Whether or not the singer was sympathetic to the political ideals and aspirations of this weaving fraternity, she could not have been ignorant of those ideals and aspirations, nor indifferent to them. The ballads collected from her, furthermore, suggest that she was deeply sympathetic. Although ballads are usually thought of as "objective," her versions reflect the social conflicts and the political realities of her own day. By making choices within the tradition and by emphasizing certain aspects of story and character she was able to express quite forcibly which side she was on in those conflicts and how she conceived those realities.

About the collector of these ballads, William Motherwell, much more is known. His biography begins conventionally: Born 13 October 1797, in Glasgow, of poor but distinguished Stirlingshire stock, he early devoted himself to literature, producing at fourteen the first draft of "Jeanie Morrison," his most popular lyric. In 1809, during a period of family financial embarrassment, William was dispatched to an uncle in Paisley to continue the education already begun in Glasgow. A bright boy, he was often assigned to tutor his duller fellows but preferred to draw pictures for them and tell them stories of dragons, knights, and quests.

At the age of fifteen, determined on a law career, Motherwell parlayed his distinctive handwriting into a post in the office of the sheriff-clerk, the principal legal administrative officer of the county. According to Campbell, the sheriff, Motherwell's political views were extremely liberal at first. As he grew older, though, he grew more conservative. In 1819, when he was Sheriff-Clerk Depute, a group of rioters in Paisley almost hurled him from a bridge into the River Cart. Some have suggested that the experience dampened his liberal ardor. But James M'Conechy, a friend of the poet-collector, argues that Motherwell's growing conservatism was but a gradual expression of his natural disposition: He was "instinctively a Tory" (M'Conechy 1865, xxiii).

About 1824 Motherwell became involved in collecting material for a new book of ballads, to be called *Minstrelsy: Ancient and Modern*. At this same time he began to collect material on his own for a second book of more high-kilted pieces and more select audience, to be called either *The Paisley Garland* or *The West Country Garland*. The first fascicles of the *Minstrelsy* appeared under unknown editorship at the end of 1824. By mid-1825 Motherwell himself had taken over the editorship, completing the book by 1827.[7] The *Minstrelsy* has often been praised for remarkable fidelity of texts to oral tradition, inclusion of tunes matched to the specific stanzas to which they were sung, unexpected insight into the oral process of ballad composition, and sound scholarship throughout.

The high-kilted garland, so far as is known, never made it to press. After the *Minstrelsy*, Motherwell went on to publish the work of an earlier Renfrewshire poet and sheriff-clerk depute, James M'Alpie. He also founded *Paisley Magazine*. From there he turned to more traditional journalistic pursuits, finally becoming editor of the Glasgow *Courier*. The move to Glasgow thrust him into the center of a congenial literary circle. Soon he published his first book of poems and found it well received. In 1835 he undertook with James Hogg to publish an edition of Burns. But a nervous breakdown in August of that year brought failing health, and he did not live to see the work completed. In the first month of his thirty-ninth year, in the early hours of the morning after Halloween, he suffered a stroke. He was dead before noon.

Part of the fascination of Motherwell and the singers from whom he collected is the paradox of the situation: a high-churchman, a Tory, a sheriff-clerk depute, so faithful in recording the ballads of covenanters, radicals, and revolutionaries. What did Agnes Lyle, elderly working-class singer from the weaving village of Kilbarchan, make of the young gentleman who came to visit again and again? She must have been aware of the religious, political, and social gulf that separated him from her. And yet she came to trust him with her bitterly subversive songs, weeping openly as she sang of forbidden love and human perfidy. They were a remarkable pair, the Radical and the Tory.

The Manuscripts and
the Songs

In quality, extent, and range, Agnes Lyle's repertoire constitutes a major piece of data for students of balladry, oral tradition, and folklore. While William Motherwell probably took down only a portion of the songs this singer knew, this surviving repertoire is still remarkably extensive for the period. Motherwell was principally interested in ballads, and he found in Agnes Lyle a singer of diversified ballad-singing technique. Her standard quatrain ballads reveal the full control of compositional elements usually associated with formulaic oral singing. Her songs in other meters reveal adaptations, adjustments, and even failures of oral technique. And a few items bear all the earmarks of aurally memorized pieces. But Motherwell's one extant notebook and his ballad collection between them authenticate each individual item, and guarantee that these items, taken together, constitute an oral repertoire, accurately recorded. The reader, then, once he understands the nature and significance of these two important documents, can have assurance that a text has been recorded accurately and attributed properly.

Motherwell housed his formal folksong collection in a single document usually called the Motherwell Manuscript. The early pages of the Manuscript are heterogeneous in character, but the last six hundred and more pages he devoted almost entirely to ballad material, each text written out with great care. In the Motherwell Notebook, on the other hand, the collector created a much more informal document. Through its pages he scattered ballad texts, lists of singers and their repertoires, statements of cash outlays and loans, outlines and notes for the "Introduction" to the *Minstrelsy*, and antiquarian matters. On page 176, to take an extreme example, he entered brief journal entries for a week in August of 1825 and for a weekend in July of 1826, followed by the detached and unexplained name "D Boone." Obviously Motherwell, like many people, used notebooks in a rather casual and unorganized way, writing notes relative to different matters in different sections of the same book.

Thanks to the efforts of Francis James Child, each of these documents survives in two versions, the autograph original and the Child-commissioned copy. The autograph Manuscript was in private hands in Child's day (M. C. Thompson, Esq., of Glasgow) but is now part of the Glasgow University collection. The Notebook may have belonged at one time to Motherwell's printer, John Wylie. In 1874, when it was copied for Child, the copyist noted that the original belonged to "Mr. J. Wylie Guild [sic.]." It has disappeared from circulation more than once but at last report was in the library of Pollock House, Glasgow (Montgomerie 1966, 5; Lyle 1975, xii). The Child copies of both documents are in the Houghton collection, Harvard.

The Manuscript is a hefty folio, its pages numbered slightly irregularly through 697. The Notebook is a small octavo of 178 numbered pages. For the Harvard copy of the Manuscript the folio has been copied onto quarto sheets and bound into two volumes. At first Child told the copyist, J.H.M. Gibbs, to make excerpts from the Manuscript. But when Gibbs had copied about fifty pages of excerpts, Child changed his mind and ordered a complete copy. Gibbs went back and added every item he had skipped, completing the copying on January 7, 1874. Child had Gibbs's work collated by M. H. Dalziel, who rearranged the pages so that the items would come in the order they fall in the folio, not in the order in which Gibbs had copied them. Interestingly enough, Gibbs received £4.1.9 for copying, but Dalziel received £.5 for collating. In 1886 James Barclay Murdock collated the copy and original a second time, inking red numbers in the margins to indicate the original pagination. Murdock was the same meticulous worker who had produced in 1875 the Harvard copy of the Notebook, an exact facsimile in size, pagination, and even the use of pencil or ink, of the autograph. For most purposes the Harvard copies of the Manuscript and Notebook are still used, as they were in Child's day, interchangeably with the originals.[1]

The Notebook offers occasional vivid glimpses of Motherwell the field collector in action, but the Manuscript offers a gauge of his development as collector over the entire period in which he was most involved with balladry. For purposes of analysis, the Manuscript divides into three segments, pp. 1–60, pp. 61–251, and pp. 252–end. The first sixty pages of the Manuscript contain songs of every description: true ballads from old women, bawdy songs for "The Paisley Garland," children's songs such as "The Frog and the Mouse," sentimental songs such as "Somebody," and historical songs such as "Captain Kidd." Though Motherwell collected many of these first songs in the field, he found others in manuscripts or printed collections. It is impossible to know precisely when Motherwell began filling in these early pages of his Manuscript. The first text, "Lady Maisry" (Child 65E), was collected from Mrs. Thomson of Kilbarchan, 25 February 1825, but the earliest dated texts are "Child Maurice" (Child 83B) and two other ballads collected from Widow M'Cormick of Paisley, 19 January 1825, entered on page 255 ff. By the end of 1824 Motherwell was involved with printer John Wylie and other friends in producing a ballad book, *Minstrelsy Ancient and Modern*. At the same time, as he confided in letters to Robert Smith and Charles Kirkpatrick Sharpe, he had in mind a pamphlet or "garland" of less edifying pieces for a more select audience. In a letter of 2 January to Smith (Montgomerie 1958, 153), he calls it "The West Countrie Garland," but in the Manuscript he changes the name to "The Paisley Garland." The change from the January title for the garland, the February text on page 1, and the heterogeneous nature of the early contents all indicate that Motherwell began the Manuscript, sometime around March 1, as a convenient repository for pieces which interested him, especially if they might be used in either the *Minstrelsy*, of which he was probably not yet the editor, or the proposed garland.

After about 60 pages, however, the Manuscript shows a change in Motherwell's conception of his collection. He includes no more "Paisley Garland" items (indeed "The Paisley Garland" never saw print, so far as is known). He now focuses exclusively on ballads, though a few of these ballads, such as Mrs. Storie's variant of "Paper of Pins" and Mrs. Birnie's variant of "Pretty Peggy O," are pieces that Child did not elect to canonize. Motherwell now seems dedicated to collection for its own sake and seeks out multiple variants of the ballads, even though he obviously can not secure publication of every single variant. Most important, he confines himself to what he considers oral texts. Although many of these are supplied by his friend Peter Buchan, more than two hundred come from his own field collecting. He gives the names of some twenty-five informants, many of whom he visited repeatedly. Thus he transforms himself from a culler of old volumes to a cultivator of old singers, and some not so old.

In the first two segments of the Manuscript, Motherwell concentrates on text rather than singer. Seldom does he give more than one song at a time from a singer and never more than two songs in succession. Instead, he attempts to organize the material by variants. Pages 196–218, for instance, contain two versions of "Clerk Saunders" (Child 69) followed by three versions of "Johnie Scot" (Child 99). Similarly, Agnes Lyle's version of "The Wee Wee Man" (Child 38) follows two versions of "Kempy Kay" (Child 33), another ballad about a creature of strange physiognomy. In these pages Motherwell is not always careful to record sources. Seventeen ballad texts in the second segment as well as a number of the songs in the first segment have no ascription of any kind.

In the third segment of the Manuscript, as in the first two segments, Motherwell is careful to preserve texts just as he heard them. But he now pays much more attention to details of singer, time, and place. In more than four hundred pages he errs occasionally, but omits ascription only twice. In each case the unascribed text follows a text sent to Motherwell by Peter Buchan, and in each case the unascribed text is probably to be understood as coming from the same source.[2] This care to identify an authentic text with a particular singer and an exact place and time is what sets Motherwell apart from the collectors of his day. And one ballad made the difference.

In the early months of 1825 Motherwell was almost fanatic on the subject of "Child Maurice" (Child 83). He saw in the ballad the basis for Home's popular tragedy *The Douglas*, widely regarded at the time as one of Scotland's greatest claims to literary distinction. Percy's version of "Child Maurice" was still a popular stall ballad of the day, but Motherwell in his youth had heard an older, more "traditionary" version from a singer now dead. He kept finding other singers who remembered having heard "Child Maurice" the old way, but none could sing it that way themselves. What a coup it would be to print in the *Minstrelsy* "the only pure traditional version" (Letter to Scott, quoted in McCarthy 1987, 301) of the ballad which had inspired *The Douglas.* Letters to friends uncovered nothing. But then, on January 19, the very day on which he had written Charles Kirkpatrick Sharpe for help, he found an old lady, Widow M'Cormick, who sang him the song. For three months Motherwell sat on the song, hoping to find other versions or extra stanzas. Finally he wrote to the great Scott himself:

> My reason for troubling you in this little matter is that if perchance any such copy may be now in your possession it would in all likelihood serve to correct some evident errors which occur in this one, and which though trifling I would rather wish to have it in my power to amend by the assistance of other recited copies than trust to my own judgment in doing so. Other copies too may possibly supply preferable readings in many places, and contain additions of material moment. . . . I mean to get this ballad inserted in a small 4to collection of Ballads now in the course of publication by John Wylie & Co. of Glasgow. Before doing so however I am anxious to learn whether you were ever acquainted with the ballad or had any copy of it which could rectify the text of the version now sent. (McCarthy 1987, 302)

Apparently Motherwell had already had one result of his collecting "inserted" into the *Minstrelsy.* The second fascicle opens (1827, 35) with a composite version of "Hind Horn" (Child 17) based on the version in Cromeck's *Select Scottish Songs,* with additions from other versions, "which, joined to the stanzas preserved by Mr. Cromeck, have enabled us to present it to the public in its present complete state." It seems safe to assume that Motherwell was responsible for the composite, since the versions from which the additions come are contained in his Manuscript. The headnote, too, has his tone and style, and promises the "Introduction" to the *Minstrelsy,* which he wrote, and the tune for the musical appendix, which he provided. This headnote betrays Motherwell's first conception of ballad editing. There is, he implies, only one correct text of a ballad, and that text is often corrupted in printed sources. Fieldwork may turn up something of value to correct a text, but the great contribution an editor can make is to take the versions with significant variants and from them print a better composite, a more "correct" version than any previous text. He sees "Hind Horn" as a keystone in the fabric connecting balladry ("Minstrelsy Modern") to romance ("Minstrelsy Ancient"), and he is obviously proud to have produced a more "correct" version or "set" for the *Minstrelsy.*

"Child Maurice" seemed such another important item because of the connection with *The Douglas.* The letter to Scott suggests that Motherwell wished to give it the "Hind Horn" treatment, but he found it more difficult to construct a composite text. Widow M'Cormick's version had many charac-

teristics, notably a more unadorned style, which made Motherwell hesitate
to piece it out with stanzas from the Percy text.

Motherwell's editorial philosophy at this point was the standard editorial
philosophy of the day, confirmed by the tremendous critical and popular
success of Scott's *Minstrelsy*, first published in 1802–1803. But Scott had had
twenty years to meditate upon that philosophy, twenty years of second
thoughts. His reply to Motherwell's letter must have come as quite a shock
to the young collector. Though the great man had nothing of substance to
say about "Child Maurice," he had a good deal to say about editing:

> Yet there are so many fine old verses in the common set [i.e., the Percy version]
> that I cannot agree to have them mixed up even with your set, though more
> ancient, but would like to see them kept quite separate, like different sets of the
> same melody. In fact, I think I did wrong myself in endeavoring to make the best
> possible set of an ancient ballad out of several copies obtained from different
> quarters, and that, in many respects, if I improved the poetry, I spoiled the sim-
> plicity of the old song. There is no wonder this should be the case when one
> considers that the singers or reciters by whom these ballads were preserved and
> handed down, must, in general, have had a facility, from memory at least, if not
> from genius (which they might often possess), of filling up verses which they
> had forgotten, or altering such as they might think they could improve. Passing
> through this process in different parts of the country, the ballads, admitting that
> they had one common poetical original (which is not to be inferred merely from
> the similitude of the story), became, in progress of time, totally different produc-
> tions, so far as the tone and spirit of each is concerned. In such cases, perhaps, it
> is as well to keep them separate, as giving in their original state a more accurate
> idea of our ancient poetry, which is the point most important in such collections.
> . . . This reasoning certainly does not apply to mere brief alterations and corrup-
> tions, which do not, as it were, change the tone and form of the original.
> (M'Conechy 1865, xxxii–xxxiv)

Hustvedt, in *Ballad Books and Ballad Men*, cautions against giving undue
credit to this letter (1930, 76–77). But the difference between the second segment of the Manuscript and the third segment indicates that the letter did
have a strong impact. The occasional dates provided in the early pages of the
Manuscript suggest that when Motherwell received Scott's letter, sometime
in May of 1825, he had filled in most of the first 251 pages, leaving only a few
pages blank in hopes of finding further variants of particular ballads. But
Scott's letter and Motherwell's own meditations seem to have shown the
collector that what he had done so far was inadequate, if not misguided. He
had overlooked the fact that a ballad is the product of a certain singer at a
certain time and place. Henceforth his collection must include such data. The
subsequent difference in the manuscript is modest but notable. The headnote on page 252 is typical: Mrs. Crum, Dumbarton, 4/7/25. In the remaining four hundred pages all items, with but two exceptions, are assigned to
identified singers, with identified residence, and most items are dated as
well.

This attention to details of ascription brought about a further shift of emphasis in the Manuscript. Gradually Motherwell became more interested in performers than in variants. Pages 255–264 contain three texts from Widow M'Cormick, with two more on pages 290–296. Pages 271–279 contain three texts from Marjery Johnston. Page 433 begins a long section of ballads from James Nicol. Page 550 begins yet another section of texts which seem to represent a single singer.

Motherwell's handling of the ballads of Agnes Lyle, his most prolific informant, shows how gradual was this shift from a variant to a performer orientation. Presumably he entered the Widow M'Cormick texts as a unit shortly after receiving Scott's letter. But two months later, when he was collecting from Agnes Lyle, he still felt the attraction of organization by variants, hence the placing of Lyle's "Wee Wee Man" (Child 38E, Ms. p. 195) following "Kempy Kay," and her "Babylon" (Child 14D, Ms. p. 174) following John Goldie's text of the same song. And yet at the same time, impressed by the sheer number of songs that Agnes Lyle knew and the uniqueness of so many of those songs, he had already begun to enter the rest of her repertoire as a unit. This unit begins on page 331 and runs, with but one interruption, to page 397.

Motherwell was not entirely unique among Scottish ballad collectors in his interest in repertoires. Jamieson before him had set about collecting the ballads of Mrs. Brown of Falkland. Peter Buchan showed a similar interest and awareness with regard to the ballads of James Nicol. And Andrew Crawfurd, Motherwell's protege, returned again and again to Mary Macqueen (Mrs. Storie) to collect as much as possible from her. Motherwell, however, collected the repertoires of a significant number of singers, noting, as Dave Harker points out "matters of performance style . . . and the importance of particular texts to particular singers" (Harker 1985, 65). He likewise understood the significance of differences in a given ballad as sung by different singers. And he recognized, influenced perhaps by Scott, that the record of a singer's full repertoire serves to authenticate individual items in that repertoire: when the repertoire as a whole shows that a singer is representative of a singing tradition, each item in that repertoire demands respect and consideration.

Motherwell began as a dilettante antiquarian especially devoted to song. In time he came to recognize the intrinsic interest and importance of certain ballads that had first attracted him because of supposed literary connections, simultaneously becoming aware of highly traditional versions of these ballads being sung everywhere around him. Scott's letter opened his eyes to the necessity of authenticating such versions by noting singer, time, and place and of publishing them in unaltered form. Finally, his experience with the singers of these versions led him to focus in his collecting not on the diachronic issue of how variants reflect the history of a ballad, but on the synchronic issues of what songs compose a singer's repertoire and how those songs differ from other contemporaneous versions. He became interested, in other words, in the individual singers and the distinctive characteristics of their repertoires. The Motherwell Manuscript, in its three segments, documents this transformation of William Motherwell from haphazard collector of popular song to serious student of ballad repertoires.

The Notebook, containing as it does explicit lists of informants and of songs in the repertoires of informants, pays tribute even more than does the Manuscript to Motherwell's awareness of the importance of individual repertoires. One section of the Notebook, pages 17–51, is especially rich in data about repertoires. This section contains Motherwell's field notes for nine days in August of 1825. It opens with Mrs. Rule's text of "Geordie" (Child 109G), collected on 16 August, and closes with Agnes Lyle's text of "Turkish Galley" ("The Sweet Trinity," Child 286Cf), collected on 24 August. Among other items included in this section are the rest of the songs collected from Agnes Lyle on 24 August, and lists of songs in the repertoires of Agnes Lyle and of another Kilbarchan singer, Agnes Laird. The Harvard copy of the Notebook bears the date "About 1826–1827" on the title page. Bibliographers usually repeat this date,[3] which was probably assigned to the volume by an early owner who had not read it carefully enough. The use of the Notebook as a field book in August of 1825, however, demonstrates that the dates on the title page are not accurate.

The texts in the Manuscript are fair copies written out neatly in that penmanship that was Motherwell's only fortune when he set out in the world to make a living. But the Notebook texts are working copies, with misunderstandings corrected, omitted words inserted, and easily understood words and stanzas abbreviated; they present, in fact, just the characteristics one would expect of texts written rapidly from oral sources. As such, they are closer to the performance, in fact, a part of the whole performance context. In transcribing these texts from Notebook to Manuscript, Motherwell, like anyone, made mistakes. In questions of disagreement, therefore, whether about a textual reading or, more importantly, about the ascription of a ballad to a particular singer, the Notebook texts take precedence over the neater Manuscript texts.

Despite Motherwell's heeding of Scott's words, there are some problems in identifying the ballads of Agnes Lyle. Child, on the basis of the Manuscript evidence, accurately identified 15. Kenneth Thigpen, the only scholar to publish a figure based on Child, finally settled on a count of 17 (1972). The actual figure seems to be 21 complete ballads, 1 nearly complete ballad, 7 fragments, and 3 titles.[4] The 22 long items are all entered in the Manuscript and are all ascribed, although not unambiguously.

The 15 ballads which Child identified as from "Agnes Lyle" are the following:

1. "The Twa Sisters" (Child 10F)
2. "Babylon" (Child 14D)
3. "Sheath and Knife" (Child 15B–16F)

4. "Hind Horn" (Child 17C)
5. "Cruel Mother" (Child 20E)
6. "Fair Janet" (Child 64B)
7. "Earl Richard" ("Young Hunting," Child 68D; 22 stanzas but incomplete, "the catastrophe wanting")
8. "Little Musgrave and Lady Barnard" (Child 81J)
9. "Johnie Scot" (Child 99G)
10. "The Baffled Knight" (Child 112E)
11. "The Gypsy Laddie" (Child 200C)
12. "Geordie" (Child 209F, and fragment 209K)
13. "Bonnie Baby Livingston" (Child 222C)
14. "Lord William" (Child 254A)
15. "The Sweet Trinity" (Child 286Cf)

Five of these ballads, "Hind Horn," "The Cruel Mother," "Johnie Scot," "The Baffled Knight," and "The Sweet Trinity" appear in both the Notebook and the Manuscript. The rest appear only in the Manuscript.

Child identified two more ballads, following the Manuscript, as from "Agnes Lile, Kilbarchan." The difference in spelling however proves to be immaterial: Motherwell was simply inconsistent in writing the name of his best informant. On page 331 of the Manuscript, for instance, he spells the singer's name *Lile*, but spells her father's name *Lyle*. Conversely, on page 367 he spells the singer's name *Lyle*, but on page 370 spells both her name and her father's name *Lile*. *Lyle* seems to be the more appropriate spelling. It is the spelling preferred for this family name in the Kilbarchan parish register, and it is the spelling Motherwell uses in the list of Kilbarchan singers on page 52 of the Notebook. The point would not need mentioning were it not for the fact that Child, by repeating Motherwell's inconsistencies, creates the impression that there might be two singers with nearly identical names. The two ballads Child attributes to the singer under the name "Agnes Lile" are

16. "Lord Derwentwater" (Child 208A)
17. "The Braes o Yarrow" (Child 214C)

For one text the Notebook and Manuscript provide conflicting ascriptions:

18. "The Wee Wee Man" (Child 38E)

This was one of six songs which Agnes Lyle sang for Motherwell on 24 August 1825. Although Motherwell correctly attributed the text to Agnes Lyle on page 40 of the Notebook, when he copied it into his Manuscript he made the understandable slip of attributing it to Agnes Laird. The confusion is not a case like the preceding case of two names for one person. Agnes Laird is not simply Agnes Lyle under a married name. She is identified as a separate singer in the list of singers on Notebook page 52, and the Notebook also includes consecutive repertoire lists for the two women. Moreover, two of Agnes Laird's six ballads are distinctive versions of ballads that Agnes Lyle also sang.[5] Motherwell made another slip of the pen, the converse of this one, in attributing Agnes Laird's "The Gay Goshawk" (Child 96D) to Agnes Lyle when he copied it into the Manuscript. Again, the Notebook evidence is clear, and the Manuscript attribution is in error.[6]

Child overlooked the fact that four other ballads which he printed from the Motherwell Manuscript also originated with Agnes Lyle. On page 331 of the Manuscript Motherwell had written:

> The six following ballads I took this day from the recitation of Agnes Lile Kilbarchan a woman verging on 50 daughter of _____ Lyle a customary weaver of Locherlip who died 14 years ago aged 80. She learned these ballads from her father.

Child correctly attributed the first two ballads, "Lord Derwentwater" and "The Braes o Yarrow," already mentioned. He published the remaining four without attribution:

19. "Sir Patrick Spens" (Child 58E)
20. "The Eastmure King" ("Fause Foodrage," Child 89B)
21. "Mary Hamilton" (Child 173B)
22. "Jamie Douglas" (Child 204G)

Of these 22 items, 6 had appeared in print before *The English and Scottish Popular Ballads*: "The Wee Wee Man," "Gypsy Laddie," "Lord Derwentwater," "Braes o Yarrow," "Bonnie Baby Livingston," and "Lord William." Motherwell had included them in his *Minstrelsy*, making minor editorial changes for the reading public in accord with the license given him by Scott's letter to correct brief "alterations and corruptions" so long as he preserved the "tone and form of the original." These corrections, of course, make the *Minstrelsy* texts less authoritative than the Child texts derived from the Manuscript and Notebook.

The 22 ballads and the "Geordie" fragment do not constitute the whole known repertoire of Agnes Lyle. The Notebook adds the first stanzas of six songs and the titles of three more, making a total of thirty-two items. This material is contained in a memorandum similar to the Agnes Laird repertoire memorandum already mentioned. This second memorandum follows immediately upon the first, and may well have been drawn up on the same day, 18 August 1825. The full text follows:

Memorandum to take from Agnes Lyle Kilbarchan the ballad she has beginning

> There was a lady she liv'd in Luke
> Sing hey alone & alonie O
> She fell in love with her fathers clerk
> Down by yon green wood sidie O

> also.
> Fair Margaret of Craignargat. got

also
Her copy of Johnnie Scot.   D°

———

Turkish Galley.   D°

———

Johnie Armstrang

———

Slippings o yarn,—a song.

———

But sixteen years of age she was
Poor soul when she began to love
But pray good people now but mind
How soon it did her ruin prove

He had so far her favour gaind
She did consent with him to lye
But this navish unthinkful act
Did prove her fatal destiny.

———

The week before Easter the day long and clear
The sun shining bright & cold frost in the air
I went to the forest some flowers to pull there
But the forest could yield me no pleasure

———

A fair maid walking in a garden
A young man there did her espy
And for to woo her he came unto her
And said fair maid can you fancy me.

———

There was two sailors were lonely walking
All for to take the cauler air
As they were walking together talking
A woman then Did to them appear

———

It was in the middle of fair July
Before the sun did pierce the sky
I saw a glint and a glancing eye
Abroad as I was walking

———

> As I went out on a May morning
> I heard a halloo so clearly
> It was some gentlemen who belong to Buckingham
> Who was going a hunting so early

This memorandum and the pages which bracket it provide a vivid glimpse of the ballad collector at work in the field. Motherwell had already made several visits to Kilbarchan, notably on 18, 19, and 27 July, when he collected a total of fifteen ballads from Agnes Lyle and one from Janet Holmes, who may have been the sister mentioned in one of the Notebook memoranda. In Kilbarchan again on 18 August, he dropped in on Agnes Laird and Agnes Lyle to find out what further songs these two women knew. In something of a hurry, apparently, by the time he got to the home of the second Agnes, he entered only the titles of familiar songs, but wrote out first stanzas of six less familiar broadside ballads. On 24 August he returned to Kilbarchan to collect full texts. The first item on his list, "There was a Lady Lived in Luke" (i.e., "The Cruel Mother"), was the first song he collected from Agnes Lyle that day. He entered it beginning on page 33 of the Notebook, immediately following the memorandum. The second song he collected, "Johnie Scot," was the third song on the list. After that, singer and collector abandoned the list altogether for "Hind Horn," "The Wee Wee Man," and "The Baffled Knight." After singing five stanzas of "The Baffled Knight," Agnes Lyle stopped. In all probability she was unable to finish the song at that time, but promised Motherwell she would work it up for a later performance. Motherwell left three pages blank to allow room to add the missing stanzas and returned to his list. The next song on the list, "Turkish Galley" ("Sweet Trinity"), was the last song collected that day. As Agnes Lyle completed this song, Motherwell discovered he had no more room for songs in that section of the Notebook; beginning on page 52 was an earlier series of notes on singers and repertoires, including the list referred to earlier of "old singing women" of Kilbarchan and other towns. Motherwell's list or memorandum would seem to indicate that he collected no more songs from Agnes Lyle that day. "Turkish Galley" is the last song marked "D°" (that is, ditto: got). According to the Manuscript he went on to collect at least three ballads from Agnes Laird that day. He was able to squeeze in "The Gay Goshawk," already referred to, between the Laird and the Lyle memoranda. For the others he changed notebooks.

Field notes from that Agnes Laird session, and indeed from the rest of Motherwell's collecting career, have disappeared. Yet these few pages provide a fascinating glimpse of the great collector. Like a good fieldworker he prepared the ground carefully and made preliminary notes. In the midst of the collecting session he could abandon those notes to let the singer sing the songs as inspiration suggested them. When inspiration failed, as it finally did, he had the list to fall back on. Furthermore, he paid Agnes Lyle a modest compensation for her help on this and other days—a total of 8/6 according to the expense account on page 156 of the Notebook. Thus the Notebook reveals Motherwell to be, in field technique as in critical understanding, a folklorist ahead of his time.

Expert though he became in field technique, Motherwell left no systematic description of his collecting. In the margin opposite stanza 10 of "Sheath and Knife," in a copy sent to Charles Kirkpatrick Sharpe, he did provide one other vignette of his experience with Agnes Lyle: "The poor old woman while singing this verse absolutely wept and the 'Adam Scrivener' who wrote and listened did all but evince similar emotion." A rather rueful footnote in the *Minstrelsy* may refer to Agnes Lyle too. Commenting on how ballad singers tend to regard their songs as true accounts, identifying for the collector the very castle, river, or oak where ballad events transpired, he says:

> I have, unfortunately for myself, once or twice notably affronted certain aged virgins by impertinent dubitations touching the veracity of their songs, an offence which bitter experience will teach me to avoid repeating, as it has long ere this, made me rue the day of its commission. (xxvii)

These affronted virgins taught Motherwell a hard lesson, but he learned it well. The *Minstrelsy* makes no further mention of fieldwork, but its editing reflects the understanding of balladry which the collector reached through his field experience.

Motherwell returned to Agnes Lyle on 25 September and secured a full text of "The Baffled Knight." The fact that he never collected—or at least never entered into the Manuscript—the broadside pieces indicates how clearly he now distinguished between older ballads and broadside texts such as these. Nevertheless, the titles and fragments in Motherwell's memoran dum, all that remain of nine songs out of thirty-two in Agnes Lyle's known repertoire, can not be ignored in any analysis of that repertoire.

"Johnie Armstrang" is doubtless "Johnie Armstrong" (Child 169). The spelling is Ramsey's. Motherwell repeats the title and spelling when he cites the Ramsey text (Child 169C) in the "Introduction" to the *Minstrelsy* (lxii). The ballad tells a tale of teachery in which the king invites Johnie to court, only to have him killed. The three Child versions use the King's Letter "theme" which Agnes Lyle uses in "Sir Patrick Spens," "Johnie Scot," and "Lord Derwentwater."

The song "Slippings o Yarn" has so far eluded identification. Clearly it is a weaving song, probably not the only weaving song in Agnes Lyle's repertoire. As a weaving song it provides a direct link between the repertoire and the Lyle family profession, and this is its principal significance. Fortunately the song traditions to which the other bits and pieces belong can be identified at least tentatively. Consequently, plot summaries can help supply the lack of full texts, while clues in the surviving stanzas can hint at particularities in this singer's treatment of these songs.

Motherwell himself identified "Fair Margaret of Craignargat," the first
title on the list, as "a common stall ballad sixty years ago." The notation
"got" is puzzling, for there is no text in the Manuscript. There is, however, a
full text printed in Charles Kirkpatrick's Sharpe's *A Ballad Book* (1823; 1976).
When Motherwell noted that he had "got" this piece, he may have meant
only that he had found the Sharpe text. This text tells in typical broadside
language the tale of a mother who dreams that a raven carries off her baby.
A wise woman tells her that the dream is a prophecy of unhappy love for the
child. When the child reaches marriageable age she passes over many suit-
able suitors to choose a young thief. She leaves with him, bearing her father's curse. The ship carrying the pair sinks, and the girl dies convinced that
her father's curse has been carried out. The ballad is unusual among ballads
of family opposition in that the opposition is justified. The catastrophe, too,
is unusual, relying as it does on coincidence rather than the evil machina-
tions of the unworthy bridegroom.

It is possible that the first fragment ("But sixteen years of age she was . . .)
represents Agnes Lyle's version of "Fair Margaret of Craignargat." The
phraseology, especially in the last line of each stanza, is reminiscent of that
of the Kirkpatrick Sharpe text, especially stanzas 1, 2, 20, and 25. If so, her
version is quite different from the stall copies and the memorized text which
Sharpe printed, despite the phraseological echoes. The long prologue is
missing, and the young man takes a more active role. It seems more likely,
therefore, that the fragment represents some one of the many songs about a
girl who loves indiscreetly and dies at the hands of her lover. There are several good candidates from this category, and the verbal parallels are even
more striking than those with "Fair Margaret." The first two lines of the
fragment, for instance, recall lines 7–8 of an American text of "The Perjured
Maid," also known as "The Gentleman of Exeter":

And at the age of sixteen years
She courted was by Lords and Peers.
(Henry 1938, 149)

The same sort of diction occurs in "The Ballad of the Ladies Fall":

Long was she woo'd e'er she was won
To lead a weeded life:
But folly wrought her overthrow
Before she was a Wife.

Too soon alas she gave consent
To yeeld unto his will.
(*Euing Collection* 1971, no. 196)

Perhaps the closest fit is "The Oxford Tragedy." The first five lines of the
fragment recall lines 13–16 of the contemporaneous Peter Buchan text:

> Her youthful heart to love inclined
> Young Cupid bent his golden bow
> And left his fatal dart behind
> Which prov'd Rosanna's overthrow.
>   (1891, 52)

The plot of the fragment too, so far as it can be guessed at, parallels that of "The Oxford Tragedy," but the parallel is not perfect. The Oxfordshire rogue must resort to threats of suicide to gain his wicked way and achieves the deed in kind while the erstwhile maid is in a swoon. The youth in Agnes Lyle's version needs nothing more than blandishments to achieve his ends, for the maid is only too ready to be deceived. But whatever ballad it represents, it clearly comes from a print tradition: the elaborate syntax—especially the use of the word *but* three times in seven lines, with two different meanings—and the sententious moralizing betray the pretensions of a broadside hack.

The second fragment, unlike the first, is easy to identify. "The Week Before Easter," or "The Forlorn Lover" as it is also known, has been popular throughout the documented history of English folk song. The Euing collection contains a broadside version from the late sixteenth or early seventeenth century (1971, no. 112). But even this early text bears evidence of previous circulation. Stanza 2 has lost the phrase "with oats," giving that stanza a rhyme scheme of *x a a b* instead of the regular scheme of *a a a b*, and a similar loss has occurred in stanza 5. Moreover, the final lines of many successive stanzas show a vestigial secondary rhyme scheme. The final lines of stanzas 1 and 2 rhyme *posies . . . roses;* stanzas 9, 10, and 11 rhyme *favour . . . ever . . . ever;* and stanzas 14, 15, and 16 rhyme *accuser . . . misuse her . . . abuser.* This rhyme scheme seems too consistent to be accidental, but too haphazard to be complete. Apparently the Euing text is an abbreviated and otherwise modified reprinting of an earlier and lengthier version in which stanzas were linked together by a pattern of rhymes in the final line of each stanza. It seems safe, therefore, to place the origins of the song somewhere in the sixteenth century.

Post-Euing printings show further effects of circulation. An eighteenth century broadside reduces the text to ten stanzas and eliminates the interlocking rhymes completely (*Roxburgh* 1966, 6: 233–235). Baring-Gould in the nineteenth century prints only six stanzas (Baring-Gould and Sheppard 1895, no. 97). Cecil Sharp, collecting in the early twentieth century, found three- and four-stanza versions in which the song, always more lyrical than narrative in tone, finally became almost pure lyric (1974, no. 59). Despite its continuing popularity in Great Britain the song has apparently not been collected in North America west of Newfoundland and has no Laws number (cf. Karpeles 1970, no. 31; Peacock 1965, 2: 441–442).

The situation in the song is clear enough. A young man has given his love to a girl who proves faithless. In a fit of masochism he forces himself to attend the wedding and watch all the details of the celebration. The usual last stanza, in which he prays to die and be buried, introduces the association of weddings with funerals which will come up over and over in the analysis of Agnes Lyle's ballads.

After these tales of faithless lovers it is a relief to turn to the third fragment ("A fair maid walking in a garden"). It is the first stanza of a classic tale of heroic fidelity. The ballad, variously known as "Pretty Fair Maid," "The Single Sailor," and "The Broken Token" (Laws N42), is widespread in both North America and the British Isles. The Cecil Sharp collection, for example, includes nine British versions (1974, no. 144). No early broadsides are known, however, and this fragment from Agnes Lyle seems to be the earliest record of the ballad. In the ballad a young man, usually a sailor or soldier, approaches a girl in a garden and asks her to marry him. She replies that she is already pledged to another, a man who has been gone for seven years now. In some versions, usually British, the man promises the girl riches if she will give up her old love, but she reasserts her fidelity. In other versions, usually North American, he suggests that her lover may be dead or even married to someone else, but she replies that if he is dead she will be true to his memory, and if he is married she wishes him happiness. In either case her intention is to marry no one else. Moved by her fidelity, the young man, in both British and North American versions, takes a love token—a ring or divided ring—from his pocket and reveals himself as the long-lost lover. In an ironic way this ballad too unites the leitmotifs of marriage and death spoken of before. But in its emphasis on fidelity and its provision of a happy ending it is unusual though not unique in the repertoire.

The fourth fragment ("There were two sailors were lonely walking") seems to belong to a comic ballad, "The Basket of Eggs." A Cecil Sharp text is remarkably similar:

> Three jolly sailors set out a-walking
> With their pockets lined with gold,
> As they were a-walking, so kindly a-talking
> Two lovely maidens they did behold.
> (Sharp 1974, 2:111)

The differences in numbers are immaterial, since one sailor and one girl are all that are involved in the subsequent plot. Agnes Lyle's phrase "cauler air" may even echo some vague aural memory of the word "gold" in the second line. In the ballad one of the sailors offers to carry a basket of eggs for one of the girls. She asks him to leave it at the inn if he walks ahead too fast for her to keep up. Arrived at the inn, the sailor thinks to treat himself to fried eggs but, uncovering the basket, discovers a baby. Of course it turns out to be his baby, and he is happily reunited with the girl he has seduced and abandoned but not forgotten. On the face of it, this would seem to be a cheery piece. But an Irish treatment of the motif is more cynical: The sailor, completely innocent, is left holding the basket (which he thinks contains a bottle of rye), and the girl disappears. Agnes Lyle, as will appear, is quite capable of darkening the usual tone of a ballad. "The Basket of Eggs," as the Irish treatment of the motif shows, offers possibilities for such an alteration.

The fifth fragment ("It was in the middle of fair July") illustrates the process of association so important in the transmission of folksongs. The stanza, though probably a ballad fragment, derives most of its diction from popular and broadside song. The first two lines are usually associated with "Two Rigs of Rye" (Laws o–11), about a man who, taking his constitutional on a July morning, overhears a pair of lovers. The boy, to test his sweetheart, declares he can not marry her because of parental opposition or some such obstacle. The girl expresses such genuine distress at the announcement that the boy, satisfied, promises to marry her. Four of the five versions of the song examined for this analysis begin with the same words as the Agnes Lyle fragment.[7] The fifth, from Gardner's Michigan collection, preserves only three lines of the first stanza, but one of these lines corresponds to the second line of all other versions and of the fragment. Despite these correspondences of diction, however, the Lyle fragment does not seem to fit with the plot of "Two Rigs of Rye," nor does the phrase "rigs of rye," or an equivalent, found in the first stanza of all five variants, appear in the fragment.

The third line of the fragment, with its "glint and a glancing eye," certainly has a formulaic ring, but it has resisted all efforts to match it to a parallel in any traceable folk song. Parallels to the fourth line, on the other hand, "Abroad as I was walking," are ubiquitous in British folksong and yet do not seem to occur in any songs which have the initial situation of this fragment. The phrase may have come to this song from "The Chain of Gold" (Sharp 1974, no. 80), which opens with two lines parallel in content to the first two lines of "Two Rigs of Rye" and which does include the phrase "Abroad as I was walking." The parallel with "Two Rigs of Rye" even extends to mention of parental hostility, but in "The Chain of Gold" the hostility is real, and the ballad ends tragically. Nevertheless it is possible that some singer familiar with both songs could have substituted the opening line of "The Chain of Gold" for the tag line of "Two Rigs of Rye."

If this is not a fragment of "Two Rigs of Rye," and certainly not of "The Chain of Gold," what song is it? A good candidate is "The Beggar-Laddie" (Child 280). The fragment preserves, in addition to the opening lines, the meter and rhyme scheme of "Two Rigs of Rye," suggesting that it is a song associated with that tune. Keith, in his discussion of "The Beggar Laddie," mentions " 'The Rigs o' Rye,' to the tune of which this ballad was sung" (1925, 228). Bronson confirms that the melodic tradition of "The Beggar-Laddie" is "perfectly distinct and unusually stable, and that this distinct and stable tradition is identical with the more popular of the tunes to which "The Two Rigs of Rye" is sung (Bronson 1959–1972, 4:250). The Child D text of "Beggar-Laddie" begins:

'T was in the pleasant month of June,
When woods and valleys a' grow green,
And valiant ladies walk alane,
    While Phoebus shines soe Clearly.

Out-ower yon den I spied a swain, *etc.*

The parallels with the fragment do not seem forced; the walk on a summer morning, the mention of the sun, and the glimpse of someone attractive. The fragment, then, may tentatively be identified as the first stanza of "Beggar-Laddie," sung as is traditional to the tune of "Two Rigs of Rye." This ballad tells the story of a girl who elopes with a beggar, learns to regret the hardship, but finally has cause to congratulate herself when her beggar reveals himself to be a great lord in disguise.

Agnes Lyle's fragment combines an introductory situation widespread in Anglo-Scottish balladry and song, a tune and two lines from "Two Rigs of Rye," and two additional formulaic lines, one of which may have been suggested by its occurrence in a somewhat similar song. The thread of associations which holds this stanza together provides an outstanding example of one of the basic compositional techniques of traditional ballad making.

The final item ("As I Went Out on a May Morning") seems oddly out of place—a Buckinghamshire local hunting song—and yet is in some ways the most exciting discovery among the fragments. It is a traditional reworking of a Stuart broadside text, "The Fox-chace or the Huntsman's Harmony by the Noble Duke of Buckingham's Hounds, etc." (*Roxburghe* 1966, 2: 360). Baring-Gould places the hunt in the reign of James I (1895, xxxvii), but Chappell (*Roxburghe* 1966, 1: 359, note) and Maude Karpeles (Sharp 1974, no. 267) each place the events in the reign of Charles II. The first record of the song, after the Stuart broadside, is this fragment collected from Agnes Lyle. Next, late in the nineteenth century, Baring-Gould collected it in Cornwall, and not long thereafter Sharp collected it right in Buckingham. This record is skimpy, but the wide geographical distribution and the persistence through nearly three hundred years would seem to indicate that the song has been more popular than the record reveals. Roger deV. Renwich, in *English Folk Poetry* (1980), mentions songs of this type and reasons why collectors have overlooked them:

The eminent Yorkshire collector, Frank Kidson, summed up the feelings of many people—including folksong collectors—when confronted with a local song pertinent only to a certain district. In his *Traditional Tunes* [1938, Oxford: Charles Taphouse], he printed but two stanzas of a North Riding hunting song, allowing a comment to fill in for the rest of the text: "I have no wish to inflict upon the readers more than two verses of this effusion. Like all songs of its class, it runs to about twenty verses, and the prowess of every fox-hunting squire and yeoman of the district is chronicled; highly interesting to those who know the descendants of the persons mentioned, but rather monotonous to the general reader."

Monotonous to the general reader, perhaps, but evidently not to the folk of the relevant district itself. (113–114)

The present song, however, has circulated far beyond its "relevant district." Furthermore, Agnes Lyle's repertoire as a whole is not particularly friendly to the squirearchy.[8] But Yorkshire, like Renfrewshire, was known for its handweaving. Renwick associates songs like this one with the Yorkshire weavers' penchant for poaching. Perhaps this item is all that remains of a similar lively hunting-song tradition in Renfrew. Both the Baring-Gould and the Sharp versions rework the catalog of dogs, which the Stuart broadside confines to one stanza, into a rollicking chorus:

> There was Dido, Spendigo,
> Gentry too, and Hero,
>> And Traveller that never looks behind him,
> Countess and Towler,
> Bonny-Lass and Jowler,
>> These were some of the hounds that did find him.
>> (Baring-Gould 1895, no. 81)

This jolly, convivial chorus surely deserves some of the credit for the broad enduring popularity of the song.

Like the preceding fragment this stanza from Agnes Lyle's version of "The Fox Chase" is remarkable as a demonstration of the recreative handling of broadside material in traditional fashion. The text derives ultimately from stanzas 1 and 2 of the broadside. It begins with a formulaic "As I walked out. . . . " It compresses the content of twelve lines into four. Finally, it shifts the meter from a rather elaborate six-line stanza to a more conventional four-line stanza with internal rhyme in the third line.

The six fragments and the one identifiable title all belong to broadside material. Even the text of "Beggar Laddie," if that is what the song is, has been shaped by a broadside hack at some point. Probably all the songs have more or less fixed texts, unlike the orally recreated pieces in the repertoire. And yet all show that the singer was no slave to any printed text. Taken line by line the fragments demonstrate varying degrees of reworking by a traditional singer or line of singers.

Twenty-two ballads, seven fragments (including the extra stanzas of "Geordie"), and three titles remain of the textual element of Agnes Lyle's repertoire. The musical element has not fared as well. In fact, a casual glance through Child might lead one to think that Agnes Lyle was not a singer at all. In the headnote of "Twa Sisters," the first Agnes Lyle ballad in *The English and Scottish Popular Ballads*, Child says, "From the recitation of Agnes Lyle, Kilbarchan." In the headnotes of "Babylon" and "Sheath and Knife" he says the same thing. The word *recitation* comes from the Manuscript, but by that word Motherwell seems to mean *oral performance*. Thirty years ago

William Montgomerie pointed out that a letter from Motherwell to his friend Robert A. Smith clarifies this usage:

> I have been long searching for some person who can *sing* the ballad of Jamie Douglas. A copy of this ballad you will find in Finlay's collection or as you may not get Finlay's book so readily you will find it in Gilchrist's ballads. Perhaps about Edinburg you may light on some one who *recites* it; hitherto in this quarter I have been unsuccessful. The reason I am so anxious to recover a *recited* copy is that I believe and have frequently been told that the *song* of "Waly Waly up yon bank" is part and portion of the same ballad but how incorporated some of my informers were uncertain others told me it was the concluding part of it. This is not improbable as you will find they assimilate in subject well, and their *tune* is the same. In one of my rambles lately . . . [I met a woman who] concurred in assuring me that she always *sang* and always had heard the ballad *sung* with Waly at the end. (1958, 154; italics added)

In the above letter Motherwell opposes a *recited* copy, obtained from oral performance or *recitation*, to a *printed* copy, obtained from a book such as Finlay or Gilchrist, and he implies that the *recitation* will have a tune, that is, it will be sung. Indeed he cites identity of tune between the ballad in question and the related song as a partial explanation of the peculiarity he would look for in a *recited* copy of the ballad.

In the case of Agnes Lyle there is really no doubt. In fact, Motherwell explicitly mentions her singing in the letter to Sharpe quoted above. At least two tunes have survived in transcriptions from her singing, and some other tunes can be identified as approximations of what she would have sung.

The two definite Agnes Lyle tunes are included among the 33 that Motherwell had fellow Paisley enthusiast Andrew Blaikie transcribe for the *Minstrelsy*. Because tunes had to be printed from engraved plates rather than from set type, Motherwell gathered these tunes into an appendix rather than affixing them to the ballads to which they fit. In each case, however, he provided a cross-reference, if one was appropriate, as well as printing the exact stanza to which the tune was sung. In emphasizing tunes as well as texts, in transcribing from some stanza other than the first, and in printing the exact stanza to which the tune fit, the Motherwell-Blaikie team was ahead of its time. The tunes from the appendix that can be assigned with confidence to Agnes Lyle texts are Tune IV to "Lord Derwentwater" and Tune XIX to "Lord William." Emily Lyle (1972) has succeeded in identifying many of the other Blaikie tunes with appropriate texts in the Motherwell and Crawfurd manuscripts. Of the eight orphan tunes in the *Minstrelsy*, Tune XXVI might be linked tentatively with Agnes Lyle's "Babylon," and Tune XIII even more tentatively with "Hind Horn." In addition, Motherwell left in his notes and Manuscript a few comments about musical aspects of her songs.[9] So few and so faint, these echoes can tell us little about Agnes Lyle the musician. But from time to time they can amplify the text and must be attended to.

Music is closely associated with metrics. In the case of Agnes Lyle's ballads, meter may be the single most important aesthetic element. Metrically, the ballads fall into four groups:

1. Ballads composed in quatrains of alternating four- and three-beat lines, with masculine rhyme *a b c b*, so-called ballad quatrains.
2. Ballads composed in couplets of four-beat lines with some sort of intertwining refrain.
3. Ballads composed in quatrains of alternating four- and three-beat lines, with feminine rhyme *a b c b*.
4. Ballads composed in quatrains of four-beat lines, with rhyme *a b c b*.[10]

Preliminary prospecting among these groups revealed a remarkable coincidence. The oral patterns discussed in the "Introduction," that is, the binary, trinary, and annular patterns of organization, and the formulaic and commonplace patterns of diction and narration, appeared in abundance in the ballads composed in ballad stanzas. But they appeared less consistently in the ballads composed in couplets or feminine-rhymed stanzas. They appeared not at all in the two ballads composed in four-beat quatrains. This remarkable pattern has suggested the basic hypothesis of the present study: The consistent way in which Agnes Lyle uses oral techniques in the standard quatrain ballads, that is, her consistent oral style, indicates that she is indeed an orally recreative, or oral-formulaic ballad singer, one whose technique depends heavily on the standard quatrain. When she sings as an orally recreative ballad singer in other meters, the strain of working in a less congenial medium shows in inconsistent technique. Finally, in singing certain songs she does not use orally recreative technique at all. She sings them instead from memory.

Determining the orality of a repertoire is really a two-step process—and of course even then the determination can not be definitive. One must first determine that in style and technique the repertoire exhibits internal consistency—in the present case, consistency in its inconsistency. Then one must demonstrate that the repertoire is distinctive of and appropriate to a single singer in a single time and place. Part Two of this study deals with the question of stylistic consistency. Stylistic success is always the result of a precarious balance of forces in the oral architectonic of the ballad. Chapter 3 will look at the standard quatrain ballads, in which that balance is constant, in order to highlight the basic forces at work in Agnes Lyle's style. Chapter 4 will look at ballads in which at least one factor is always upsetting the balance. In couplet ballads the factor is uncongenial meter, and the singer has to compensate, with varying degrees of success. In feminine-rhyme quatrain ballads, not only does the singer have to deal with an uncongenial meter, but in each case there is a further complicating factor for her to handle. Chapter 5 will look at ballads in which, despite complicating factors, she has achieved notable aesthetic success, suggesting why this should be so. Part Three will deal with the question of whether these assembled versions exhibit characteristics of a single controlling personality. Chapters 6 and 7 will show how Agnes Lyle's distinctive treatment of two ballad leitmotifs, love and perfidy, is characteristic of this daughter of a weaver, singing in southwestern Scotland in the mid-1820s.

PART TWO

The Ballads of Agnes Lyle
Technique

THREE

The Weaver's Daughter Sings

Agnes Lyle's collected repertoire includes ten pieces in standard ballad meter. These ten pieces reveal the singer at her most competent, consistent, and controlled. They demonstrate her technique of traditional patterning on all levels of articulation, from phoneme to piece. In particular, they demonstrate her exploitation of traditional rhyme, alliteration, and assonance, her reliance on formulaic diction at the levels of phrase, line, stanza, and stanza cluster, and her achievement of organization through the annular, binary, and trinary principles of the Western oral aesthetic (see Introduction). There are other ballads in which Agnes Lyle is more than competent, consistent, and controlled, in which she transcends her technique. But understanding how she transcends her technique requires a precise understanding of what her technique is, based on detailed analysis of some of those ballad quatrain pieces in which her technique is most clear.

"Johnie Scot" (Child 99G)

1   Johnie Scott's a hunting gone,
      To England woods so wild,
    Until the king's old dochter dear
      She goes to him with child.

2   "If she be with bairn," her mother says,
      "As I trew weel she be,
    We'll put her in a dark dungeon,
      And hunger her till she die."

3   "If she be with bairn," her father says,
      "As oh forbid she be!
    We'll put her in a prison strong,
      And try the veritie."

4   The king did write a long letter,
      Sealed it with his own hand,
    And he sent it to Johnie Scot,
      To speak at his command.

5 When Johnie read this letter long,
   The tear blindit his ee:
"I must away to Old England;
   King Edward writes for me."

6 Out and spak his mother dear,
   She spoke aye in time:
Son, if thou go to Old England,
   I fear thou'll neer come hame.

7 Out and spoke a Scotish prince,
   And a weel spoke man was he:
Here's four and twenty o my braw troops,
   To bear thee companie.

8 Away they gade, awa they rade,
   Away they rade so slie;
There was not a married man that day
   In Johnie's companie.

9 The first good town that they passed thro,
   They made their bells to ring;
The next good town that they passed thro,
   They made their music sing.

10 The next gude town that they passed thro,
   They made their drums beat round,
The king and a' his gay armies
   Admiring at the sound.

11 When they came to the king's court,
   They travelled round about,
And there he spied his own true-love,
   At a window looking out.

12 "O fain wald I come down," she says,
   "Of that ye needna dout;
But my garters they're of cauld, cauld iron,
   And I can no win out.

13 "My garters they're of cauld, cauld iron,
   And it is very cold;
My breast-plate is of sturdy steel,
   Instead o beaten gold."

14 Out and spoke the king himsell,
   And an angry man was he:
The fairest lady in a' my court,
   She goes with child to thee.

15 "If your old doughter be with child,
   As I trew weel she be,
I'le make it heir of a' my land,
   And her my gay lady."

16 "There is a Talliant in my court,
   This day he's killed three;
And gin the morn by ten o'clock
   He'll kill thy men and thee."

17 Johnie took sword into his hand,
   And walked cross the plain;
There was many a weeping lady there,
   To see young Johnie slain.

18 The Talliant never knowing this,
   Now he'll be Johnie's dead,
But, like unto a swallow swift,
   He flew out owre his head.

19 Johnie was a valliant man,
   Weel taught in war was he,
And on the point of his broad sword
   The Talliant stickit he.

20 Johnie took sword into his hand,
   And walked cross the plain:
Are there here any moe of your English dogs
   That's wanting to be slain?

21 "A priest, a priest," young Johnie cries,
   "To wed my bride and me;"
"A clerk, a clerk," her father cries,
   "To tell her tocher wi."

22 "I'm wanting none of your gold," he says,
   "As little of your gear;
But give me just my own truelove,
   I think I've won her dear."

23 Johnie sets horn into his mouth,
   And he blew loud and schrill:
The honour it's to Scotland come,
   Sore against England's will.

Agnes Lyle's "Johnie Scot" belongs to a line in the tradition of this ballad which has usually been ignored. In her version Johnie does not know of his true-love's plight, nor of the king's anger. Indeed, he may not even be aware that his beloved is the king's daughter. The king writes a moving—and treacherous—letter asking for Johnie's services. With tears in his eyes Johnie hastens to obey the summons. Drawing near the court he spies his true-love in a high window. Overjoyed, he asks her to come down, but of course she can not. She is a prisoner. Among the many tales of treachery in the repertoire, this one is unique in the glorious outcome of events. Perhaps the special glee the singer took in singing it accounts for the text's absolute perfection of annular, binary, and trinary structure on every level.

DIAGRAM 1

Stanzaic and Tonal Structure of "Johnie Scot"

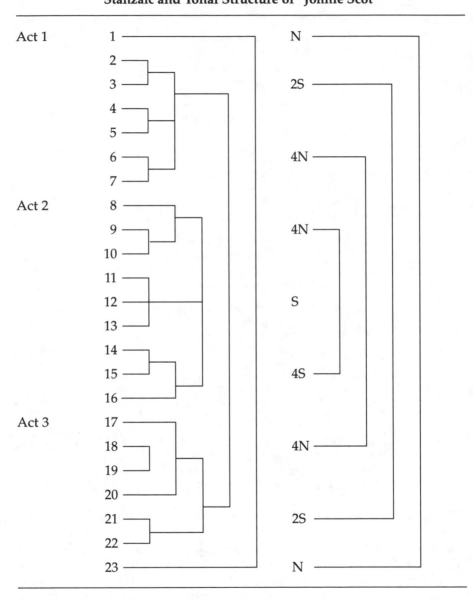

The easiest place to see the annular forces at work organizing a piece such as this one is in the act and stanza structures (Diagram 1). Classic ballads, such as those of Agnes Lyle, tend to focus on individual scenes, with very little transition between scenes ("leaping and lingering").[1] This technique produces an over-all dramatic structure which can be analyzed in terms of acts, as David Buchan has done. Within the acts the narrative technique is stanzaic. That is to say, action moves stanza by stanza. As the diagram makes clear, the repertoire text of "Johnie Scot" is overwhelmingly annular in its act and stanza structure. The piece falls into three acts of 7, 9, and 7 stanzas respectively. Stanzas 1 and 23 frame the intervening stanzas. Stanzas 2–7 balance stanzas 17–22, though the internal pattern of 17–22 counterpoints rather than duplicates the pattern of 2–7; stanzas 2–7 form a triad of balances (pairs of adjacent stanzas), with two of the balances forming a further balance, while stanzas 17–22 form a framed balance and a balance. The central 9 stanzas form three groups of three, but the outside groups of three are composed of a singlet and a balance each, whereas the middle group is a triad. Moreover, as annular technique dictates, stanzas 8–10 are mirrors of 14–16, rather than parallels. That is to say, in 8–10 the singlet comes before the balance, and in 14–16 it follows. The stanzaic structure of this ballad, then, exhibits annular organization overall, in the framing function of the first and last stanzas, and in the internal structure of Act II.

In "Johnie Scot" the tonal structure reinforces the stanzaic structure. The framing stanzas are narrative. The pattern of two speech and four narrative stanzas in Act I is mirrored in the pattern of four narratives followed by two speech stanzas in Act III. The central act is divided as evenly as nine stanzas can be divided, with four narrative stanzas balancing five speech stanzas. The extra speech stanza is the pivotal stanza 12, the precise turning point in the ballad, in which Johnie learns that he has been tricked and that his true love is in chains.

In a ballad as complex as "Johnie Scot" it is sometimes difficult to be sure what constitutes the essential narrative structure. But on this level too there does seem to be an annular principle at work (Diagram 2). As has been pointed out, the pivotal point in the narrative structure is the exact center of the ballad, when Johnie is disabused.

Examination of the character structure reveals that the ballad is built around three encounters between hero and heroine, at the beginning, middle, and end of the ballad (Diagram 3). This structure, though rather diffuse, mirrors the stanzaic and narrative structures closely. Most of the Lyle ballads are not so relentless in their congruence on various levels of analysis.

Analysis of the annular patterns in the stanzaic structure serves as well to bring out the binary organization of the ballad. "Johnie Scot," in fact, illustrates nearly all of the pairing techniques that Agnes Lyle relies upon. Stanzas 2 and 3 form a balance paired by incremental repetition, the fifth type in Andersen's typology (see Introduction). This type is incremental, or "progressive," as Andersen prefers to dub it, because in the succeeding stanza(s)

DIAGRAM 2
Narrative Structure of "Johnie Scot"

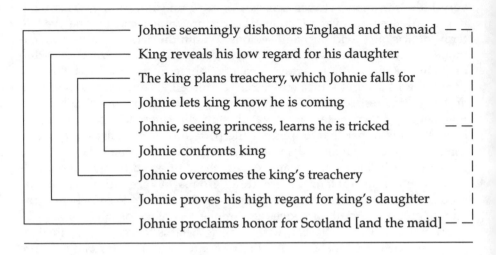

Johnie seemingly dishonors England and the maid

King reveals his low regard for his daughter

The king plans treachery, which Johnie falls for

Johnie lets king know he is coming

Johnie, seeing princess, learns he is tricked

Johnie confronts king

Johnie overcomes the king's treachery

Johnie proves his high regard for king's daughter

Johnie proclaims honor for Scotland [and the maid]

DIAGRAM 3
Character Structure in "Johnie Scot"

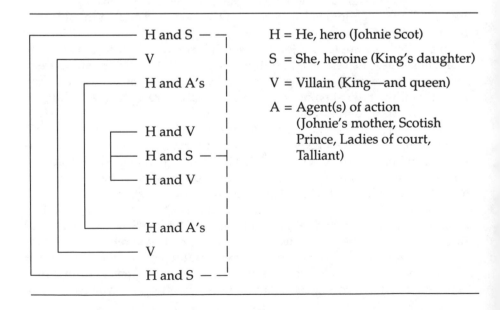

H and S

V

H and A's

H and V

H and S

H and V

H and A's

V

H and S

H = He, hero (Johnie Scot)

S = She, heroine (King's daughter)

V = Villain (King—and queen)

A = Agent(s) of action
(Johnie's mother, Scotish
Prince, Ladies of court,
Talliant)

the plot progresses beyond the point at which it has stood in the precedent stanza. Thus, stanza 3 is modelled on stanza 2, but substitutes "king" for "queen". The plot progression, in this case, is minimal, but measurable: the king decides not to kill the girl but rather to entrap her lover.

Stanzas 4 and 5 unfold his trick and its success. These stanzas are paired by a binary principle which might be called action-reaction. In 4 the king writes a long letter, and in 5 Johnie reacts to that long letter. This stanza also includes a minor example of Andersen's second type of repetition, the causative. Line 1 of stanza 5 is determined not only in action but even in diction by line 1 of stanza 4. The action in the rest of the stanza is a response to the action in stanza 4, but there is no verbal repetition. In stanzas paired by action-reaction, as distinguished from stanzas paired by causative repetition, the action of the succeeding stanza is caused by the action of the precedent stanza. On the level of wording or diction, however, the two stanzas are independent and substantially different.

Stanzas 6 and 7 provide a second example of progressive or incremental repetition. Stanza 6 presents the misgivings of Johnie's mother. Stanza 7 moves the plot forward by providing Johnie with a troop of horsemen to ride with him. Because this example, like the example of stanzas 2–3, is only two stanzas long, rather than three, it does not provide the sense of "lingering" over the scene that Andersen usually finds characteristic of incremental repetition. It does, however, manage to create the characteristic suspense about what is to come next.

The repetition in stanzas 9 and 10 is essentially static ("The first gude town . . . The next good town . . . The next gude [sic] town"), as in emphatic repetition, Andersen's first type. Making drums beat in the third repetition does not move the plot beyond making bells ring in the first. The word *emphatic* describes the effect precisely. The last two lines of stanza 10, however, indicate that the retinue has arrived at London. That *is* progress.

Action and reaction unite stanzas 18 and 19. The Talliant attacks Johnie; Johnie kills the Talliant.[2] The framing stanzas 17 and 20 provide an example of narrative repetition, Andersen's third type. In 17 Johnie strides out, the presumed victim. In 20 he strides back, the proven hero. The irony of presenting a situation and its reversal in language which is as nearly as possible identical must have delighted singer and listener alike.

An unusual annular pattern unites stanzas 21–22. In 21 Johnie calls for a priest to give him his bride, and the king calls for a clerk to tell Johnie the tocher. In 22 Johnie, taking up the two in reverse order, rejects the tocher and calls again for his bride.

Repetition of one sort or another is obviously the most common way that binary organization is achieved. This version of "Johnie Scot" offers examples of pairings based on emphatic, causative, narrative, and progressive (incremental) repetition. Andersen's remaining type of repetition, recurrent (which he places fourth), involves two or more occurrences within the text but independent of each other. Obviously this type can not form pairs and

balances. Andersen considers it the most common of the five types, however, and "Johnie Scot" includes at least two examples. The first is found at
the beginning of stanza 14:

> Out and spoke the king himsell,
> And an angry man was he,

which echoes the beginning of stanza 7 (itself an echo of stanza 6):

> Out and spoke a Scotish prince
> And a weel spoke man was he.

The second example, involves stanza 14 again, stanza 15, and stanzas 1
and 2. When Johnie comes to court, the first two stanzas of the scene describing his encounter with the king closely echo the first two stanzas of the
ballad. Stanza 14 repeats the substance of stanza 1 and ends with formulaic
reworking of the final line of that stanza. Stanza 15 begins with an ironic
echo of stanza 2.

> "If she be with bairn," her mother says,
> "As I trew weel she be,"

becomes:

> "If your old doughter be with child,
> As I trew weel she be."

The mother continues:

> "We'll put her in a dark dungeon,
> And hunger her till she die."

Johnie, however, pledges:

> "I'll make it [the child] heir of a' my land,
> And her my gay lady."

The ironic repetition, as in stanzas 17 and 20, serves to emphasize the contrast. Furthermore, recurrent repetition here, while not creating a stanzaic
pair or balance, does contribute to an overall binary organization alongside
of and counterpointing the trinary act structure. This repetition, this echo,
not found precisely in any other collected text, is an example of the kind of
control Agnes Lyle exercises at her most competent.

Because framing creates rings or frames by pairing, it is a binary as well
as an annular principle. Accordingly, Agnes Lyle's technique seems to allow
counting the four stanzas of a framed balance as the metrical equivalent of
the four stanzas of a pair of balances. "Lord Derwentwater," discussed in
the introduction, exemplifies this pattern in stanzas 1–4 and 9–12. In the

present ballad, stanzas 17–20 coordinate with stanzas 4–7 in an annular pattern that matches the three balances of stanzas 2–7 with a framed balance and a balance in stanzas 17–22 (see diagram 1).

The first and last stanzas of "Johnie Scot" are likewise paired by framing, as Diagram 2 makes clear, even though there is no verbal repetition. In the first stanza shame is implied. In the last stanza honor is proclaimed. In the first stanza Johnie goes hunting in England. In the last stanza he returns to Scotland with his prize. In the first stanza he secretly impregnates the girl. In the last stanza he openly celebrates his bridal with the blast of a horn.

The horn itself likewise frames the ballad even though it is not explicitly mentioned in the first stanza. This first stanza seems to represent a more or less regional variation found only in this text, in Mrs. Thomson's Kilbarchan text (99C), in two Paisley texts (99Da and b), and in one text (99L) from the Campbell MS of border county ballads. The stanza is formed by compressing a widespread commonplace and the 3-stanza incipit which is almost standard for the ballad into a single quatrain. The incipit is discussed below, in connection with "Mary Hamilton." The commonplace in question runs thus in the form in which Agnes Lyle realizes it more completely, at the beginning of "Earl Richard":

> Earl Richard has a hunting gone,
>   As fast as he can ride
> He's a hunting-horn about his neck
>   And a broadsword by his side.

One advantage the singer gains by using a commonplace is that the audience, once it has heard the first line or two, can supply the rest of the stanza from its own memory, leaving the singer free to skip to something else. Economy of language is thus secured. In the present case the audience, having supplied the horn at the beginning of the ballad, is ready to hear it blow at the end. Agnes Lyle's tightly compressed incipit has the further artistic advantage of setting up the recurrent repetition in stanza 14, already discussed.

The trinary organization of the ballad exhibits the same forms of repetition as the binary but also exhibits some features peculiar to itself. The first and most obvious trinary pattern is the three-act structure. This is also the most arbitrary and "intuitive" pattern. Nevertheless, analysis into three acts does seem to make good sense in most of Agnes Lyle's ballads. And the clear stanza structure which surfaces when these act divisions are posited confirms the basic validity of the intuition.

In "Johnie Scot" the action falls into three fairly clear divisions. Stanzas 1–7 depict Johnie's summons to England, including the reason for the summons, Johnie's straightforward but naive reaction, and the more canny reactions of those about him. Stanzas 8–16 bring Johnie from Scotland to England and indicate what he found there. In these middle stanzas the reversal of appearances which is apparent to the singer and her audience, and suspected by the mother and Scottish prince, becomes evident to Johnie. Similarly, Johnie's noble attitude toward the pregnancy is a reversal of the ignoble royal attitude. The final seven stanzas contain the great scene in which Johnie defeats the king's champion (a kind of counter-reversal) and claims the princess for his bride.

On the act level the stanzaic structure also reveals trinary organization. The first act (disregarding the prologue) is organized around three balances. This is a fairly common pattern in the repertoire, reappearing, for example, in "Mary Hamilton," "Little Musgrave," "Sir Patrick Spens," "Babylon," and, in equivalent form, in the third act of this very ballad. Indeed, the longer acts in the repertoire generally preserve some kind of trinary structure. Act II of this ballad, for instance, though longer than Act I, preserves the trinary division by expanding the primary stanza groups from pairs to triads. As with balances, the principle of unity at work in these triads is not the same in every case. Admittedly, each of the three triads is unified by subject matter: the triad 8–10 describes the journey, the next triad describes the meeting with the princess, and the third describes the meeting with the king. The internal consistency of each triad, however, goes beyond mere unity of action.

In the first triad stanza 8 is an introduction to the balance formed by 9 and 10. In the balance, a triple repetition, largely static, is distributed over six lines, leaving the final two lines of the second stanza free for additional matter. Thus, in 9 and 10, trinary and binary organization overlap or counterpoint each other, as they do when this two-stanza formulaic cluster occurs three other times in the repertoire.

The middle triad in the act, and the exact middle of the annular pattern as well, subsumes a different sort of binary pattern. Stanza 12 serves a double function, relating to stanza 11 in action and to stanza 13 in diction. It forms a balance with the preceding stanza as answer to the question implied therein, and as reaction to Johnie's action of looking up. It forms a balance with the following stanza through repetition and through identity of speaker. The repetition in stanza 13 is based on lines 3 and 4 of 12, while lines 1 and 2 look more to stanza 11. Hence, the triad could be diagrammed as follows:

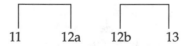

This pattern too will be met in other ballads.

The third triad is a mirror image of the first, though the internal principles at work are not the same. In 14 and 15 an exchange that echoes the diction of the first two stanzas of the ballad occurs between the king and

Johnie. In 16 the king springs his trap. This triad, incidentally, is also united by the rather unusual reliance on a single rhyme, *ee*.

Trinary patterns are not nearly as common on other levels of analysis as they are on the stanzaic. But this ballad, like one other in the repertoire, "Lord William," includes an important trinary feature in the character structure (see diagram). Hero and heroine meet only three times in this ballad, in the first stanza, in the middle three stanzas, and in the final stanza. The intervening stanzas are used first to draw up the lines of opposition and set the trap and then to spring the trap and bring opponents face to face.

In "Johnie Scot," as in all the quatrain ballads, the annular, binary, and trinary patterns form a rhetoric, enabling the singer to organize her piece on all levels of articulation from half stanza up. And immersion in this rhetoric creates a system of rhetorical expectations in the traditional audience, helping it to follow the ballad storyline. Because of the highly compressed nature of the art of balladry, the audience finds very little redundancy in a ballad, and so needs this special skill to follow a singer as she weaves tune and text into a story. "Johnie Scot," for example, tells a moderately complex story, though generally the divisions of scene and action are marked clearly enough:

> Johnie Scott's to England . . .
> The king's old dochter dear goes to him with child . . .
> Her mother says . . .
> Her father [the king] says . . .
> The king did write a long letter . . .
> When Johnie read this letter . . .
> "I must away . . . "
> Spak his mother . . .
> Spoke a Scotish Prince, "Here's Four and twenty o my braw
>   troops . . . "
> Away they gade . . .
> When they came to the king's court . . .
> He spied his own true-love . . .
> She says . . .
> Out and spoke the king . . .
> "Gin the morn by ten o'clock . . . "
> *Johnie took sword . . .
> The Talliant stickit he . . .
> "A priest, a priest," young Johnie cries . . .
> Johnie sets horn . . .

The asterisk marks the one ambiguous transition in the narrative. The action of taking sword in hand and walking across the plain, while the women weep, could easily be taken as some kind of immediate response on Johnie's part to the king's threat. Nothing in this stanza tells the audience that a night has passed and all have gathered for the tournament. But for the skillful audience there are hints. The annular trinary structure of Act II will have prepared such an audience for the narrative change of direction at precisely this point. The sudden shift away from the *ee* rhymes of the last triad will confirm that change—a welcome bit of redundancy. In this way a subliminal sensitivity to the structuring principles of ballad rhetoric helps the experienced and skillful audience follow the singer.

It would obviously be tedious to analyze text after text with the kind of minute attention to detail here lavished on "Johnie Scot". But equally obviously, one example does not prove a case. Further examples can strengthen the case, show aspects of this singer's technique not exemplified by the first example, bring out the expressive range of the technique, and help allay fears that this kind of analysis implies a monolithic technique for engendering mechanical and bloodless texts.

Certainly it would take a hardhearted person to call Agnes Lyle's "Mary Hamilton" bloodless, or even mechanical, though it is extremely well constructed, and many of the stanzas have close formulaic affinity with stanzas elsewhere in the repertoire.

Like "Johnie Scot," "Mary Hamilton" easily divides into three acts, which might be titled "Mary and the Queen," "Mary and the Burghers," and "Mary on the Gallows." Stanzas 1–3 form a pure prologue, without dialogue, the longest such incipit in the repertoire.

> 1   There were ladies, they lived in a bower,
>   And oh but they were fair!
> The youngest o them is to the king's court,
>   To learn some unco lair.
>
> 2   She hadna been in the king's court
>   A twelve month and a day,
> Till of her they could get na wark
>   For wantonness and play.
>
> 3   Word is to the kitchen gane,
>   And word is to the ha,
> And word is up to Madame the Queen,
>   And that is warst of a',
> That Mary Hamilton has born a bairn,
>   To the hichest Stewart of a'.

These stanzas imply a characteristic irony: Mary has come to the king's court as to a school of wisdom, and there the king teaches her supreme folly. But by the end of the ballad she has acquired wisdom and concomitant stature. In stanza 22 the king offers her pardon and food. The initial stanzas of other versions (Child D, E, F, J, U, W, Y, and BB) attribute Mary's downfall to the corrupting influence of rich meat, bread, wine, spices, and so on. Even the present prologue has a reminder of food in the mention of kitchen and hall. But now Mary, in her new-found wisdom, rejects the king's double

offer and rebukes him for his folly. Though a continuation of the scene on
the gallows, this episode is in effect a kind of epilogue.

> 22 By and cum the king himsell,
>   Lookd up with a pitiful ee:
>   "Come down, come down, Mary Hamilton,
>   This day thou wilt dine with me."
>
> 23 "Hold your tongue, my sovereign leige,
>   And let your folly be;
>   An ye had a mind to save my life,
>   Ye should na shamed me here."

Prologue and epilogue, united by motifs of luxury, royalty, and folly, frame
the three intensely dramatic scenes that lie between.

The first scene or act is composed of three pairs of stanzas, the narrative
proceeding by incremental repetition. Stanzas 4, 6, and 8 follow a common
model, but by changes of wording move the plot forward. Stanzas 5, 7, and
9, in answering these three stanzas, eschew repetition. Stanza 5 answers 4
with false words:

> "It was a shouir o sad sickness
>   Made me weep sae bitterlie."

Stanza 7 answers 6 with true words:

> "I put it [the sweet babe] in a piner pig,
>   And set it on the sea."

And 9 answers 8 with action.

> She put not on her black clothing,
>   She put not on her brown,
> But she put on the glistering gold,
>   To shine thro Edinburgh town.

The progression from false words to true words to action is noteworthy. Presumably the action in stanza 9 expresses the deepest truth of all. At any rate,
Mary's response to the announcement of her execution is to dress for the
occasion.

Act II, describing a judicial procession not unlike the one which accompanied the trials of 1820, is also composed of balanced stanzas. The incremental repetition is not so strong as in Act I. Stanza 12 changes the pitying
bailie's wife of stanza 10 to *bailie's son,* a non-incremental change, since it
does not advance the plot. But this stanza also changes *Edinburgh town,* of
stanza 10 to *Tolbuith stair,* an incremental change indicating that Mary is
being incarcerated. Stanza 13, however, simply repeats stanza 11, with no
change at all:

> "Gie never alace for me," she said,
> "Gie never alace for me!
> It's all for the sake of my puir babe,
> This death that I maun die."

Act III takes place on the gallows. As in "Johnie Scot," the transition from Act II is weakly marked. The connective *"But"* could easily link the following action in time and place with the preceding; the abandonment of the unified diction and treatment which prevail in Act II is all the listener has to go on. This final scene, like the first two, proceeds by a series of balances. But incremental repetition, attenuated in Act II, is now eliminated entirely. The second member of each balance simply restates the idea of the first in the static form of repetition that Andersen dubs emphatic, as in the following example:

> 17   "Little did my mother think,
>   First time she cradled me,
>   What land I was to travel on,
>   Or what death I would die.
>
> 18   "Little did my mother think,
>   First time she tied my head,
>   What land I was to tread upon,
>   Or whare I would win my bread."

Narrative progression is confined to the two framing stanzas which likewise serve to enhance and enlarge the scene. The mood created by this series of statements and restatements is quiet and reflective.

The tone changes abruptly in stanza 22. The unwary listener may even expect that Mary, who now evokes pity and even admiration, not repugnance, is to be reprieved. But such is not the case. Mary realizes that king and court have nothing to offer her, and she wisely refuses to reinvolve herself. The story is over. This final half-scene, as already indicated, is but an epilogue, harkening back to the prologue and tying the ballad together.

The placing of this half-scene is the result of several forces at work in the ballad. First, it makes a final comment on topics first touched on in the opening of the ballad, and in doing so it expresses the annular principle on a conceptual level. Second, it expresses a need or at least a preference on Agnes Lyle's part to end a song with an angry denunciation. "Mary Hamilton" is but one of many ballads in the corpus in which characters become involved with their betters only to find in the moment of crisis that they have been abandoned. Mary has been the king's mistress, but the king, making no provision for her, leaves her to solve for herself the problem of her pregnancy. Mary is also the queen's special maid, even washing the queen's feet, but the queen has her executed. Mary's final speech, however, like the final speeches in "Gypsy Laddie," "The Eastmure King," "Fair Janet," and many other pieces in the repertoire, gives the wronged party the last word, a word of bitter and ironic reproach. Third, the scene serves to bring on stage the third character of the drama, the king. In English and Scottish romantic ballads the deep character structure, like other structures, usually observes the rule of three, focusing on two sexual partners and a third oppositional figure. This rule of three is not always obeyed by Agnes Lyle, but it does seem to exert an influence. In this ballad a certain built-in irony enhances the character structure. None of the characters quite fit the standard roles. Mary, who plays the heroine role, starts out as a bit of a slut, though she grows in dignity as the song progresses. The queen is the closest thing to villain, but surely she has some reason to feel aggrieved. The king is the heroine's lover but hardly a hero. The audience expects three characters, but after 21 stanzas only two have come on stage. Tension and suspense is achieved by playing on the rhetorical expectations associated with the standard character structure of romantic ballads. The appearance of the king resolves that suspense and prepares the audience for a further resolution—the rescuing of Mary. But she has grown in strength and heroism and refuses such an easy solution.

Finally, the half-scene is here because it has been forced out of an earlier place in the story by the strong 3-2-3 annular pattern dividing the stanzaic structure into three acts, and especially by the binary principles governing the internal structure of each of these acts. In reliance on paired stanzas as the main narrative vehicle in all three acts, "Mary Hamilton" is the most binary of all the standard quatrain ballads in the repertoire. A total of nineteen stanzas (including stanza 23, which is a variation of stanza 5) out of twenty-three are members of balances, frames, or repetitions of one sort or another. This extraordinary formalism gives the ballad a sense of restraint and dignity which underlines the tragic horror of the story.

A ballad that relies so much on doubling will exhibit many formulaic relationships among its stanzas, but "Mary Hamilton" shares formulaic relationships with other Agnes Lyle ballads as well. The establishment of this type of relationship among lines and stanzas from different ballads is important. In the first place it helps confirm that the corpus is a single repertoire and not a collection of texts that Agnes Lyle memorized from a variety of singers, broadsides, or chapbooks. In the second place, it helps clarify how her oral recreative technique works. As might be expected, most of the parallels are with other ballad-quatrain pieces. But these parallels are not simply verbal repetitions. The second stanza can illustrate the point:

> She hadna been in the king's court
> A twelve month and a day,
> Till of her they could get na wark
> For wantonness and play.

This stanza parallels, among others, the third stanza of "Fair Janet":

> They had not sailed one league, one league,
> One league but only three,

> Till sharp, sharp showers fair Janet took,
>   She grew sick and like to die.

On the level of diction only five repetitions occur: *hadna* (written *had not* the second time), *till, she, and,* and *they.* The last three of these are merely coincidental. Only the first two are significant, articulating as they do the deep structure of the two stanzas, which is identical in the two stanzas, and can be expressed thus:

> line 1: something positive does not progress more than
> line 2: a certain distance in time or space
> line 3: before [*till*] something negative surfaces
> line 4: and proves even worse (here, unwanted pregnancy).[3]

This deep structure may properly be called a formula, a recipe for composing a stanza, just as the recipe for what goes into a baby's bottle may be called a formula. Each stanza in question, too, may properly be called a formula, composed as it is according to the recipe, just as the fluid mixed according to a prescribed recipe and put into a baby's bottle is called a formula. The recipe is one that Agnes Lyle uses at "Eastmure King" 15, in a positive inversion at "Sir Patrick Spens" 2, and several other times in "Fair Janet," as well as in the quoted "Mary Hamilton" stanza. "Fair Janet" 19, for instance, is a particularly close parallel, the principal difference being that in the final line of 19 the something worse is death from overexertion too soon after childbirth:

> She hadna danced the floor once owre,
>   I'm sure she hadna thrice,
> Till she fell in a deadly swound,
>   And from it neer did rise.

Stanza 10 and the first four lines of six-line stanza 15 are other examples:

> Fair Janet was nae weel lichter,
>   Nor weel doun on her side,
> Til ben and cam her father dear,
>   Saying, Wha will busk our bride?
>   . . . .
> Supper scarslie was owre,
>   Nor musick weel fa'n to,
> Till ben and cam the bride's brethren,
>   Saying, Bride, ye'll dance wi me.

The last two lines of these stanzas from "Fair Janet" form a subformula used independently in stanzas 11, 16, and 17 of the ballad as well as in stanza 22 of "Mary Hamilton." Indeed, "Fair Janet" 11–13, "Mary Hamilton" 4–9, and "Mary Hamilton" 22–23, seem to belong to a stanza cluster or "theme" in which the deep structure is even deeper and freer of determined diction than in the formulas considered thus far. The elements seem to be:

a. "Ben and cam" someone
b. who asks a question or gives an order
c. involving physical ascent or descent
d. and is rebuked for folly
e. and given an explanation.

In "Mary Hamilton" 4 the line "ben and cam Madame the Queen" (cf. Child A, C, D, E, K, L, and M, to cite only texts with connections to Motherwell or Renfrewshire) has been suppressed for reasons of structure and balance, but the "tension" of its "essence" can be felt, especially in the rebuke of the queen for "folye." At this same point there is a triple order to rise up, followed twice by questions and once by an order. In "Fair Janet" 11 there are two questions, only the second of which pertains to ascent, in this case to a horse's back. The repeated question allows the "theme" to be expanded by a double rebuke and explanation in "Fair Janet"— repetition which is emphatic as well as incremental—and by ever more truthful responses in "Mary Hamilton."

On the level of line and couplet, as on the level of stanza and stanza-cluster, the formulaic diction of "Mary Hamilton" is widely echoed in the repertoire. Some samples:

> Some unco lair to learn ("Lord William" 1b)
> Word is to the city gone / And word is to the town
>   ("Eastmure King" 12a–b)
> Rise, oh rise, my bonnie Jeanie Faw / Oh rise and
>   do not tarry ("Gypsy Laddie" 11a–b)
> O hold your hand, you minister ("Lord William" 15a)
> As he came in by Stirling town ("Geordie" 5a)

The list could be extended to several times this length by citing multiple occurrences of these formulas and adding others.

In "Mary Hamilton" Agnes Lyle uses her formulaic resources with great freedom. The first stanza of the incipit, for example, is echoed in the openings of "Twa Sisters" and "Babylon," and the other two stanzas, as has been shown, are echoed elsewhere in the repertoire. All three stanzas are likewise echoed widely in the "Mary Hamilton" tradition. But the particular configuration of this incipit is unique in both Agnes Lyle's repertoire and the "Mary Hamilton" tradition. The singer seems to have imported it from the "Johnie Scot" tradition. Child 99I, from the Kinloch Mss., provides an especially striking parallel (but cf. the K and M texts):

> Johnie is up to London gane,
>   Three quarters o the year,
> And he is up to London gane
>   The king's banner for to bear.

> He had na been in fair London
> A twalmonth and a day,
> Till the king's ae daughter
> To Johnie gangs wi child.
>
> O word is to the kitchen gane,
> And word is to the ha,
> And word is to the king himsel
> Amang his nobles a'.

There is a clear stanza-for-stanza correspondence between this incipit and Agnes Lyle's "Mary Hamilton" incipit, indicating that this is a well-known "theme." Versions of "Johnie Scot," such as that of Agnes Laird (also of Kilbarchan), which do not begin with this particular form of the "theme" often begin with a compressed or expanded version of it. Agnes Lyle herself, as was pointed out, begins "Johnie Scot" by compressing the "theme" and combining it with a commonplace about hunting. But here, in an entirely new context, she uses the whole "theme" and makes it work.

Not only the incipit, but nearly every stanza in Agnes Lyle's version of "Mary Hamilton" has parallels in versions of that ballad by other singers. Nevertheless, the way she orders and uses these stanzas here and develops parallel stanzas in other songs of the repertoire indicate that she did not simply memorize this ballad. She totally assimilated it so that its vocabulary became her ballad vocabulary; its narrative form became her narrative form. The result is that when she sang "Mary Hamilton" it was a unique rendition stamped with her aesthetic, her "themes," and her point of view. When she sang other ballads they were consistent with "Mary Hamilton"—and "Johnie Scot"—in diction and narrative technique.

The narrative technique of "Fair Janet" has already been discussed in connection with "Mary Hamilton." But the diction of this ballad also merits close study. "Fair Janet" is a fairly rare item, not reported in this century nor outside the British Isles. It may in fact have died out entirely from tradition. Child gives seven versions, all from the late eighteenth or early nineteenth century. Agnes Lyle's version is particularly repetitive on both the deep and surface levels, as the preceding discussion would indicate. This repetitive diction makes it possible to discuss linguistic features of her style without constant bouncing from ballad to ballad to find comparative data.

Eighteen out of twenty-two stanzas in "Fair Janet" are close formulaic matches on the deep level to one or more other stanzas in the text, usually stanzas immediately adjacent. Only stanzas 6–9 do not share in this stanzaic matchmaking. But even these stanzas share in the surface repetition of words and phrases. Over the course of the ballad "If you do love me weel," or its mate "He did love her weel," occurs four times. A mother's bower is mentioned three times. The ringing of Lincoln's bells is likewise mentioned three times, in three successive stanzas. Janet and Willie's "auld son" is so identified three times. At the fourth mention, the "auld son in your arms" becomes "a son into my arms." People "ben and cam" five times. Busking the bride is mentioned thrice and thrice she is asked to "dance wi me."

An examination of the poetic resources drawn upon for this formulaic language reveals a heavy reliance on alliteration to achieve tone color:

> weel, Willie
> build a bonnie ship
> set her on the sea
> sharp sharp showers (i.e. pains)
> large and lang
> sere her son
> busk our bride
> fair and full
> saddle saft
> come to Mary's Kirk
> supper scarselie
> ben and cam the bride's brethren
> gien me the gecks
> bell . . . birds . . . [a]bove

In general this alliteration is functional as well as decorative, serving to associate related words and ideas and to emphasize important points. This use of richly varied alliteration is typical of the repertoire as a whole. One notable exception is "Bonnie Baby Livingston," which is laced with alliteration on one letter, *l*: a total of twenty-eight accented *l*'s occur in forty-four lines, in addition to the many buried *l*'s in words like *playing* and *flower*. In that ballad the emphasis on one alliteration seems to have been suggested by the names of the heroine and villain, *Livingston* and *Linlyon*, respectively.[4]

Unlike the alliteration, the rhyme pattern of "Fair Janet" is atypical, relying heavily on the *ee* rhyme. In the corpus as a whole, this rhyme occurs only twenty-eight percent of the time, but in this text it occurs fifty percent of the time, and in *trulie* the accent is wrenched to make the word rhyme with *sea*. Such heavy dependence on a single rhyme reflects the extreme reliance on repetition in the ballad as a whole. Rhyme and alliteration are rather blatant sound devices, but there are other more subtle uses of sound in the text. Notable, for instance, is the orchestration of broad Scots *oo* and *ee* in the first two lines of the ballad. In the formula line, *"And an angry man was he,"* the four-fold repetition of short, nasalized vowels is beautifully balanced by the final long open vowel of *he* (pronounced almost like *hay*). Assonance, in fact, is frequent (e.g., "It's I'll provide him five," and "I'll cut my glove"), as is internal rhyme (e.g., "to her . . . bower," and "fair . . . hair"). Sound patterns even combine to create a binary sound structure in the line "She hadna danced half owre the floor." The two clusters of *a*'s, *n*'s, and *d*'s are balanced by the two rhymes of *owre* and *floor*. Such patterns of assonance, internal rhyme, and alliteration lend the language an aphoristic quality which doubtless makes the phrases come more readily to the tongue in the heat of performance.[5]

Not surprisingly, given the rich tone color, "Fair Janet" contains what is probably the most tender scene and most tender single stanza in the repertoire:

> "Willie, lay the saddle saft,
>   And lead the bridle soun,
> And when we come to Mary's Kirk
>   Ye'll set me hooly down.

As in some of the best English (and Scots) poetry, this stanza relies on understatement to achieve an aching poignancy. There is no scene of Janet tearing her hair and crying "Willie, Willie, what are we to do!" or "I can't ride a horse so soon after having a baby." It is simply, "Willie, lay the saddle saft." The emotion is expressed through concrete detail and direct action, the whole tied together with alliteration, assonance, and the gentle rhyme of *soun* and *hooly down*. It is a fine moment, a touch of human feeling breaking through the inevitable march of the ballad to its pitiful catastrophe.

Concluding this chapter with a consideration of the several levels of articulation in a single ballad will help clarify the interrelationships of these levels. The ballad "Lord William" is the rarest item in Motherwell's Agnes Lyle collection. According to Bronson it is the only complete version, text and tune, ever collected. Two texts from Peter Buchan, the Child B and C, seem to be the only other versions to have reached print. It is one of the happy ironies of fate that although only two known tunes from Agnes Lyle have survived, one is such a rare item.

"Lord William" (Child 254A)

1 Sweet William's gone over the seas,
       Some unco lair to learn,
   And our gude Bailie's ae dochter
       Is awa to learn the same.

2 In one broad buke they learned baith,
       In one broad bed they lay;
   But when her father came to know
       He gart her come away.

3 "It's you must marry that Southland lord,
       His lady for to be;
   It's ye maun marry that Southland lord,
       Or nocht ye'll get frae me."

4 "I must marry that Southland lord,
       Father, an it be your will;
   But I rather it were my burial-day,
       My grave for to fill."

5. She walked up, she walked down,
    Had none to make her moan,
    Nothing but the pretty bird
    Sat on the causey-stone.

6 "If thou could speak, wee bird," she says,
    "As weell as thou can flee,
    I would write a long letter
    To Will ayont the sea."

7 "What thou wants wi Will," it says,
    "Thou'll seal it with thy ring,
    Tak a thread o silk and anither o twine,
    About my neck will hing."

8 What she wanted wi Willie
    She sealed it wi a ring,
    Took a thread of silk, another o twine,
    About its neck did hing.

9 This bird flew high, this bird flew low,
    This bird flew owre the sea,
    Until it entered the same room
    Wherein was Sweet Willie.

10 This bird flew high, this bird flew low,
    Poor bird, it was mistaen!
    It let the letter fa on Baldie's breist,
    Instead of Sweet William.

11 "Here's a letter, William" he says,
    "I'm sure it's not to me;
    And gin the morn gin twelve o'clock
    Your love shall married be."

12 "Come saddle to me my horse," he said,
    "The brown and a' that's speedie,
    And I'll awa to Old England,
    To bring home my ladie."

13 Awa he gaed, awa he rade,
    Awa wi mickle speed;
    He lichtit at every twa miles' end,
    Lichtit and changed his steed.

14 When she entered the church-style,
    The tear was in her ee;
    But when she entered the church-door
    A blythe sicht did she see.

15 "O hold your hand, you minister,
    Hold it a little wee,
    Till I speak wi the bonnie bride,
    For she's a friend to me.

16   "Stand off, stand off, you braw bridegroom,
         Stand off a little wee;
      Stand off, stand off, you braw bridegroom,
         For the bride shall join wi me."

17   Up and spak the bride's father,
         And an angry man was he;
      "If I had pistol, powther and lead,
         And all at my command,
      I would shoot thee stiff and dead
         In the place where thou dost stand."

18   Up and spoke then Sweet William,
         And a blithe blink from his ee;
      "If ye neer be shot till I shoot you,
         Ye'se neer be shot for me.

19   "Come out, come out, my foremost man,
         And lift my lady on;
      Commend me all to my good-mother,
         At night when ye gang home."

The ballad is "Fair Janet" with a happy ending. A hero named William loves a heroine named (although not in the present text) Janet. Her father opposes the love match and sponsors a high-born suitor as a more proper bridegroom. As in "Fair Janet," hero and heroine seem to come from the people, rather than the gentry; he is a student (despite the Child title), and she is a bailiff's daughter. Janet elopes without benefit of clergy but is dragged back to her father's house and a forced wedding. At the wedding she rejects the high-born bridegroom and gives herself to her first love, William. In the final stanzas the spirit of "Johnie Scot" prevails over that of "Fair Janet." Sweet William tweaks the nose of his new father-in-law, sets his bride before him, and gallops away. Similarities of plot and character help explain why the ballad shares much imagery with "Fair Janet" but can not explain why both ballads should include horses and saddles, sympathetic birds, an overseas voyage, mothers-in-law, or even—one ending happily—the identification of wedding with funeral. Thematically, both ballads deal with human perfidy and the failure of those the heroine should be able to trust, her own family. Both ballads resolve the issue on an ambivalent note of scorn and triumph. The interloping bridegroom is a more active agent in "Fair Janet" and the object of the final denunciation. In "Lord William" the bridegroom is a mere cipher and the family itself, as in "Johnie Scot" receives the hero's final rebuke. The many correspondences between this ballad and others in the repertoire, including "Fair Janet" and "Johnie Scot," help to clarify the singer's method of oral recreation and to show that there is a single mind at work shaping the ballads.

"Lord William" appears to be a late addition to Scottish balladry. Its newness shows in complexity of stanzaic, narrative, tonal, and character

DIAGRAM 4
Stanzaic, Tonal, and Narrative Structures in "Lord William"

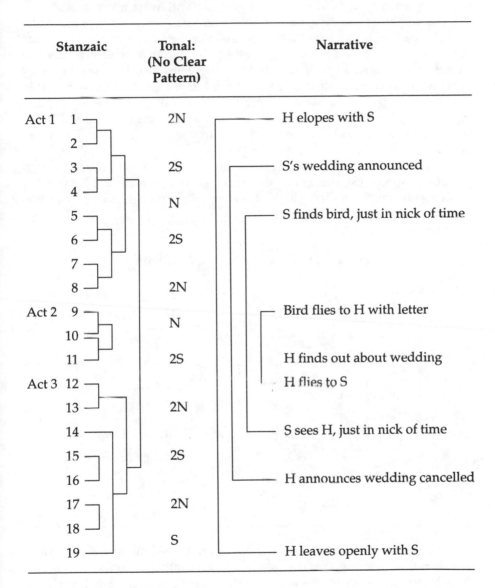

Stanzaic	Tonal: (No Clear Pattern)	Narrative
Act 1 1	2N	H elopes with S
2		
3	2S	S's wedding announced
4		
5	N	S finds bird, just in nick of time
6	2S	
7		
8	2N	
Act 2 9	N	Bird flies to H with letter
10		
11	2S	H finds out about wedding
Act 3 12		H flies to S
13	2N	
14		S sees H, just in nick of time
15	2S	
16		H announces wedding cancelled
17	2N	
18		
19	S	H leaves openly with S

structures (Diagram 4). The stanzaic structure falls into three acts, which might be named "Separation," "Summons," and "Reunion." The first and third acts have eight stanzas apiece, and the second act has three. Within this pattern every stanza is a member of a pair, stanzas 14 and 19 framing, and the rest balancing. As in Johnie Scot the three middle stanzas form two balances, stanza 10 pairing with 9 in formula and 11 in content. Examples of causative repetition occur in stanzas 3–4, 7–8, and 17–18; incremental repetition in 3–4 and 9–10; and emphatic repetition within stanzas 3 and 16.

The narrative structure supports the stanzaic. The pivotal point in the annular pattern is at stanzas 9–11, the exact center of the stanzaic structure and of the ballad as a whole. The rest of the narrative structure does not correspond quite so meticulously but is never more than one stanza out of sync with the stanzaic structure. In 7–8 the heroine (S) asks the hero (H) to come, and in 12–13 he answers the request. In 4–6 she finds the bird, and in 14 she finds her lover. In 3–4 her father announces her marriage, and in 15–18 her lover announces the cancellation of that marriage. In 1–2 she elopes, and in 19 her lover takes her away again.

The tonal structure randomly alternates stanzas of narrative (N) with stanzas of speech (S), confirming that this level of articulation is not consistently significant in the technique of Agnes Lyle although it is in the technique of Mrs. Brown of Falkland.

DIAGRAM 5
Character Structure in "Lord William"

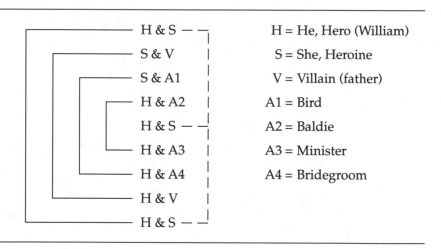

The character structure, on the other hand, is well defined and counterpoints rather than supports the stanzaic and narrative patterns (Diagram 5). The pivotal point occurs at stanza 14 rather than stanza 10. Moreover, both hero and heroine deal with secondary agents in the first half of the song; in the second half the number of these agents is the same, but only the hero deals with them. As in "Johnie Scot," the hero and heroine are paired at the first, the pivotal, and the final points in the pattern. As in "Mary Hamilton," the principle at work in the character structure is strong enough to push an unexpected figure, Baldie, onto the scene. This mysterious character is probably William's tutor or perhaps an old man-servant. He serves no plot exigencies but serves to balance the minister in the character structure.

The ballad, then, exhibits a high degree of formal symmetry. The narrative structure harmonizes with the basic stanzaic structure, and the character structure provides a pleasing counterpoint. This persistent formality is perhaps the principal aesthetic value of the ballad text, but individual happy touches likewise occur. Although, like "Johnie Scot," the piece is built up from commonplace or commonplace-like stanzas, these stanzas have been freely recomposed; 13 and 19 are particularly vigorous. The euphonious line about "an angry man" reoccurs in 17. Especially happy uses of alliteration include "pistol, powder, and lead," "a blithe blink," "bonnie bride . . . braw bridegroom," and:

> In one broad buke they learned baith,
> In one broad bed they lay.

In Sweet William, moreover, Agnes Lyle has provided a rare example of a ballad character with a sense of humor. He assures the minister that yes, he and the bride have been friends for some time now. He winks at his future father-in-law when the old man threatens violence. And he sends best wishes to his new good-mother (mother-in-law) when he abducts her daughter. He is, in short, a man who refuses to take himself too seriously. It is no wonder his Janet found him so charming.

The analysis conducted in this chapter suggests that a particular ballad version is a product of two factors, tradition and technique. These two are related somewhat like the scholastic's act and potency. The potential principle is the tradition of the particular ballad as it reaches the particular singer. The actualizing principle is the performer's particular technique, which shapes the tradition to create a performance under particular circumstances in a particular time and place.

Agnes Lyle's own ballad technique includes a vocabulary of formulas for phrase, line, stanza and commonplace, and stanza cluster and "theme," though as the next chapter will show, the metrics of the ballad quatrain operative in these formulas make them difficult to use in other meters. Her formulas are realized and organized according to the annular, binary, and trinary principles of the western oral aesthetic. These principles tend to create rather simple, harmonious patterns on the stanzaic, narrative, character, and even verbal and phonemic levels, though with some counterpointing. But they are rather attenuated on the tonal level. Formulaic vocabulary and traditional methods of organization are essential elements of the technique she brings to the singing of a ballad.

But a ballad singer, even when orally recreating, is never wholly independent of the ballad's antecedents. As David Buchan puts it:

> Sounds, syntactic patterns, and formulaic constructions all adhere to the ballad-story. They do not necessarily occur in the same place but, like burrs, they stick

to the ballad and appear somewhere within it. The tenacity of these patterns illustrates how strongly developed is the oral poet's aural memory, and how his aural sense operates in the process of composition quite differently from the literary poet's. (1972, 161)

These burrs of sound, syntax, formula, and pattern are as important in the ballad's tradition as are the characters and plot they cling to. They too are part of the overall "essence" of the ballad and exert "tension." Richness of language, then, does not come to balladry in the lifetime of a single singer. The singer, rather, exercises the ballad craft by being alert to such possibilities and beauties of language wherever they may be found and assimilating the best of them into a personal ballad vocabulary that will enrich the subsequent tradition of the ballads this singer performs. The preservation and enrichment of the traditional formulaic technique and of the individual ballad traditions depends, therefore, on the sensitivity and taste of a whole long chain of singers or bricoleurs. Agnes Lyle is a significant link in that chain. Assimilating a vocabulary of phrases and lines, and, as in the case of "Mary Hamilton," transposing "themes" and formulas freely, she has indeed enriched ballad tradition with her creative technique.

The Weaver's Daughter Nods

The preceding chapter showed how Agnes Lyle developed her distinctive yet traditional oral technique and used it to enrich the tradition of ballads she sang. There were times, however, when her technique failed her or was unavailable to her, and she sang ballads without her customary well articulated oral architectonic. All of the ballads here in question exhibit maverick features which help explain the failure, if failure it can be called. Some give evidence of being from the singer's inactive or even passive repertoire. Some seem to be fixed-text songs sung more or less from memory. Some, because of the popularity of the ballad in a variety of forms, seem to suffer from conflicting models. All are in meters other than the standard ballad meter. And one goes to a familiar air which seems to drag lyric stanzas with it into the ballad. Yet these imperfect specimens, no less than the perfect specimens of the preceding chapter, can teach the investigator much about the way of a maid with a ballad.

This inconsistency should not cause surprise. A singer's repertoire is not a homogeneous whole, each piece assimilated identically, learned equally expertly, and performed equally often. Kenneth Goldstein addresses this matter in an essay on active and inactive folksong repertoires:

> When we read about the size of a particular tradition bearer's repertory, we somehow get the impression that each item has the same import as any other item, and that after the informant has accumulated the body of tradition we recognize as his total repertory he has equal command and recall of every item in it. . . . Only when we note that certain items exist in fragmentary form or are otherwise imperfectly remembered while others are performed completely and without hesitation, do we even begin to realize that items of repertory are not all of the same import to the tradition bearer. . . . Some hold greater memories for the singer than do others. . . . Some are occasionally performed, while others represent only a memory of tradition. And there lies our cue. At any particular time in the life of a tradition bearer (and not only when he is working with a collector), some of the items in his repertory are active and others are inactive. (1971, 63)

Goldstein's comments would seem to describe Agnes Lyle's repertoire aptly. While songs such as "Mary Hamilton" and "Johnie Scot" surely represent her active repertoire, songs such as "The Twa Sisters" and "The Golden Vanity" almost as surely represent her inactive or even passive repertoire. All other things being equal, the collector is likely to gain a more complete and developed text of a song in the singer's active repertoire than of one in the inactive repertoire.

Still, the status of the song in the active repertoire is only the first of several variables that affect, whether positively or negatively, the texture and integrity of the song as collected. A second such variable is the creative stance the singer takes toward the song. Eleanor Long (1973) has described four such stances, the perseverating, the confabulating, the rationalizing, and the integrative.[1] The singer taking the perseverating stance "insists upon faithful reproduction of his text," that is, he sings it from memory, as nearly as possible to the way he learned it. The singer taking the confabulating stance, "in no particular awe of received tradition . . . may *add* narrative themes, . . . creating 'crossed' texts, . . . may *revise*, . . . may simply *improvise*" freely, fluidly, and with flourish. The singer taking the rationalizing stance "[makes] the text conform to a previously-adopted, extra-textual system of values that is of significance to the singer," whether that system be political, religious, moral, or aesthetic. Finally, a singer taking the integrative stance "goes beyond [the other three] by *creating* texts that are unique and as often as not memorable. He makes use of traditional verbal formulae and narrative themes, but he is not enslaved by them: his value-system is that of the poet, or 'maker,' not that of the craftsman, decorator, or free-style artist" (232–233; all italics in original).

If the ballad analysis in the preceding chapter is accurate, Agnes Lyle took an integrative stance toward the ballads there analyzed, creating the unique and memorable texts of an oral poet. But, as the Goldstein article suggests, *a singer is capable of taking different stances at different times, especially toward different materials.* Thus, the ballads considered in the preceding chapter, all products of the integrative stance, present an oral texture. But others, memorial products of the perseverating stance, preserve the literary texture of the original penned pieces. It should come as no surprise, therefore, to discover that Agnes Lyle's text of "The Wee Wee Man" is, word for word, much like other versions or that her text of "The Baffled Knight" exhibits essentially literary principles of organization. Consciously or unconsciously, she memorized these pieces.[2]

A third factor that may affect the texture or integrity of a song is how popular the song is. The word *popular* is used here in its popular sense of *current and widely accepted*. Popularity can have either a positive or negative effect. If a singer has too many conflicting models she may produce a diffuse and formless text, like Agnes Lyle's text of "The Twa Sisters." Of that ballad Motherwell writes that it "is very popular in Scotland and occurs in all possible shapes." On the other hand, the popularity of the "Yarrow" group (Child 214–215) seems to have had a favorable influence. The multiformity and richness within this distinctive ballad tradition have provided a variety of models for stanza building and an adequate store of appropriate commonplaces, thus offsetting the tradition's stringent metrical and rhyme demands (see Chapter 5).

Such demands of rhyme and especially of meter constitute a fourth factor affecting the texture and integrity of a text. As the evidence of the preceding chapter suggests, Agnes Lyle's art is stanzaic art and the most congenial medium for that art is the standard ballad quatrain. Ballads such as "Hind Horn" or "The Gypsy Laddie" exhibit the same structural and compositional principles as the standard quatrain ballads, but because of the difference in medium these principles express themselves in somewhat different ways. As a consequence, the singer exercises less consistent control over them.

An intrusive tune is a fifth factor that can affect the texture and integrity of a ballad. Such a tune can create an all but irresistible urge to incorporate stanzas from some other context associated with that tune. Thus Agnes Lyle, like practically all known singers of "Jamie Douglas," incorporates stanzas from the haunting lyric "Waly Waly." But she is more successful than most at integrating the lyric stanzas into the texture of the ballad, using a framing pair at the beginning and end of the ballad to express the essential mood of the piece and a nonce reworking of the cockle shells/silver bells commonplace (usually an explicit!) in the pivotal stanza 8 to express Jamie Douglas's rejection of his wife.

"Jamie Douglas" and the fragment "It Was in the Middle of Fair July" (influenced by "Two Rigs of Rye;" see Ch. 3) are the only definite cases in the repertoire of influence by an intrusive tune. The rest of this chapter will examine how the texture and integrity of the non-standard-meter texts show a negative influence of the other four factors, taking up those factors in reverse order.

The most decisive of these factors for Agnes Lyle seems to be meter. Analysis of couplet ballads such as "Hind Horn" or "The Twa Sisters" reveals the results of reliance upon a less congenial medium.

"Hind Horn" (Child 17C)

1   Young Hyn Horn's to the king's court gone,
      Hoch hey and an ney O
He's fallen in love with his little daughter Jean.
      Let my love alone, I pray you.

2   He's bocht to her a little gown,
    With seven broad flowers spread it along.

3   She's given to him a gay gold ring.
    The posie upon it was richt plain.

4   "When you see it losing its comely hue,
    So will I my love to you."

5   Then within a little wee,
   Hyn Horn left land and went to sea.

6   When he lookt his ring upon,
   He saw it growing pale and wan.

7   Then within a little [wee] again,
   Hyn Horn left sea and came to the land.

8   As he was riding along the way,
   There he met with a jovial beggar.

9   "What news, what news, old man?" he did say:
   "This is the king's young dochter's wedding day."

10   "If this be true you tell to me,
   You must niffer clothes with me.

11   "You'll gie me your cloutit coat,
   I'll gie you my fine velvet coat.

12   You'll gie me your cloutit pock,
   I'll gie you my purse; it'll be no joke."

13   "Perhaps there['s] nothing in it, not one bawbee;"
   "Yes, there's gold and silver both," said he.

14   "You'll gie me your bags of bread,
   And I'll gie you my milk-white steed."

15   When they had niffered all, he said,
   "You maun learn me how I'll beg."

16   "When you come before the gate,
   You'll ask for a drink for the highman's sake."

17   When that he came before the gate,
   He calld for a drink for the highman's sake.

18   The bride cam tripping down the stair,
   To see whaten a bold beggar was there.

19   She gave him a drink with her own hand;
   He loot the ring drop in the can.

20   "Got ye this by sea or land?
   Or took ye't aff a dead man's hand?"

21   "I got na it by sea nor land,
   But I got it aff your own hand."

22   The bridegroom cam tripping down the stair,
   But there was neither bride nor beggar there.

23   Her ain bridegroom had her first wed,
   But Young Hyn Horn had her first to bed.

"Hind Horn" comes the closest of the couplet ballads to the style and structure of the standard quatrain ballads. The stanzaic structure falls into three clear acts of separation, return, and recognition. On this level perfect annular symmetry prevails, Acts I and III containing seven stanzas each and the central Act II nine. The first and last stanzas neatly frame the ballad and summarize the story.

The structure one level down, however, is not quite so neat. Stanzas 2–7 of Act I admit of analysis as three balances, as two triads, or as a balance and a balance of balances. In addition, stanzas 3 and 4 form a distinct balance which does not articulate with any of the three patterns just described. Act II consists of a rather complex framed structure which overlaps for one transitional stanza with Act III. Framed by stanzas 10 and 15, stanzas 11–14 form an interrupted triad (a b x c). Buchan (1972, 92) describes a similar pattern in connection with the ballads of Mrs. Brown, but the interrupted triad is unusual in Agnes Lyle's repertoire, occurring only here and in "Geordie." Stanza 17 balances with stanza 16 to form the last balance in Act II and with stanza 18 to form the first balance in Act III. From yet another point of view, stanzas 18 and 22 frame the intervening triad, which also includes one balance. The symmetrical tonal pattern supports the general stanzaic structure with only slight discrepancies, as does the character structure. The character structure itself is extremely simple, like the character structures of most couplet ballads, regardless of singer. But even though the character and tonal structures are less contrapuntal and the stanzaic structure is more ambiguous than the corresponding structures usual in quatrain ballads, these structures still demonstrate the same organizing principles, the same decisive influence of annular, binary, and trinary forces at work.

The narrative point of view, on the other hand, is more objective and impersonal in this ballad than in any text so far examined. If, for example, the listener asks why the bride marries another, there is no hint of an answer. The ballad never touches on motives. This means as well that it remains remarkably free of villainy. Neither the king nor the bridegroom is a "heavy" in the plot. Of the lady herself the listener knows nothing beyond the bare outline of her actions. Indeed, the most lively figure in the tale is the beggar who niffers clothes with the hero.

"The Twa Sisters" (Child 10F)

1   There was two ladies livd in a bower,
        Hey with a gay and a grinding O
    The youngest o them was the fairest flower
        About a' the bonny bows o London.

2   There was two ladies livd in a bower,
        An wooer unto the youngest did go.

3   The oldest one to the youngest did say,
        "Will ye take a walk with me today,
        And we'll view the bonny bows o London.

4   "Thou'll set thy foot whare I set mine,
    Thou'll set thy foot upon this stane."

5   "I'll set my foot where thou sets thine:"
    The old sister dang the youngest in,
        At, etc.

6   "O sister dear, come tak my hand,
    Take my life safe to dry land."

7   "It's neer by my hand thy hand sall come in,
    It's neer by my hand thy hand sall come in.

8   "It's thy cherry cheeks and thy white briest bane
    Gars me set a maid owre lang at hame."

9   She clasped her hand[s] about a brume rute,
    But her cruel sister she lowsed them out.

10 Sometimes she sank, and sometimes she swam,
    Till she cam to the miller's dam.

11 The miller's bairns has muckle need,
    They were bearing in water to bake some breid.

12 Says, "Father, dear father, in our mill-dam,
    It's either a fair maid or a milk-white swan."

13 The miller he's spared nae his hose nor his shoon
    Till he brocht this lady till dry land.

14 I wad he saw na a bit o her feet,
    Her silver slippers were made so neat.

15 I wad he saw na a abit o her skin,
    For ribbons there was mony a ane.

16 He laid her on a brume buss to dry,
    To see wha was the first wad pass her by.

17 Her ain father's herd was the first man
    That by this lady gay did gang.

18 He's taen three links of her yellow hair,
    And made a string to his fiddle there.

19 He's cut her fingers long and small
    To be the fiddle-pins that neer might fail.

21 The very first spring that the fiddle did play,
    "Hang my auld sister," I wad it did say.

22 "For she drowned me in yonder sea,
    God neer let her rest till she shall die,"
        At the bonny bows o London.

"The Twa Sisters" offers an interesting comparison with "Hind Horn."

As has already been suggested, Agnes Lyle's text of "The Twa Sisters" seems to be adversely affected by the third factor affecting texture and integrity, namely overpopularity. Along with "Barbara Allen" it has been one of the most persistently popular ballads in the Anglo-American tradition. But no ballad, not even "Barbara Allen," exists in such an array of versions. When fashioning a rendition of "The Twa Sisters" a singer like Agnes Lyle was probably bombarded by versions in what Motherwell calls, in the phrase already quoted, "all possible shapes." Having too many ideas to work with, she produced a text in which the stanzaic structure admits of a dizzying number of alternative interpretations. Even the overall structure can be seen as consisting of two acts, or of three.[3] On the character, narrative, and tonal levels these structures are even more ambiguous. In short, the annular, binary, and trinary forces are never decisive in their influence.

In some ways, then, "The Twa Sisters" is the exact opposite of "Hind Horn." One is relatively formless, the other fairly intricately structured. Furthermore, one is tragic, the other comic; one bitter, the other mellow. But the two ballads also share common features from their venerable narrative tradition. The first feature the ballads share is a reliance on narrative agents not actually involved in the main conflict. The beggar in "Hind Horn" has already been mentioned. He has the longest scene in the text, and the only one developed almost exclusively through dialogue. He is jovial (stanza 8), up on gossip (stanza 9), canny (stanza 13), and skilled in his craft (stanza 18). Like the nameless sergeant in *Antigone* he manages to steal the show. In "The Twa Sisters" the miller who finds the body and the herdsman who makes the fiddle likewise resemble minor figures of Greek tragedy, for example the two herdsmen of *Oedipus* who unwittingly trigger the denouement.

The second feature the two ballads share is employment of a magical item as an important plot device. In "Hind Horn" the item is the ring, while in "The Twa Sisters" it is the hair-strung fiddle. In each case the magical item is a recognition device, the ring in two different ways, and in each case the device acts to reveal unfaithfulness and perfidy.

The third feature the ballads share is a fairy-tale richness of imagery. In "Hind Horn" these images are especially lush: first of all, the magic ring with its "richt plain posie;" rich wearing apparel, including the gown with seven broad (embroidered?) flowers, clouted and velvet coats, clouted pock, and purse and knapsack; a fairy-tale king and his young daughter; a milk-white steed; gold and silver; the castle gate and stairs; a dead man's hand; sea voyages; and wedding and bedding. In "The Twa Sisters" the lush imagery includes yellow hair, fingers long and small, cherry cheeks and white breastbone, a milk-white swan, ribbons many, silver slippers, a bower, the sea, the stone, the mill-dam, bread, water, children, hands and feet, broom bushes, and finally, the magic fiddle. One is apt to assume that these traditional images are found everywhere in balladry. Not so. They are the proper legacy of certain ballads only within the larger ballad tradition. Of Agnes Lyle's ballads, these two are sole inheritors of this legacy of fairy-tale imagery.[4]

Like the couplet ballads, others in Agnes Lyle's repertoire show the strain of working with overpopular material in an uncongenial medium. "The Gypsy Laddie," for example, is composed in feminine rhyming quatrains in the meter that hymnists call 8's and 7's. Rhymes on *Davy/lady*, occurring in seven of the fourteen stanzas, seem preferred but not obligatory. Agnes Lyle uses this meter in only one other preserved ballad, "Braes o' Yarrow," again with a more or less required rhyme scheme. Overpopularity of the ballad is probably as much of a factor in the formation of Agnes Lyle's text of "Gypsy Laddie" as uncongenial meter. Bronson comments on the perennial popularity of the piece, provides 130 tunes (though most are from the twentieth century), suggests that it belongs more properly with the older ballads in the first hundred Child numbers, and cites the stability of the Class A tune family since before 1630, as "one of the longest traditional sequences observable in all British balladry." It is impossible to know on manuscript evidence how popular this item was in Kilbarchan in 1825, but if popularity elsewhere, before and since, is any indication, it was probably quite popular. The paucity of manuscript evidence may simply indicate that the song was so popular it was regarded as a species of weed.

Overpopularity, as in the case of "The Twa Sisters," can produce too many conflicting models, so that the singer produces essentially amorphous texts. In the present case the stanzaic structure shows very few signs of binary, much less annular or trinary forces at work. The story falls into three acts, describing flight, pursuit, and vengeance, but unambiguous balances occur only in stanzas 13–14 (see below) and in stanzas 5–6:

> "Yestreen I rode this water deep,
>   And my gude lord beside me;
> But this nicht I maun set in my pretty fit and wade,
>   A wheen blackguards wading wi me.
>
> "Yestreen I lay in a fine feather-bed,
>   And my gude lord beyond me;
> But this nicht I maun lye in some cauld tenant's barn,
>   A wheen blackguards waiting on me."

The tonal structure reveals binary and trinary patterns, but in a very uncharacteristic way. Three stanzas of narrative at the beginning are matched by three stanzas of narrative at the end. But the remaining eight stanzas consist of 4 stanzas of speech balanced by 4 stanzas of alternating narrative and speech. The character structure is even more informal. Gypsy Davy does not become differentiated from the gypsies as a group until stanza 7 (see below). Immediately thereafter he melts back into the crowd, emerging only as a convenient rhyme. The Lord of Cassillis, too, blends with a mysterious "they" in stanza 10. No clear hero, heroine, or villain roles emerge at all. The Lord at least acts with dispatch. But Jeanie Faw is a "wanton lady," not unlike Lady Barnabas in this singer's "Little Musgrave." And Gypsy Davy is a deceiver and braggart, selling Jeanie's clothes to buy drink (see stanza 12, below) and swearing that he will never let her husband come near her, a boast he is powerless to make good (see stanza 7, below).

Unlike the stanzaic, tonal, and character structures, the narrative structure does achieve a reasonable symmetry. But in the final three stanzas even the narrative technique is unorthodox:

> 12   They drank her cloak, so did they her goun
>   They drank her stockings and her shoon
> And they drank the coat that was nigh to her smock
>   And they pawned her pearled apron.

> 13   They were sixteen clever men,
>   Suppose they were na bonny;
> They are a' to be hanged on ae tree,
>   For the stealing o Earl Cassilis' lady.

> 14   "We are sixteen clever men,
>   One woman was a' our mother;
> We are a' to be hanged on ae day,
>   For the stealing of a wanton lady."

Stanza 12 summarizes a series of events, instead of dramatizing an action. Stanzas 13 and 14 resolve the plot in a style more characteristic of broadsides and may in fact stem from a broadside text. Ballad-like or not, however, these final stanzas contain the singer's judgment on the inequities represented in the story: the lady gets off scot-free, the gypsies hang; such is ever the way of the world, at least as Agnes Lyle sees it.

Although the texture of "Gypsy Laddie" reflects unresolved pressures felt by the singer, it also reveals effective oral touches. The repetition of stanzas 5–6, for instance, provides an ironic glimpse of the naivete and pretentions of a lady who imagines that even in a tenant barn she will have people to wait on her. These same stanzas give the modern reader one of the few glimpses in this repertoire into actual life in the Scotland of 1825. The tenant barns where the fraternity of the road found refuge are well described from personal experience by William Thom in *Rhymes and Recollections of a Handloom Weaver* (1844, passim).

Stanzas 7 and 11 provide an example of the singer's way with formulas:

> "Come to thy bed, my bonny Jeanie Faw,
>   Come to thy bed, my dearie,
> For I do swear, by the top o my spear,
>   Thy gude lord'll nae mair come near thee."
>
> . . . .
>
> "Rise, oh rise, my bonnie Jeanie Faw,
>   Oh rise, and do not tarry!
> Is this the thing ye promised to me
>   When at first I did thee marry?"

In her use of formulaic language Agnes Lyle is never enslaved by words;
the underlying concept is the important thing. Here in stanza 11 she takes the
concepts of stanza 7, idea by idea, and turns them upside down. The gypsy
would keep husband from wife, but wife should not leave husband. Having
gone to the gypsy's bed, she must now rise from it. The gypsy's adulterous
promise can not annul her wedding promise. The same stanza 7 provides an
ironic contrast to stanza 8.

> When her good lord came hame at nicht,
>   It was asking for his fair ladye;
> One spak slow, and another whispered out,
>   "She's awa wi Gipsey Davy!"

The effect is like a cross-cut in a film (cf. Buchan 1972, 98–99). At the
very moment that Davy is swearing that the Lord will never come near
Jeanie, the Lord is setting out to bring home the bride and string up the
braggart. Thus, despite failure to achieve a fully symmetrical oral architectonic, this ballad manages to tell the complete story clearly, with some graceful touches, and with a final note of irony.

One of the advantages of Agnes Lyle's repertoire for studying classical
balladry is that it seems to be a rather typical repertoire, with the variety of
pieces that Goldstein's and Long's comments would lead one to expect. In
particular, among the pieces in non-congenial meters are one or two that do
not seem to have active status in the repertoire, and one or two that seem
memorized.

The most important memorized piece is "The Baffled Knight." Significantly enough, it is the one piece for which there is evidence that Agnes
Lyle, the oral ballad singer, could not sing the whole song straight through
the first time she tried. Motherwell got only five stanzas on August 24 and
had to return a month later for the rest of the song. A second piece of evidence that this is a fixed-text piece, sung from memory, is that there is a
mistake in it of the sort one might make in singing such a song. The rhyme
scheme indicates that stanza 2 should begin with the first two lines now
printed with stanza 4. The stanza would then go:

> "What if I should lay thee down,
>   Amang the rigs of corn, maid?
> Sheets nor blankets have I none,
>   To keep thy clothing clean, maid."

With the switch completed, stanza 4 would read:

> "What if I should lay thee down,
>   Amang the quiles of hay, maid?
> Then the king's life-guard will come
>   And steal our steeds away, maid."

What has happened is that the singer, herself seduced by the *hay* rhyme, has jumped from stanza 1 to stanza 4. Realizing immediately that clothes come before horses in the song, she has completed the stanza with the lines from stanza 2, saving the unused lines to begin stanza 4. This kind of mix-up and subsequent correction, involving similar stanzas, is quite common when people sing from memory (Cf. Lord 1981, 460).

The ballad belongs properly with those fixed-text broadside fragments that Motherwell did not bother to finish collecting.[5] In this particular case, however, recognizing a piece which was important to him because of the literary connection to Percy's *Reliques,* he persisted until he had the whole song. It is different from the rest of the repertoire in a number of ways. Though highly organized, with binary and trinary patterns occurring, the overarching structure is linear, rather than annular, parallel rather than chiastic. The first part of the ballad (stanzas 1–5), and the third part (stanzas 14–20), each consist of an introductory stanza, followed by two or three pairs of parallel stanzas. The effect is linear, like a paragraph with its topic sentence followed by points developed in parallel structure and unlike an oral ballad scene with its annular structure of internal balances framed by opening and closing stanzas. In the middle scene the use of parallel structure is even more pronounced. The pattern established in 6–9 is repeated in 10–13 in forward, not reverse order, in a linear, not an annular pattern.

In subject as in style the song bears little relationship to the more ballad-like pieces in the corpus. The closest analogy, perhaps, is "Geordie," in which the heroine likewise proves herself capable, no matter how hopeless the situation. The lady who contends with the knight, however, has no outside interference, and the kind of broad farce that surfaces in the treatment of her situation surfaces nowhere else in the repertoire. She, unlike the heroines in most versions of this ballad, seems quite willing at first. The knight worries about her gown and her horse, but she assures him that she can wash her gown or ransom her horse, if need be. By the middle of the song, however, she has grown weary of his cautious ways and is simply leading him on, literally and figuratively.

> "But see ye na yon fair castel,
>   Over yon lily lea, sir,
> Where you and I may crack a while,
>   And never one may see, sir?"

Far from defending her own virtue, she is making a fool of her would-be seducer. Once inside the castle, she shuts the gate in his face, telling him through the grate:

> "There is a flower in my father's garden,
>   The name o't marigold, sir,
> And he that would not when he might,
>   He shall not when he wold, sir.

"But when eer ye meet a pretty maid,
And two miles from a town, sir,
Ye may lay her down," she says,
"And never mind her gown, sir."

This song is clever and well-structured, as one expects naughty Scots songs to be, but the structure is such as one would expect in literary, not oral texts. Indeed, certain types of ribald songs, relying as they do on verbal wit, do not lend themselves to the process of oral recreation. Popular handling may wear them smooth, but once all rough edges are smoothed, the texts tend to fix. Child's judgment on this variant may be the final one: "E [Agnes Lyle's text] is, in all probability, a broadside copy modified by tradition." If this is a fixed-text song, it is not surprising that the singer mixed up two of the stanzas and could not at first remember all twenty.

Agnes Lyle's difficulties with "The Baffled Knight" indicate that the piece was not only memorized but also inactive in her repertoire, as Goldstein says pieces often are. "The Golden Vanity" suggests a further refinement on Goldstein's refinement of Von Sydow. *Not only may an active ballad-tradition bearer know ballads which are currently inactive in her repertoire, she may serve as passive tradition bearer for yet other ballads.* Only seven stanzas long, Agnes Lyle's text of "The Golden Vanity" is both short and fragmentary. The stanzas are composed of two four-beat lines with an internal refrain, almost as if the singer were trying, not totally successfully, to mold the piece into a couplet ballad. Though the tale of the perfidious shipmaster would seem to be a naturally appealing one for this singer, the perfidy of the shipmaster is the very point about which the version is unclear. The song ends:

5   He had an instrument, made for the use,
     He bored nine holes in her water-sluice,
         Left her sinking in the Lowlands, low, low, low,
         Left her sinking in the Lowlands low.

6   Some took their hats, and some took their caps,
     All for to stop her watery leaks.
         She was sinking, etc.

7   They took him up by their ship-side,
     They sewed him in an auld cow's-hide,
         Left him sinking, etc.

The transition from stanza 6, in which the enemy sailors are trying to stop the holes in their ship, to stanza 7, in which the boy's body is being sewed up in a cow's hide, is anything but clear. Had the song been a regular part of this singer's repertoire, she would hardly have forgotten how to sing the part where the master refuses to rescue the heroic little cabin boy. Nevertheless, like many others in Scotland in her day, she "knew the song" for, like "The

Twa Sisters," "The Golden Vanity" seems to have been popular in South-west Scotland in the 1820's. At the end of the Lyle text in the Notebook, Motherwell lists five other singers who he knows can sing the song, three of them from the one city of Glasgow.

Some idea of the wide variety of forms this song may assume at a given time in a given region may be gained by examining the 36 Flanders texts collected in New England between 1930 and 1960 (1960–1965, vol. 4). A person familiar with the song, who tried to sing it without any preparation, would discover that "The Golden Vanity" is capable of almost infinite expansion or contraction. The whole story can be over in 4 or 5 stanzas, or it can be stretched out for 15 or 20. What the singer puts in or leaves out is likely to depend on the inspiration of the moment, the patience of the audience, the promptings of memory, and personal inventiveness. The traditional tune of this ballad, like the text, is no more than an outline, capable of expansion and contraction, doubling and curtailing, according to the talents and whims of the singer, but quite defying any attempt at stabilization. Such seems to be the meaning of the 36 versions of the ballad in Flanders, or the 111 versions in Bronson, or the one version in Agnes Lyle's repertoire. This was a song anyone could sing who had heard it often enough. At times in its history it has been so popular that any singer in a given region would have heard at least a dozen versions.

The fate of such songs is very different from the fate of a rarer and more complex ballad such as "Fair Janet." The rarer ballad is passed along from singer to singer like a precious heirloom. To be its custodian takes special talents, special interests, and a special personality. But "The Golden Vanity," like the Biblical corn (or the pearls before swine?), has been scattered broad-cast. It springs up in good ground and hard ground, among thorns and by the wayside. No two straws are alike, but no two are very different either. Anybody can sing the song, and anybody is likely to. Agnes Lyle probably would not take such a song very seriously. She could sing it of course, if the gentleman insisted. Who couldn't, after all? But her "Golden Vanity" bears little resemblance to those ballads she brooded over for forty years. The least assimilated and integrated item in her repertoire, it is valuable for that very reason. It illustrates the state of a ballad just getting started, as opposed to a finished and perfected work.

In her standard-quatrain ballads Agnes Lyle achieved a symmetrical oral architectonic by means of a distinctive and consistent oral technique. In the ballads in non-standard meter her technical facility was compromised by competing factors—always an uncongenial meter, often overpopularity, sometimes lack of practice, and once an intrusive tune. It is impossible to know, in the case of ballads like "The Twa Sisters" or "Gypsy Laddie," whether the singer had any higher aesthetic ideals or criteria. Realizing consciously or not the difficulties involved, Agnes Lyle may have framed for herself a freer, more linear aesthetic. Or she may even have contented herself with gathering up the pieces of the story as she had heard them, passing them on in that imperfect form rather than assimilating them and then reissuing them in a finished ballad in her own style. Certainly ballad singers today, in New England, Appalachia, Scotland, wherever ballads are still heard, seem to be preservers of pieces, not oral recreators. Their songs are like heirloom pitchers, glued back together and passed on to the next generation. Some of Agnes Lyle's ballads, such as "The Gypsy Laddie," "The Twa Sisters," and "The Golden Vanity," seem to be those cracked and glued heirlooms, ballads much like the ones being collected today. But many are pieces fresh from the potter's wheel, the design traditional but the item itself bearing the mark of the potter's hand.

FIVE

The Weaver's Daughter Soars

The repertoire of ballads collected from Agnes Lyle of Kilbarchan demonstrates that this singer brings to her ballads not only her competence in a traditional oral technique but also the ideals and genius of her personal aesthetic. To some extent this aesthetic finds expression in traditional ballad structure and ballad language, the common vehicles of oral technique. Especially in her quatrain ballads, she relies on such elements as formulaic phrasing, commonplace stanzas, repetition, the three-act structure, and annular, binary, and trinary structures of other sorts. In exploitation of these traditional resources Agnes Lyle is competent and more than competent. In her "Mary Hamilton," for instance, she frames the essential action with a prologue presenting Mary's arrival in court and an epilogue presenting her final encounter with the king. Within this frame she moves the story through three dramatic and well-organized scenes or acts. The first of these acts consists of a triad of paired stanzas. The second consists of a pair of paired stanzas. The third consists of another triad of paired stanzas, but, to make the act longer and fuller since it is the most important of the three, the triad is framed by a ring. There is a nice irony built into the character structure, with none of the characters quite fitting standard roles of hero, heroine, or villain. Tension and suspense, achieved by the delayed appearance of the king, resolve not in the rescue of the heroine but in her heroic refusal of such an easy solution. In this fine version of "Mary Hamilton" the singer expresses her aesthetic impulse almost entirely by the nuanced use of the traditional resources of oral ballad technique. What is true of "Mary Hamilton," in this regard, is true of the quatrain ballads as a group, as Chapter 3 has demonstrated.

Though Agnes Lyle is quite responsive to the peculiarities of each separate ballad tradition, her ballads, like those of Mrs. Brown, often give the impression of being assimilated into a generic narrative structure which exists independent of the particular ballad. Mrs. Brown's couplet ballads, in particular, have much of the complexity usually reserved for quatrain ballads. But when Agnes Lyle struggles with the couplet or some other uncongenial metrical medium she sometimes produces an unsatisfactory, amorphous rendition. In three cases, however, the struggle has led her to the discovery of unique narrative and aesthetic potential in the material of a particular ballad tradition. In these three cases she goes beyond mere responsiveness to deep intuition. Each of these three ballads grows organically, not stretched over a generalized narrative framework, but informed by an intuited narrative principle inherent in the very concept of the ballad in question. For "Babylon" the singer had to go beyond standard ballad technique to discover an adequate primary narrative principle. But for "The Cruel Mother" and "The Braes o Yarrow" she found within the common resources of balladry a pair of techniques that she could elevate to primary narrative principles.

Because "Babylon" has a unique structure it would seem to belong to a somewhat different genre from that of the ballads considered so far in this study. The analysis of those ballads indicates that there is some sense in talking about a genre of Anglo-Scottish classic oral ballads. This genre admits a structural definition analogous to the structural definitions of *märchen* based upon Propp's analysis. The definition can be formulated in terms of the characteristic structuring forms and patterns identified in earlier chapters. Agnes Lyle's quatrain ballads, such as "Mary Hamilton," "Johnie Scot," and "Lord Derwentwater" exhibit these characteristic structuring forms and patterns and belong to this genre, as do all the ballads of Mrs. Brown, even the couplet ballads. And many of Agnes Lyle's other ballads likewise aspire to membership in this genre, whether or not they achieve it.

There are, however, ballads in the English-language tradition which have always troubled scholars. Certainly the riddle or wit-combat ballads (Child 1, 2, 3, and 46), "Edward" (Child 13), "The Maid Freed From the Gallows" (Child 95), and "Our Goodman" (Child 274) do not derive their fundamental structure from a complex of annular, binary, and trinary stanzaic, narrative, and character patterns, though they may admit some of these patterns incidentally.[1] Hence, they do not conform to any definition of ballad which uses such structures as defining criteria. Because these troublesome ballads have unique particular structures, each seems to constitute its own genre. The idea of a one-member genre or genus is not new. The medieval scholastics held that among angels there is no species or individuation within genus: each angel, exhausting the possibilities of its own kind of being, is a genus unto itself. In the more sublunary genera, on the other hand, there are often several possibilities of species (e.g., *Canis canis, Canis lupus,* and *Canis latrans*), and innumerable possibilities of individuation. So within balladry. Versions of specific ballads, such as "Mary Hamilton," "Fair Janet," "Little Musgrave," or "Sir Patrick Spens," while remaining individual and distinctive, exhibit at the same time (in all orally recreated renditions, at least) the common generic structure of oral classic ballads. But "Edward," "The Maid Freed from the Gallows," and certain other ballads do not exhibit this common generic structure. In each case the underlying and defining structural principle is unique and so limited in its narrative possibilities that it can give rise to only one ballad or ballad group. "The Maid Freed from the Gallows," for instance, demonstrates astonishing uniformity not only in English tradition, but throughout Europe, from the Magyar plains to the Scandinavian fjords, as Eleanor Long has shown (1971). Whatever the language, a person in trouble calls upon a succession of relatives, who disappoint, and a lover, who usually succeeds. This narrative idea does not produce multiple stories. All realizations are so similar as to be identified with one another. "The Maid," surprisingly enough, turns out to be an angel. In the case of some of these ballads, the genre or genus proves a little more versatile, admitting of differentiation into two or three individual ballad types. The group of wit-combat ballads, for example, may constitute a distinctive genre, but clearly that genre admits of little speciation, the possibilities for structuring narratives around this particular sort of verbal duel being limited.

"Babylon" seems to be such another ballad, differentiating into a limited number of sub-types. In the English-language tradition this ballad divides into two main sub-traditions, differing principally in the denouement. In one sub-tradition the three sisters are accosted by an outlaw, who offers either marriage or death. The first two sisters, the meek ones, simply choose death. But the third sister says, in effect, "You're not going to get away with this; my brother will avenge me." The outlaw asks her brother's name, and she says it is Baby Lon, or some such outlandish name. Recognizing his own name, and too late recognizing his sister, the brother kills himself. The second sub-tradition, to which the Lyle "Babylon" belongs, is like the first, up to the point where the third sister starts making threats. In this sub-tradition she says she has not one but three brothers to avenge her. The outlaw asks about the brothers, and she says that one is such and such (usually a minister), the second is such and such, and the third is an outlaw in these very woods. Recognizing the description of himself and his brothers, the outlaw then kills himself. The essential difference, then, is that in the first sub-tradition the anagnorisis of the tragedy is consequent upon revelation of the name, whereas in the second, it is consequent upon revelation of the livelihood of the three brothers.[2] As often happens with ballads, individual renditions seldom realize fully the Platonic essence of the ballad. In the case of "Babylon," however, two of the Child versions are quite Platonic. The A version is a fully realized rendition of the first sub-type, with the outlaw recognizing his own name. And the Lyle text is a fully realized rendition of the second sub-type, with the outlaw recognizing the description of himself and his brothers. From this point of view the Lyle text is the only "perfect" version of the second sub-type in either Child or Bronson.

"Babylon" (Child 14D)

1   There were three sisters, they lived in a bower,
      Sing Anna, sing Margaret, sing Marjorie
    The youngest o them was the fairest flower.
      And the dew goes thro the wood, gay ladie

2 The oldest of them she's to the wood gane,
To seek a braw leaf and to bring it hame.

3 There she met with an outlyer bold,
Lies many long nights in the woods so cold.

4 "Istow a maid, or istow a wife?
Wiltow twinn with thy maidenhead, or thy sweet life?"

5 "O kind sir, if I hae't at my will,
I'll twinn with my life, keep my maidenhead still."

6 He's taen out his we pen-knife,
He's twinned this young lady of her sweet life.

7 He wiped his knife along the dew;
But the more he wiped, the redder it grew.

8 The second of them she's to the wood gane,
To seek her old sister, and to bring her hame.

9 There she met with an outlyer bold
Lies many long nights in the woods so cold.

10 "Istow a maid, or istow a wife?
Wiltow twinn with thy maidenhead, or thy sweet life?"

11 "O kind sir, if I hae't at my will,
I'll twinn with my life, keep my maidenhead still."

12 He's taen out his we pen-knife,
He's twinned this young lady of her sweet life.

13 He wiped his knife along the dew;
But the more he wiped, the redder it grew.

14 The youngest of them she's to the wood gane,
To seek her two sisters and to bring them hame.

15 There she met with an outlyer bold,
Lies many long nights in the woods so cold.

16 "Istow a maid, or istow a wife?
Wiltow twinn with thy maidenhead, or thy sweet life?"

17 "If my three brethren they were here,
Such questions as these thou durst nae speer."

18 "Pray, what may thy three brethren be,
That I durst na mak so bold with thee?"

19 "The eldest o them is a minister bred,
He teaches the people from evil to good.

20 "The second o them is a ploughman good,
He ploughs the land for his livelihood.

21　"The youngest of them is an outlyer bold,
　　Lies many a long night in the woods so cold."

22　He stuck his knife then into the ground,
　　He took a long race, let himself fall on.

In this second sub-tradition the structure grows out of the cast of characters: a father (implicit here, explicit in the Child E version), three daughters,
their three brothers. The incipit, establishing that there are three daughters,
unfolds into a story of encounters between three sisters and an outlaw or
"outlyer," and this third encounter in turn unfolds into three parts as the third
sister describes her three brothers (see Diagram 1). This unfolding technique,
though uncommon in balladry, is an old ploy. A highly specialized type of
incremental repetition, it can be defined as follows: A single narrative element
unfolds to reveal a repetitive series of n elements. The last of these elements in
turn unfolds to reveal a new series of n elements. And so on.

DIAGRAM 1
"Unfolding" in "Babylon"

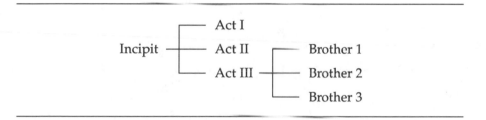

In the *New Testament* book of *Revelation*, for instance, the great book has
seven seals. The breaking of the seventh seal introduces a new group of
seven—in this case angels with trumpets. And so on.

In *Revelation* the device is a pre-existent structure into which John has
assimilated his vision,[3] a framework upon which he has hung his narrative.
In "Babylon" the device is part of the very concept of the ballad. Without
the three daughters there would be no ballad, without the triple encounter
there would be no plot, and without the triple identification of brothers
there would be no denouement.

Although the controlling structure in the Lyle version is the unfolding
structure, the trinary principle is at work as well, determining that there shall
be three sisters, not two or five, and three brothers, not two or one. The
binary principle is at work balancing stanzas in question and answer sticho-
mythia. These forces, however, are not the fundamental narrative forces in
the ballad. Nor is the fundamental narrative force the stanzaic structure, in
which a prologue describing the three sisters, introduces the three acts corresponding to the triple encounter of maidens and outlaw (see Diagram 1). But

an examination of this act structure will show how the unfolding principle dominates it.

The ballad unfolds the first time when the prologue opens into the three-act triple encounter. The first two acts are composed of three pairs of balanced stanzas. Each balance is connected by action more than by any of the principles of repetition so common in the quatrain ballads. The first balance of each act describes one of the sisters being accosted by the outlaw. The second balance contains the dialogue. The third balance describes the murder followed by the prophetic reddening of the knife as the outlaw tries to clean it. Act II consists of a simple repetition of Act I, with the second sister substituted for the first (see Diagram 2).

DIAGRAM 2
Narrative Structure of "Babylon"

ACTS I AND II	ACT III
Balance 1: Girl goes to wood	Girl goes to wood
Girl meets outlaw	Girl meets outlaw
Balance 2: He: Marry or die?	He: Marry or die?
She: I choose death	She: My brothers will kill you
Balance 3: Outlaw kills girl	He: Who are your brothers
	She: Ploughman
	Minister
	Outlaw
Wiped blade reddens	Outlaw falls on blade
(Omen of death)	(Omen fulfilled)

The first balance and a half of Act III repeat the corresponding stanzas of the first and second acts. But the second couplet of the second balance, in which the last sister mentions the brothers who would protect her honor, prepares for the second unfolding. This unfolding occurs in the third balance when the outlaw, in one stanza, asks who her brothers are, and the maiden, in three stanzas, tells him they are a minister, a ploughman, and an outlaw.

A narrative unfolds when the last item in a series opens out into a new series of the same size. In the Lyle "Babylon" the series which unfolds is, to be very precise, the series of killings which is narrated in the first member of the third balance in each act. In Act I and II the outlaw kills his sisters. In Act III the sister kills the outlaw brother. Her weapon is the triple revelation.

Thus the four stanzas in which the girl kills her brother by telling him who she is and who he is, correspond structurally to the first member of the third balance in the other two acts, in which the outlaw literally kills his sisters. The final stanza of the ballad, in which the outlaw falls on his own knife, completes the balance and fulfills the prophecy contained in the second member of the balance in the preceding acts (see Diagram 2).

The irony of the concept and the structural perfection of the realization are the two principal aesthetic claims of this rendition. Like many of the pieces in Agnes Lyle's repertoire this couplet ballad is in a meter she finds intractable, but by abandoning the effort to conform its irony to the shape of the quatrain ballads, she is able to find its true individual structure. Her genius shows in her ability to intuit the essence of this ironic tragedy and realize that essence perfectly. Although not a ballad of the same kind as the quatrain ballads discussed in chapter 4, it is, of its own kind, equally competent, and deserves to be ranked with those pieces.

In "Babylon," as in the quatrain ballads, Agnes Lyle expresses her aesthetic in a traditional structure, although in this case not a generalized structure but a structure particular to the tradition of this ballad. In other ballads, however, she sometimes expresses her aesthetic in ways particular to the singer herself, not to the tradition. Especially does this happen when her grasp of traditional technique proves inadequate to the task at hand, and she must leap beyond the limitations of her own technique. Because her technique is based on the standard ballad quatrain, she is not forced to make that leap in her songs in this meter. But her two most successful pieces, "The Cruel Mother" and "The Braes o Yarrow," admirably illustrate this leap to originality. Each of these pieces is in a meter which is, for her, not standard. In each case the success of the piece demanded that the singer go beyond mere mechanical mastery of technique to a total understanding of that technique at some deeper level, beyond mere mechanical mastery of plot to an understanding of the inherent tensions and conflicts in that plot. For "The Cruel Mother" this success required the intuition that the ballad could be seen as a story of transformation in the life of the woman. The technique of transformation from narrative to speech which has always been a part of ballad style provides the perfect vehicle for expression of that intuition. For "The Braes o Yarrow" this success required the intuition that the ballad was about action and reaction, that is, about exteriority and interiority. The objective, concrete narrative technique which has always been a part of ballad style, by focusing on different kinds of things to narrate in the two halves of the ballad, could in this case provide the proper vehicle for the intuition. In neither of these cases is the core of the ballad the standard three-act stanzaic structure, harmonized by supporting or contrapuntal narrative and character structures, that is so well articulated in the ballad-meter ballads. Rather, in each case the singer has developed a unique structure based on some other characteristic ballad technique. And in each case this technique provides a symbolic correlative for the major thematic idea of the ballad in question.

In "The Cruel Mother" the narrative principle, causative repetition, is one commonly but not universally found in the Child 20 tradition. That tradition includes three basic narrative elements: the description of the murder, the accusation by the ghostly boys, and the prediction of punishment. Some texts, such as the Child O text, include all three elements. Some texts, such as the Child J, include or stress only two. And some, such as the Child L, stress only one of the elements, to the exclusion or near exclusion of the other two. The Lyle version stresses the murder and the accusation, and reduces discussion of the punishment to a single line, repeated once. Causative repetition is traditional in versions that include both murder and accusation: The wording of the stanzas describing the murder and burial determines the wording of the stanzas presenting the boys' accusation. The Lyle text takes this narrative technique and pushes it to its logical ultimate. Using the transforming technique of causative repetition as an organizing principle, she has produced a perfectly symmetrical song of considerable psychological subtlety.

"The Cruel Mother" (Child 20E)

1 There was a lady, she lived in Lurk,
    Sing hey alone and alonie O
  She fell in love with her father's clerk.
    Down by yon greenwood sidie O

2 She loved him seven years and a day,
  Till her big belly did her betray.

3 She leaned her back unto a tree,
  And there began her sad misery.

4 She set her foot unto a thorn,
  And there she got her two babes born.

5 She took out her wee pen-knife
  She twind them both of their sweet life.

6 She took the sattins was on her head,
  She rolled them in both when they were dead.

7 She howkit a grave forenent the sun,
  And there she buried her twa babes in.

8 As she was walking thro her father's ha,
  She spied twa boys playing at the ba.

9 "O pretty boys, if ye were mine,
  I would dress ye both in silks so fine."

10 "O mother dear, when we were thine,
  Thou neer dressed us in silks so fine.

11 "For thou was a lady, thou livd in Lurk,
  And thou fell in love with thy father's clerk.

12 "Thou loved him seven years and a day,
    Till thy big belly did thee betray.

13 "Thou leaned thy back unto a tree,
    And there began thy sad misery.

14 "Thou set thy foot unto a thorn,
    And there thou got thy two babes born.

15 "Thou took out thy wee pen-knife,
    And twind us both of our sweet life.

16 "Thou took the sattins was on thy head,
    Thou rolled us both in when we were dead.

17 "Thou howkit a grave forenent the sun,
    And there thou buried thy twa babes in.

18 "But now we're both in [the] heavens lie,
    There is pardon for us, but none for thee."

19 "My pretty boys, beg pardon for me!"
    "There is pardon for us, but none for thee."

As Diagram 3 shows, the song divides into matching units of nine stanzas each. The foci of the annular structures of the two units are the killing itself and the description of the killing, stanzas 5 and 15 respectively. The focus of the annular structure of the ballad as a whole is stanza 10, in which the pretty boys reveal themselves to be the murdered children of the lady of Lurk.

Part I of the song describes a lady leading a double life with great success for seven years. She has a secret lover but long escapes pregnancy. When she finally does become pregnant she manages to conceal the fact and dispose of the infants. Since she gave birth without the help of a midwife, she has no reason to suppose that her actions will ever become known. So secure is she in her immunity that she can even allow herself to make conventional sentimental remarks about (as she supposes) other people's children.

Part II is a transformation, stanza by stanza, of Part I. The pretty little boys whom the lady did not take seriously now describe to her, incident by incident, her whole secret life. Each detail, exactly as it happened, is thrown back in her face. The ballad technique is especially effective here: a few simple adjustments transform an objective statement of fact into a damning accusation.

This transformation of Part I into Part II is mediated by a single stanza, the tenth, set squarely in the middle of the song. All the lady's security crumbles when she hears the boys address her as "Mother dear!" A simple word uncovers a hitherto unsuspected relationship and transforms the whole reality of the woman's life. The effect on the listener, too, is electrifying. Who has not had the eerie feeling of being watched under circumstances in which there was no way anyone could be watching? Who has not had the

DIAGRAM 3
Causative Repetition as Structuring Principle in "The Cruel Mother"

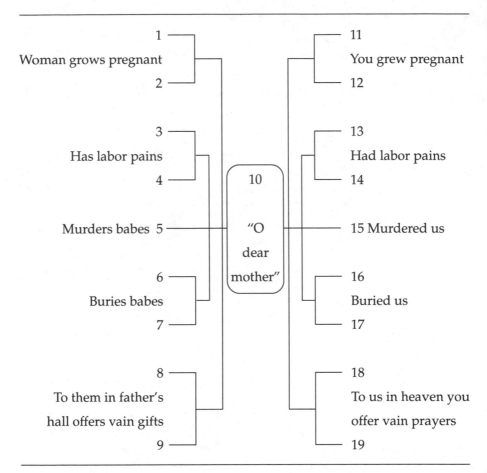

experience of being observed doing something they did not really want anyone to see them doing, even if it was no more than picking their nose or
scratching their rear end? The motif of the secret action observed is used
with chilling effect in suspense films such as Hitchcock's *Rear Window*, as
well as in this ballad.

The course of events in the lady's life, as narrated in Part I, transforms
her from a simple girl in love with a man below her station into a har-
dened murderess of infants, incapable of remorse. The recapitulation of
this course of events, in Part II, transforms this monster into a cringing
wretch, begging to be saved by the very children she has murdered. The
subject of the ballad, then, is transformation: the transformation of innocence into arrogance, of arrogance into abjection, of fact into accusation, of
immunity into culpability, of living soul into ghost, of victim into aggres-

sor, of concealment into revelation, of object into word, of event into discourse, of objectivity into subjectivity. Causative repetition serves as the ideal vehicle for expressing this transformation. But in the last two stanzas of Part II, when plot considerations do not demand exact correspondence and wording does not permit it, the transformation still occurs on the conceptual level: the "father's ha[ll]" becomes "heaven hie" (our Father's house, where there are many mansions), the facetious offer of fine silks becomes a desperate plea for prayers, and the sentimental epithet "pretty boys" becomes, by the addition of a simple "my," an appeal to kinship that is self-damning. It was the unique achievement of Agnes Lyle to discover in the logic of a ballad technique, causative repetition, the ideal vehicle for this song of transformation.

For "The Braes o Yarrow" this singer's artistic task is formidable. She must fashion an effective and controlled text in an uncongenial medium with severe rhyming restraints. The meter is a feminine-rhyming quatrain of alternating four- and three-beat lines. The rhyme-scheme admits only words that rhyme with *Yarrow*. Agnes Lyle, however, is more than equal to the task and produces here perhaps the single most powerful piece in the repertoire.

"The Braes o Yarrow" (Child 214C)

1   There were three lords birling at the wine
     On the dowie downs o Yarrow;
   They made a compact them between
     They would go fight tomorrow.

2   "Thou took our sister to be thy bride,
     And thou neer thocht her thy marrow;
   Thou stealed her frae her daddie's back,
     When she was the rose o Yarrow."

3   "Yes, I took your sister to be my bride,
     And I made her my marrow;
   I stealed her frae her daddie's back,
     And she's still the rose o Yarrow."

4   He is hame to his lady gane,
     As he had dune before! O;
   Says, "Madam, I must go and fight
     On the dowie downs o Yarrow."

5   "Stay at hame, my lord," she said,
     "For that will cause much sorrow;
   For my brethren three they will slay thee,
     On the dowie downs o Yarrow."

6   "Hold your tongue, my lady fair,
     For what needs a' this sorrow?
   For I'll be hame gin the clock strikes nine,
     From the dowie downs o Yarrow."

7   She wush his face, she kamed his hair,
       As she had dune before, O;
    She dressed him up in his armour clear,
       Sent him furth to fight on Yarrow.

8   "Come you here to hawk or hound,
       Or drink the wine that's so clear, O?
    Or come you here to eat in your words,
       That you're not the rose o Yarrow?"

9   "I came not here to hawk or hound,
       Nor to drink the wine that's so clear, O;
    Nor I came not here to eat in my words,
       For I'm still the rose o Yarrow."

10 Then they a' begoud to fight,
       I wad they focht richt sore, O,
    Till a cowardly man came behind his back,
       And pierced his body thorough.

11 "Gae hame, gae hame, it's my man John,
       As ye have done before, O,
    And tell it to my gay lady
       That I soundly sleep on Yarrow."

12 His man John he has gane hame,
       As he had done before, O,
    And told it to his gay lady,
       That he soundly slept on Yarrow.

13 "I dreamed a dream now since the streen,
       God keep us a' frae sorrow!
    That my lord and I was pu'ing the heather green
       From the dowie downs o Yarrow.

14 Sometimes she rade, sometimes she gaed,
       As she had dune before, O,
    And aye between she fell in a soune,
       Lang or she cam to Yarrow.

15 Her hair it was five quarters lang,
       'Twas like the gold for yellow;
    She twisted it round his milk-white hand,
       And she's drawn him hame from Yarrow.

16 Out and spak her father dear,
       Says, What needs a' this sorrow?
    For I'll get you a far better lord
       Than ever died on Yarrow.

17 "O hold your tongue, father," she said,
       "For ye've bred a' my sorrow;
    For that rose'll neer spring sae sweet in May
       As that rose I lost on Yarrow."

The success of the ballad is made possible in part by compensating factors that help offset the limitations imposed by meter and rhyme. The "Yarrow" tradition is very rich in Scotland. There are three or four separate ballads, and perhaps a lyric song as well, subsumed under Child 214–215. These pieces exchange stanzas among themselves rather freely and generate a good stock of model stanzas. The rhyme requirement is interpreted rather freely. Among acceptable rhymes for *Yarrow* are, from this ballad, *yellow*, *sorrow*, *sore O*, and *thorough*. The word itself seems to have at least three distinct usages: (1) the name of a plant; (2) a geographical name—river, village, or region; (3) a metonym for fields or downs. As a result of all these factors—the number of songs based on the *Yarrow* rhyme, the multitude of stanzas generated in these songs, the liberal interpretation of what constitutes a rhyme, and the several meanings of the word to be rhymed—the restraints on the singer are rather less stringent than might at first be imagined. Indeed, as with the "Mary Hamilton" tradition, there is almost an embarrassment of riches to choose from in the form of formulas and commonplaces (or "context-bound formulaic stanzas," as Andersen would prefer to call them, since they are particular to one tradition). It is this richness within the *Yarrow* tradition itself that compensates for the fact that the singer can not draw upon her standard quatrain repertoire of commonplaces and formulas.

Nevertheless, the necessity of solving the special artistic problems of "The Braes o Yarrow" has affected the over-all architectonics. The character structure is relentlessly annular, but the strain shows in the stanzaic structure. Strain here is perhaps to be expected because the metrical and rhyming restrictions are in effect stanzaic restrictions. The ballad has, in fact, two stanzaic structures, not one, corresponding to the external-internal split operative in the ballad and to the narrative and supra-narrative functions of the stanzas (see Diagram 4). The first of these is a three-act structure framed by a one-stanza prologue and two-stanza epilogue reminiscent of "Mary Hamilton." Most of the balances consist of statement and response, usually in the form of causative repetition, though in the balance at stanzas 12–13 the statement is in indirect discourse, and the causative repetition links 12 with 11 instead of 13. The three acts divide the narrative cleanly into preparation, battle, and mourning.

This three-act structure is counterpointed very strongly by a two-part stanzaic structure corresponding to the movement of the ballad on the affective or supra-narrative level. The annular character structure reinforces this two-part structure, pivoting as it does on the very point between stanzas 11 and 12 which serves as the break point for the alternate stanzaic structure (see Diagram 5). The differences between Part I and Part II are multiple and fundamental. The first half of the ballad concentrates on the hero, the second half on the heroine. The first half concentrates on the action: the stanzas are there to tell what parties are involved and what these parties do; all is for the sake of story. The second half concentrates on feelings; the stanzas are there to tell

DIAGRAM 4
"The Braes o Yarrow": Complementary Stanzaic Structures

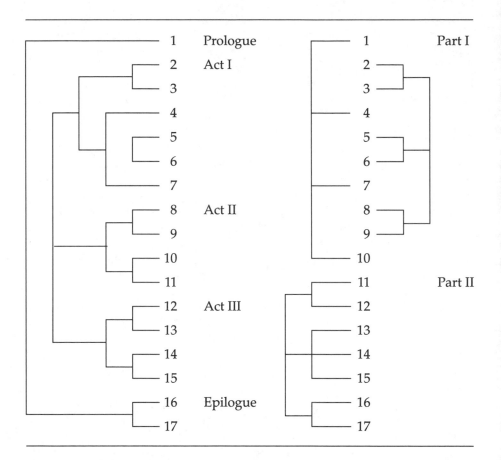

what the parties feel; all is for the sake of character revelation. The difference between the two parts is the difference between epic and lyric, between plot and character, between doing and feeling, between the physical and the spiritual, between action and contemplation. This difference between the two parts corresponds to a fundamental duality in worldview. And in the worldview of Scottish balladry that duality includes the difference between male and female, as the character structure emphasizes.

Part I of the ballad provides rather conventional action and confrontation scenes. First the brothers threaten the hero and he defies them. Then the hero announces to the heroine his heroic intentions, to which she, like the mother in "Johnie Scot" and the boy in "Sir Patrick Spens," responds with misgivings. Finally the hero confronts the three brothers and is treacherously slain. All action is clearly motivated, but the focus is on action and not on character. What is explicitly stated to happen constitutes the message being

DIAGRAM 5
"The Braes o Yarrow": Character Structure

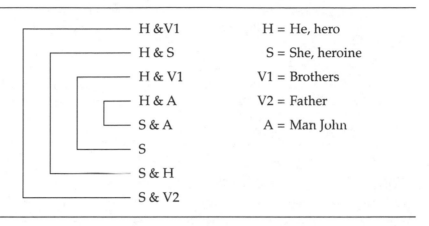

H & V1	H = He, hero
H & S	S = She, heroine
H & V1	V1 = Brothers
H & A	V2 = Father
S & A	A = Man John
S	
S & H	
S & V2	

conveyed. Of course the stanzas have a supra-narrative function, as in all ballads. But this supra-narrative function is primarily foreshadowing. The commonplace stanza used as an incipit, for instance, "signals violent confrontation," often about a woman, according to Andersen (1985, 124; for more on supra-narrative function see chapter 6). And according to Rogers (1980, 96), hair combing, a symbolic act performed in stanza 7, often indicates waiting for a beloved, perhaps in vain.[4] The principal connotation of the action in the context of this ballad concerns plot: The hero won't come back. Throughout Part I, then, the principal information conveyed, both explicitly and by implication, concerns external action.

In Part II, however, the actual message of each stanza goes far beyond the external action portrayed. The shift in emphasis occurs right in the middle of a scene, when the stabbed hero calls his man John to his side. He is very careful about how John is to tell the heroine of his death:

> Tell it to my gay lady
> That I soundly sleep on Yarrow.

At the moment of death his thought is directed more to her than to himself. Tell her not to grieve, he says. His sleep will be peaceful and "sound." The sentiment is hardly original, but then, neither are love and death. The reason for pointing to the stanza is to indicate the precise point at which the ballad begins to concentrate on how people feel and react rather than on what they do. The hero in this stanza confirms that indeed he loves his wife, and it was conjugal love, not stubborn pride, which motivated him to fight. The sleep image of stanza 11 is carried over into stanza 13. There the heroine reveals how closely in tune with her husband she is. At the moment he "falls asleep" she too is sleeping, but far from soundly;

disturbing images of pulling heather with her husband (as for a marriage bed?) fill her dreams.

In Part II of "Braes o Yarrow" the heroine reveals herself by what she says, but much more by what she does. Edith Randam Rogers, in her study of ballad symbolism *The Perilous Hunt* (1980), comments on this aspect of ballad style:

> The "real" quality of symbols is closely related to the eminently visual nature of ballad diction. Occidental culture, as it is, tends to communicate through the eyes; ballads, however, go even beyond the customary proportions in translating into visual terms many phenomena normally associated with any of the other four senses, or none of them. . . . The pleasure of touch is communicated in visual terms when we watch a girl comb her lover's hair. We shall further see that various psychological processes also become visible. (2)

Stanzas 14 and 15 demonstrate striking use of visible actions to render psychological processes visible. In stanza 14 the girl leaps on her horse, a conventional ballad response that indicates anxiety to be at the scene of trouble. But her anxiety breaks all conventional bonds. She pushes her horse to the utmost. When it can do no more she leaps off and runs ahead on foot. "Sometimes she rade and sometimes she gaed." Her anxiety has a manic quality, however. Sometimes she has to run because she can't sit still on her horse; but sometimes she can not even stand, for "aye between she fell in a soune." The manic action continues in the next stanza. Variants of stanza 15 appear in a number of the *Yarrow* ballads, but never to such effect. The grotesque image of a young woman riding home with her lover's body dragging in the road behind her, tied by its hand to her long yellow hair, is a compelling icon of abandonment and grief.

As Rogers suggests, this process of expressing inner states by visible actions, which may be called *objectifying,* is a standard ballad practice. Indeed, objectivity is one of the hallmarks of balladry, as of much of Western folk narrative. In an objective narrative style objectifying through speech or action is almost the only way to reveal inner states (See the next chapter). Usually the technique appears consistently throughout a piece. But in the Lyle "Braes o Yarrow" there is a polarization. The first part concentrates on action, with no hint of the significance of the action. At the end of Part I, in fact, the true plot is complete. The ballad could have ended here, for "Sir Patrick Spens" does end at just this point, with the betrayed hero dead and his wife waiting in vain for his return. The *Yarrow* ballad goes on, however. In the second half all is interiority, all is significance. The words and actions are meaningless apart from their emotional effect. They accomplish nothing, but they express much. And objectification, a kind of incarnation without which the internal can not be externalized, here becomes a symbol of the duality that structures this ballad and the worldview out of which it grows.

The central stanzas of Part II express the heroine's grief in manic and grotesque terms. The final two stanzas take a more conventional turn. In these stanzas the woman's father rebukes her for the excess of her grief. She replies that he has no right to speak. He himself is the cause of her grief. These stanzas describing such an exchange between a father and a bereaved child constitute a stanza cluster or "theme," and both "Sheath and Knife" and "Jamie Douglas" end with realizations of the same "theme." This "theme" in "Braes o Yarrow" resonates with the echo of its use wherever it occurs. Thus, in the last two stanzas the woman's grief, previously expressed in all its particularity, is now subsumed to the universal through the use of narrative material familiar from other contexts. Her story becomes one more chapter in the universal history of infamy.

The cliché has it that great art is born out of struggle. In the case of Agnes Lyle the struggle was at least in part with the ballad medium itself. When her medium refused to conform to the standards she set for herself in the quatrain ballads, her material sometimes defeated her. But in "Babylon" her struggle with the material yielded a highly competent ballad, fully realizing the unique narrative structure informing its tradition. And in "The Cruel Mother" and "The Braes o Yarrow" the struggle yielded something more: ballads which elicit the kind of emotional involvement and reward the kind of close analysis that great poetry and great song elicit and reward. For:

> What is called oral tradition is as intricate and meaningful an art form as its derivative "literary tradition." . . . It is not simply a less polished, more haphazard, or cruder second cousin twice removed, to literature. (Lord 1960, 141)

PART THREE

The Ballads of Agnes Lyle

Leitmotifs

Love and Death

Students ballad-hunting in the southern Appalachians used to be advised to ask for "old-timey love songs" (on the theory that mountaineers would not know what "ballads" were). When they came back home and sang the pieces they had learned in their wanderings, families and friends often asked, "But why are they so sad?" This combination of clichés, that ballads are "love songs," but "sad," is not entirely inaccurate. Recent scholarly work from diverse critical schools confirms the impressionistic conviction that love and death are the great ballad subjects.

Three post-Lord, post-Buchan books, in particular, give serious attention to ballad meaning and to the leitmotifs in which that meaning often finds expression. Roger deV. Renwick, in *English Folk Poetry: Structure and Meaning* (1980), takes a structuralist approach to the ethic and world view expressed in traditional verse. Edith Randam Rogers, in *The Perilous Hunt* (1980), takes a literary approach to the use of symbols in European balladry. Flemming G. Andersen, in *Commonplace and Creativity* (1985), takes a narratological-linguistic approach to the connotations of commonplaces in Anglo-Scottish balladry. Application to Agnes Lyle's ballads confirms the insights of these authors into the thematic roles of love and death in traditional English-language ballads and also suggests ways in which her repertoire is distinctive. Renwick's analysis of the social structure of "euphemistic" ballads helps to explain why certain Lyle ballads end with love or, alternately, with death. Rogers's analysis of six classes of symbols, all dealing with both love and death, casts light on obscure points in Lyle ballads. And Andersen's analysis of the supra-narrative function of commonplace stanzas brings out subtleties in the narrative handling of love and death in the Lyle ballads. This analysis of leitmotif from these several points of view will tend to confirm the unity and especially the traditionality of the Lyle repertoire by demonstrating how the singer consistently frames her ballads within traditional limits. And it will confirm the creativity of the singer by demonstrating how she achieves nuance through exercise of choice within those limits.

Renwick touches on love and death in his chapter on "The Bold Fisherman" (e.g., 26, 41). But a more useful chapter for students of balladry is probably the chapter on "The Semiotics of Sexual Liaisons," in which the love-death opposition is related to the comic or tragic outcome of the love affair. In this chapter Renwick sets up a three-part classification for those

English folksongs which include sexual acts as part of their content. He calls the three types the symbolic, the metaphoric, and the euphemistic.[1] In the first type, the sex act is represented symbolically and somewhat abstractly, as in the following two examples from among many he cites:

> The cuckoo is a fine bird,
> She sings as she fly,
> And the more she sing Cuckoo
> The summer draw nigh;
> (63; from Sharp 1974, 1: 623)

and (a little more explicit):

> Down in the meadows the other day
> Gathering flowers both fine and gay,
> Gathering flowers both red and blue,
> I little thought what love can do.
> (65–66; from Sharp 1974, 1: 171)

The first piece is probably not about cuckoos, and the second is not about flowers, at least not primarily; flowers and cuckoos function as symbols in these songs. There is, accordingly, no one-to-one correspondence of elements in the symbolic action with elements in the symbolized sexual action; it makes no sense to ask what is the singing, and what is the flying, and what is the red, and what is the blue. In metaphoric songs, another of Renwick's types, there is such a correspondence, as the following example illustrates:

> O come, said the soldier, 'tis time to give o'er
> O no, says the fair maid, please play one tune more
> I do like your playing and the touching of the long string
> And to see the pretty flowers grow, hear the nightingale sing.
> (93; from Kennedy 1975, 415)

In this example music is not a symbol but a metaphor, and the one-to-one correspondence between musical references in the dialogue and aspects of the sexual encounter is quite clear. The third type (which Renwick places second), is euphemistic in that it uses the "reasonably decorous" speech of ordinary conversation, in which the sex act is represented by a euphemism, as in "The Baffled Knight" and "The Basket of Eggs," two of Renwick's examples, or in the following stanza from Agnes Lyle's "Lord William":

> In one broad book they learned baith,
> In one broad bed they lay;
> But when her father came to know
> He gart her come away.

In euphemistic songs girls indulge in "wantonness and play," until they "go with child." Young men "lie with" their partners, or even, as in "Bonnie Baby Livingston," they "stow them clean away."

Drawing on analysis of 92 English euphemistic songs, Renwick builds a model of the sexual code expressed in songs of this type (72). The signifiers in the model are five oppositional pairs of personal traits related to territory, experience, social status, personality, and motive: Is the character acontextual (e.g., a sailor), or does the character have a particular territorial context (e.g., a village maid)? Is the character older and more experienced or younger and more innocent? Is the character high-born or lowly? Is the character blessed with a strong and innovative personality or a weak and conventional one? Finally, does the character court over the strong opposition of some authority figure, or does the character court for intrinsic motives (i.e., for pure love)? Renwick labels his oppositions masculine and feminine, but the terms assertive and passive will serve the purpose here.[2] The basic message of the model is that a character who exhibits passive traits will have a tragic (or at least unsuccessful) experience in a sexual liaison with one who exhibits assertive traits. The experience can become comic (ending happily), if the passive one can exhibit at least one assertive trait—though even that may not be enough.

Since one signifier suffices for a euphemistic song, although some include more, the possible combinations of elements from the model are many. Renwick identifies 13 applications ("precepts") among his 92 songs. Though his first group of applications, to songs about prostitutes, does not apply to Agnes Lyle's songs (none of hers are about prostitutes), his other two groups of applications are quite apt. The second group of applications is to songs about the eternal triangle of husband, wife, and lover. Here Renwick observes that the husband who is passive in his relationship to his wife will have a tragic experience. "Little Musgrave" would seem to be a weak application of this principle: Lord Barnabas, the husband, has a definite context, and is out of that context, a "feminine," or "passive" trait according to the model, when his wife, taking an active role, seduces Mossgrey. A stronger example is Jamie Douglas, who passively accepts what people tell him about his wife and locks himself in his room. So too, Linlyon is conventional and passive enough to let Barbara Livingston write to her lover, trusting to his defined context for protection. Other weak husbands are the bridegrooms in "Fair Janet," "Hind Horn," and "Lord William." A sad example of this principle is the King of Onorie, who loves the fair maid "passively," motivated by intrinsic reasons, "for womanheid / And for her fair beautie."

Adulterous lovers, Renwick observes, will likewise come to grief if they stray out of their defined context. Mossgrey is the most obvious victim of this principle. Though Renwick frames the principle in terms of wife and lover, "Mary Hamilton" demonstrates its applicability to "the other woman" as well as to "the other man." Besides straying out of her proper context, Mary Hamilton makes other "passive" mistakes, such as engaging with someone older, more experienced, and higher-born, and getting pregnant.

But Renwick discusses these latter applications of the model in connection with man-maid relationships, not in connection with adultery. This principle has an "escape clause," as Sweet William and Hind Horn demonstrate at their lovers' weddings: Innovative action can turn tragedy to comedy.

The Lyle ballads suggest further applications of the Renwick model to triangular love relationships, applications not covered in his list of "precepts." In "Little Musgrave" and again in "Gypsy Laddie" a low-born man who indulges in adultery with a high-born lady comes to grief. Lady Barnabas seems to come to grief because she initiates the liaison for intrinsic reasons (Mossgrey is good looking), and because she remains passive when the warning horn blows. "Bonnie Baby Livingston" suggests two more applications: that the innovative wife can circumvent her husband and that if she loves for intrinsic reasons, she may come to grief nonetheless.

Renwick's final set of precepts concerns relationships between a man and a maid. In his folksong sample the most important principle of all is that a liaison with an acontextual man will lead to grief, unless the maid can be resourceful, like the girl in "Basket of Eggs," who hands her lover the baby in an egg basket. But except for the "Basket of Eggs" and "Broken Token" fragments, none of Agnes Lyle's ballads clearly demonstrate this principle. It may have some application to "Babylon," in which the outlyer seems at first an acontextual man. A second important principle is that a rape or seduction attempt will be unsuccessful for the man if the maid can be innovative. A version of "The Baffled Knight" is Renwick's example of this principle at work. The strongest example in the repertoire is "Babylon," in which the two weak sisters are destroyed but the innovative sister escapes death. The love ballads that end tragically illustrate other applications of the model. "Fair Janet" and "The Cruel Mother" (along with "Mary Hamilton") have heroines who make the conventional passive mistake of becoming pregnant, and "Fair Janet," "Twa Sisters," and "The Braes o' Yarrow" have heroines who love for intrinsic reasons. The unambiguously happy love ballads in the repertoire also conform to Renwick's model. "Johnie Scot" is a complex example. The heroine exhibits the passive traits of love for intrinsic reasons as well as pregnancy. But she, to quote Renwick, "succeed[s] in escaping the tragedy by means of a sanction—by possessing the masculine trait of *social status* at least equal to, or even higher than, her male partner's" (81). "Lord William" demonstrates Renwick's final principle, that a liaison "in a neutral context with a partner of equal age, experience, and social status" (82) can end happily. William and his beloved are beyond the sea, both young and innocent, and of modest station. In terms of the model, they are made for each other.

Renwick's sample tends to focus on women in songs of courtship and on men in songs of adultery. Consequently, he says very little about the conditions under which a man may love successfully or unsuccessfully. The tragic husband in "Sheath and Knife," at least marginally a euphemistic sexual song, demonstrates only "passive" qualities: he loves for intrinsic reasons, he takes the trip at his wife's suggestion, and he goes hunting, again at her suggestion, while she has her baby. Hind Horn, on the other hand, succeeds by being innovative. Johnie Scot, finally, is innovative, acontextual (a Scots soldier in England), and doubly defiant, (since the authority figure is both father and king).

This analysis of the Lyle repertoire in terms of the Renwick model for euphemistic folksongs reveals things about both balladry and the model and suggests several conclusions. In the first place, all seventeen of the ballads with explicit sexual content are consistent with the model. This statistic is somewhat surprising in view of Renwick's statement in the following chapter of his study that "the Child ballads would have had little referential function, being antique pieces referring to a world past and gone, quite beyond the reach of the company's [i.e., the company assembled in a pub in the late nineteenth century] experiential present" (117). This consistency between the Renwick model, derived from English folksongs, and these seventeen ballads, representative of the Lowland Scots tradition, suggests that the model applies to classic ballads as well as to broadside ballads and "folksongs" in the narrowest sense of that term and to Lowland Scots songs as well as to English songs. If the model articulates a worldview, as Renwick holds, then this conclusion reinforces the impression that Lowland Scotland and England share a common set of sexual mores and attitudes. The next thing to notice is that Renwick's 13 precepts do not exhaust the applications of the model. Beyond the world of "folksong," in the world of balladry, further types of situations are imagined, and the implications of the model in these further situations are worked out. Finally, matching the model to the Lyle ballads reveals that the two components which figure most often in this repertoire are social disparity and love for intrinsic reasons.[5] The next chapter will return to this bit of data.

In *The Perilous Hunt* Edith Rogers examines six motifs or symbols common to international balladry from Britain to Russia. The book, though weak in over-all impact, is rich in individual insights into both Spanish and Anglo-Scottish ballads. Her thesis is that visual images are signalers of the emotional content of a ballad:

Deceived by the seeming simplicity of style, we may fail to give due credit to the subtle means of implying, suggesting, or insinuating; but thinking back on a ballad we have heard, we find that somehow we know much more than we were told in words. We are aware, for example, of the intentions, expectations, emotions, sufferings, strengths, or failings of a girl. Or again, we know, long before the narrative reaches that point, whether the hero is going to triumph or to die. Should we now have the ballad repeated, we are likely to find that the explicit information in the text is about the girl's dress or the man's dog, and that there is no mention of the girl's mood or the man's imminent fate.

My point is that the verse about the dress or the dogs is precisely what made us aware of all the things unsaid. . . . The literal meaning of the image is not displaced by, but coexists with its figurative meaning. This, while not the exclusive property of the poetic diction of ballads, is one of its essential characteristics. (2)

Because Rogers, like Andersen, is discussing connotations and because the symbols she identifies are sometimes encapsulated in English ballad commonplaces, there is some overlap between the Rogers and Andersen studies.

Rogers finds that the hunt, her first symbol, usually functions as a hint, a prelude to what is to come, usually either love or death. The Lyle repertoire provides several examples of hunts with such a presaging function. In the first stanza of "Johnie Scot" the association of hunting with love is almost metaphorical:

> Johnie Scott's a hunting gone.
>   To England's woods so wild,
> Until the king's old dochter dear
>   She goes to him with child.

In "Earl Richard" associations of hunting with love and with death combine as Earl Richard, out hunting, stops to visit his old girlfriend on his way to see the new one, and the scorned lady stabs him. Hunting is likewise a prelude to death in "Sheath and Knife," but this time it is the beloved who dies. The association of hunting with death by murder, as Rogers points out, is easily understood. Her examples, three Danish ballads, could almost be variants of the repertoire version of "The Braes o Yarrow":

> In Danish ballads family feuds reach a bloody settlement when the hostile parties meet in the woods. Three ballads end with a fatal clash between the hero and the lady's brothers, whose permission to court their sister he has failed to ask (DgF 303, 415, 416). (21)

In stanza 8 of "The Braes o Yarrow" the brothers even ask, "Come you here to hawk or hound?" The hero's statement in stanza 9, implying that he has left hawks and hounds at home, corresponds to a second function of hunting imagery in balladry: A successful hunt, as in "Johnie Scot," indicates the integrity of a hero, but an unsuccessful hunt indicates the hero's disintegration. In stanza 9 the unsuccessful hunt motif has been reduced to its simplest form, absence of hawk and hound. A hero without his hawk and hound is a hero doomed (Cf. Rogers 1980, 36). Note that this motif, signalling the reversal of the hero's fortunes, is introduced in the exact center of the ballad; in emotional structure as in stanzaic structure, annular symmetry sometimes prevails.

Rogers's next symbol, the game, is rare in the Lyle repertoire. The most common connotation of games is love. The commonplace about 24 ladies playing ball, as both Rogers and Andersen assert, singles out one player as the flower of them all. The implication would seem to be that she will be a flower at the game of love, just as she was at the game of ball. Her free ballplaying is too attractive to resist. Ballplaying is thus a prelude to sexual activity, usually adultery or abduction. Andersen is puzzled by a second use of ball playing, that in "The Cruel Mother" and "The Twa Brothers." Rogers clarifies the confusion: games, with their highly controlled structure, serve as symbols of fate (54). Thus, when the cruel mother spies her boys playing at ball, fate enters the story. In Agnes Lyle's version, the relentless march of the second half of the ballad reinforces this interpretation of the function of the ball playing. Similarly, the twa brothers playing a game of ball can not avoid their sad fate in Child 49. Indeed, the primary function of games in all ballads may be as symbols of fate: their function as symbols of love may be a special case, an indication of the fated and fatal quality of the love to come.[4]

Clothing, the third symbol which Rogers analyzes, is one of the most ubiquitous symbols in ballads as in life. It frequently indicates the beauty of the wearer. Thus, when Hind Horn gives his beloved a broad gown, he is acknowledging her beauty, and when the miller admires the younger sister's silver slippers and ribbons many, he is admiring the girl's multiple charms. Rich clothes, in addition to symbolizing beauty, often symbolize wealth, status, and love (60). When the Lady of Cassillis leaves with the Gypsy Laddie, she trades her silken cloak for a plaidie. In putting off her silk, she is putting off wealth, status, and the love of her husband. But not completely. She retains her gown, stockings, and shoes. When the Gypsy Laddie sells these he is selling what is left of her wealth, beauty, status, and what is left of her love for him. Another subtle example of this sort of clothing symbolism occurs in "Hind Horn." Returning to his own land on his sweetheart's wedding day, Hind Horn discovers that his beauty, wealth, and status have not served to secure love. So he niffers clothes with a beggar. To gain all, he is willing to lose all. His act of disguise, functional on the level of plot, is a kind of a death on the level of meaning; and unless the grain of wheat die it remains itself alone.

Giving clothing can serve as a kind of expiation (66). Thus, when the cruel mother sees the pretty boys in her father's hall she wants to dress them in silks so fine. But it is too late. The boys reject this act of expiation. But at least the cruel mother had wrapped her dead sons in the "sattins was on her head." Mary Hamilton does not even do so much. She signals her initial cruelty by putting her child in a piner pig—a small pot—instead of wrapping it well.

While much of the poetic excellence of a ballad comes through manipulation of the singer's resources, poetic qualities also arise through the accidents of transmission (Coffin 1961, 250 ff.). "Mary Hamilton" offers a striking example. In those texts of the ballad in which the dead baby remains undiscovered and unadmitted, Mary believes she is going to a wedding or other pageantry in the Capital. She dresses accordingly. Not until she gets to the courtroom, or even the gallows, does she realize that, fooled herself, she has fooled no one. In Agnes Lyle's version, and not in hers alone, Mary knows clearly that she is going to her execution. When stanzas about going to and dressing for a wedding become attached to a version like this one in which Mary has admitted murdering her child, the effect is startling. The wedding is her execution, her wedding with death. And the care with which she dresses for the occasion is a commentary on the great internal strength of this woman who is also a child-murderess. The fascination of the ballad centers on the great drama with which the protagonist plays out the scene of her own death. She dresses in a wedding dress of gold.[5] She rebukes those who weep. She drinks a toast to all travellers who sail the sea between her birthplace and her deathplace. And finally she refuses a reprieve from the king himself, existentially choosing the hand which fate has dealt her:

> "And had ye a mind to save my life
> Ye should na shamed me here."

Ironically her manner of bearing the shame of her death gives her a dignity which is immortal.

Some of the drama which attaches to this execution scene may come from the association, supposed or real, of the heroine with the court of Mary Queen of Scots. That Mary too played her execution to the hilt. The drama with which she conducted herself in her final hours was well known, and some of her reputation doubtless rubbed off on her maid-in-waiting. At the moment of execution Mary Stuart dropped off her gown of coal black and stood exposed in bodice and petticoat of blood red (Fraser 1970, 538).

> "Cast off, cast off my goun," she said,
> "But let my petticoat be."

Mary Hamilton by casting off her gown expresses symbolically her renunciation of the luxurious life she has led, a renunciation she will confirm by her words to her paramour in the final stanza. According to Andersen, the one who dresses herself in splendor is usually seeking to regain her lost love. Mary's choice of vesture is thus doubly ironic. She dons the glistering gold only to doff it; she goes seeking her paramour only to reject him.

Fair Janet is a second character in the repertoire who dresses for a wedding which is simultaneously her own funeral. Unlike Mary, however, Agnes Lyle's Janet rejects finery from the beginning: "Sma busking will serve me."[6] As Rogers suggests, dressing well would symbolize expectation of a happy marriage. Such, Janet knows, is not to be. Rejecting finery, Janet rejects hope (77).

Like clothing, hair is often used to signify physical beauty. In this northern European tradition it is most often yellow hair, as in "The Twa Sisters," "Earl Richard," and "Braes o' Yarrow." More specifically, as Andersen and Rogers both point out, combing hair expresses sexuality and sexual longing, whence the poignancy of references to hair juxtaposed with references to death. In "Braes o' Yarrow" the wife combs her husband's hair one last time before he rides off to be murdered beside the River Yarrow.

Andersen points out that references to sewing are functional equivalents to references to combing and convey the same message of sexual longing (1985, 109; cf. 112). Accordingly, Agnes Lyle sings:

> Young Patrick's lady sits at hame,
>   She's sewing her silken seam;
> And aye when she looks to the salt sea waves,
>   "I fear he'll neer return,"

where the A, F, and H versions of "Sir Patrick Spens" mention combs or combing. Whether sewing or combing, the lady yearns for her husband sexually and every other way, but her yearning is in vain.

If combing hair down indicates sexual longing, what is indicated by putting hair up? Mary Hamilton puts up the queen's hair with gold combs. Does this detail indicate the queen's sexual coldness? Does it indicate that in some way Mary saves the queen's marriage by servicing her husband? Certainly the detail has endured in tradition persistently enough to indicate that it is a significant element in the affective structure of the ballad.

The motif of yellow hair combines in "The Twa Sisters" with the motif of magic music, another important ballad symbol. In this ballad the song of the hair-strung fiddle has a clear narrative function, to effect the denouement by exposing the murderess. But the dramatic effectiveness of the song depends as much on its "supra-narrative function," to borrow Andersen's phrase. As Rogers puts it, "Allowing for all the variety in the character of the musicians and in the development of the stories, the music in the ballads discussed up to now can be said to express an ideal concept—supreme beauty or supreme love, or a fusion of both" (127). The cruel sister has deprived the heroine of life, of love, of all. But nothing, not even death, can deprive her of her yellow hair and her voice, this final double symbol of her beauty and her love (Cf. 125).[7]

The final symbol Rogers discusses is transformation, specifically the transformation of lovers into birds. Within the Lyle repertoire this sort of vestigial metempsychosis survives only in "Earl Richard." The text is an instructive one to consider when reflecting on the vagaries of ballad transmission. Apparently the ballad "Young Hunting," of which this text is a variant, has quite died out in Scottish and British tradition and never gained a foothold in northeastern North America. But in the southern United States it still flourishes in a truncated form. Like the southern American versions, Agnes Lyle's text is also truncated. Motherwell closes his transcription with a line of x's and the comment: "The catastrophe is wanting, but the lady's treachery was discovered and she was burned." In the missing final portion of the ballad the hero's father accuses the girl of killing Richard. Divers or "duckers," sent to look for the body, are unsuccessful until the bird tells them to try by night, floating candles on the water to discover the location by the brightness of the flame. When the murderess is confronted with the recovered corpse, the wounds of the corpse break out afresh. The murderess asserts that her maid, not she, is the guilty party, and the maid is sent to the stake. The flames refuse to do more than singe the maid a little for her complicity in the cover-up operation. But when the lady is tied to the stake, they consume her eagerly. No wonder Agnes Lyle had trouble with this "catastrophe," and American singers dropped it completely! It is hard to see how such a complex denouement ever developed in balladry, but easy to see how it disappeared, especially in the simpler style of balladry which the nineteenth century came to prefer.

What seems to have happened is that singers like Agnes Lyle had trouble with the ending and tended to break off before the ballad was finished. The next "generation" of singers, knowing the song only up through the dialogue with the bird, fashioned from what they remembered a new and intriguing conclusion. Already in the long version of "Young Hunting," the symbolic bird, like the birds in the Spanish ballad of "Conde Olinos" which Rogers discusses, has dropped the metempsychotic role and functions as instrument of revenge. In the Lyle version the refashioning has progressed a step further: the bird is now an incipient symbol of conscious guilt. In more recent American versions the refashioning is complete. These versions end with the bird confronting the murderess. This conclusion has an unsettling ambivalence about it. Though the body is safely out of sight, a little bird knows all, and the lady will never be able to enjoy an easy night's sleep. Thus tradition has refashioned the bird. No longer the metempsychotic soul of the murdered lover, nor simply an agent of discovery, it is now the full-fledged embodiment of conscience. But what Rogers says of the birds in "Conde Olinos" still applies to the bird in "Young Hunting/Earl Richard":

> The changes in the function of the motifs suggest some reasons for . . . longevity. Whether a popular ballad lives or dies depends not so much on the quality of its ancestors as on its ability to evoke new associations that touch the values and concerns of successive generations. Those who would use the word "traditional" to denote something that has not kept up with the times fail to recognize that tradition—at least popular tradition—sustains only what is alive. (148)

The bird as symbol of guilt can find a place in a Christian worldview that does not allow much room for metempsychosis.

In addition to the bird, Agnes Lyle's "Earl Richard" contains many other fine touches. The traditional language is often felicitous. Alliterative phrases include many classic epithets: "hunting horn," "bow bendit," "water wide," and the oath by "grass-green growing corn." The oath has intrigued scholars, including Child and Wimberly, who both considered it a survival of pagan practices (Child 1882–1898, 2: 137; Wimberly 1928, 362). At times the formulaic technique produces a gnomic quality, as in:

> Keep thou thy cage of beaten gold,
> And I will keep my tree;

a chilling effect, as in:

> Till the blood seep from thy bane;

or effective ballad understatement, as in:

> But little thocht of that penknife.

The story contains scenes of high drama, and this version preserves the best of them: the murder/kiss, the ride with corpse booted and spurred, and the discovery that the bird knows all and can not be tricked. The final scene of more complete versions, when the fire singes the maid but consumes the lady, is ironic but not essentially dramatic, and requires a tiresome amount of exposition to prepare it. The candles floating on the water are the only redeeming element in that tiresome exposition. They appeal to the folklorist and to the comparative mythologist, but obviously to the traditional singer they have not been worth the trouble. The story of the knight, the scorned lover, and the bird has proved to be alive and evocative; the sequel to that story is now dead.

As the above analysis demonstrates, all six major ballad symbols exhibit, in the usage of Agnes Lyle as well as in the usage of the larger European ballad community, associations with love and associations with death. The hunt is a prelude to love, or to death. Games, too, are preludes to love, but that love usually eventuates in death. Clothing is a gift of love, but shedding clothing is a kind of death. The act of combing hair expresses longing for love, a longing especially poignant if the love object is already caught in death. Magical music can induce love, and transcend death. Finally, violent death can transform the beloved into a bird of rumor or of conscience.

Like Rogers, Andersen emphasizes the connotative or affective aspects of ballad language, especially in Part III of *Commonplace and Creativity*, where he discusses the supra-narrative function of ballad formulas. This supra-narrative function is related to the emotional value of the narrated action:

> Formulas typically serve as *forewarning* or as *personal characterization:* they will often signal the dramatic development towards the narrative climax, or they may be employed to portray the characters at the moment of crisis, outline their reaction to dramatic events. In either case the stylistic overtones derive from expressions of *people acting*. It appears that the formulas' emblematic potential provides the only widespread instances of character portrayal in the tightly structured ballad genre, preoccupied as it is with getting the story told. The alternation between presaging and characterizing formulas is one of the decisive factors for the ballad's peculiar dramatic narrative presentation. (288; italics in original)

Andersen goes on to point out that from the point of view of subject matter as opposed to function, the two main divisions are formulas of love and formulas of death. In some cases, the two subjects overlap.[8]

Fifteen of the Lyle ballads are included in Andersen's tabulation of commonplace occurrence, but only four or five appear more than twice (see Table 1). Andersen himself is doubtful of the status of the "Mary Hamilton" stanza which begins: "She put not on her black clothing." He suggests that it may be a variant of the "She dressed herself in scarlet red" commonplace. Or it may be a context-bound, formula-like stanza, by which he means a formula-like stanza which appears in only one ballad tradition (251). The same formula, however, seems to lie behind the following stanzas found in "Fair Janet" tradition:

> Some put on the gay green robes,
>   And some put on the brown;
> But Janet put on the scarlet robes,
>   To shine foremost throw the town.
>   (Child 64A 19)
>
> . . . .
> "I will not hae't of the berry brown,
>   Nor yet o the holly green;
> But I will hae't of the crimson red,
>   Most lovely to be seen."
>   (Child 64E 8)

The formulation is found, then, with comparable connotations in at least two traditions and so qualifies as a commonplace according to Andersen's definition.

In these fifteen ballads Agnes Lyle utilizes, one or more times according to Andersen's citations, a total of eighteen of the commonplaces (counting "She dressed herself in scarlet red"). In general, Agnes Lyle's use is wholly traditional as Andersen defines the tradition. The present chapter has already suggested a number of the ways that an awareness of supra-narrative function can clarify a text. It only remains to make a few observations on the particular role of supra-narrative function in the Lyle technique.

When a commonplace has more than one supra-narrative function, Agnes Lyle may exploit this option. Thus, the commonplace "He mounted her upon a steed," may have either positive or negative overtones. The one mounted may go freely and happily or may be forced. The aura the commonplace brings with it from its many uses to describe elopement lend it a special charm when it is used to describe Geordie's lady carrying her love from the gallows. But its negative aura lends a note of foreboding to the scene in which the Eastmure King seems to rescue the threatened widow; the listener knows that, despite his kindly words, he is up to treachery. The commonplace "When Johnie looked the letter on" has a similar oppositional set of connotations. In "Geordie" the letter is an honest summons to help; in the three other ballads in which it occurs, it is a treacherous summons to entrapment.

The commonplace "Sat drinking at the wine" has slightly different func-

TABLE 1
Andersen Commonplaces in Lyle Ballads

BALLADS	COMMONPLACES
"Johnie Scot" (99G)	She lookit over her father's castle wa'
	He set his horn to his mouth
	When Johnie looked the letter on
	The first town he came to
"Geordie" (209F)	Where will I get a bonny boy
	When Johnie looked the letter on
	Go saddle to me the black, the black
	He mounted her upon a steed
"Sir Patrick Spens" (58E)	Sat drinking at the wine
	Where will I get a bonny boy
	When Johnie looked the letter on
"The Eastmure King" (89B)	When bells were rung and mass was sung
	But word's gane up and word's gane doon
	He mounted her upon a steed
"Mary Hamilton" (173B)	He hadna been . . . a month but barely ane
	But word's gane up and word's gane doon
	She dressed herself in scarlet red (?)
"The Cruel Mother" (20E)	Playin at the ba
	She's set her back untill an oak
"Little Musgrave" (81J)	Playin at the ba
	He set his horn to his mouth
"Lord Derwentwater" (208A)	When Johnie looked the letter on
	Go saddle to me the black, the black
"Bonnie Baby Livingston" (222C)	Playin at the ba
	When he came to fair Ellen's gates
"Fair Janet" (64B)	He hadna ridden a mile, a mile (2 times)
"Hind Horn" (17C)	What news, what news, my bonny boy
"The Baffled Knight" (112E)	He mounted her upon a steed
"The Gypsy Laddie" (200C)	Go saddle to me the black, the black
"The Braes o' Yarrow" (214C)	Sat drinking at the wine
'Lord William" (254A)	Go saddle to me the black, the black

NOTE: "Twa Sisters" (10F), "Babylon" (14D), "Sheath and Knife" (15B–16F), "The Wee Wee Man" (38E), "Jamie Douglas" (204G), and "Sweet Trinity" (286Cf) contain none of the commonplaces singled out by Andersen. The list is not surprising. These six are anomalous in other ways as well, as the discussion in Chapters 5 and 6 brings out.

"Earl Richard" ("Young Hunting" 68D), contains several phrases that seem to be more distant multiforms of Andersen commonplaces: "He louted owre his saddle-bow" (He looked over his left shoulder); "They booted and spurred him" (He mounted her upon a steed); and "As they were coming hame again" (He hadna ridden a mile, a mile); in each case the narrative and supra-narrative functions are as Andersen defines them, but the wording, though in appropriate ballad style, is not characteristic of the formula. Probably Andersen was deliberately conservative in identifying realizations of his formula-families (commonplaces) in order to prevent quibbling criticisms based on whether a particular realization was close enough to the main branch or not.

tions, depending on context. In sea ballads, it presages a violent storm; in land ballads it presages a violent confrontation. Both uses are found in the repertoire, in "Sir Patrick Spens" and "Braes o' Yarrow," respectively. "Where will I get a bonnie boy" has a similar division of functions according as the context is sea or land. Thus, Young Patrick Spens seeks a bonnie boy to climb the mast and look out for land, but Geordie seeks a boy to carry a message. In "Fair Janet" the double function of the "He hadna ridden/ sailed" formula is exploited in a single ballad. Andersen describes this double function as "ominous transition towards *disaster* at sea, or *violent confrontation* on land, in either case leading to imminent danger for the person engaging in the formula's action" (260). The disaster at sea presaged in the stanza beginning "They had not sailed one league, one league," is death from childbirth. This disaster, averted at sea, eventuates on dry land from the confrontations signalled by the second occurrence of the formula (in a form not noted by Andersen) in stanza 10, beginning "Fair Janet was nae weel lichter." At the third occurrence of the formula, in stanza 19, the disaster can no longer be delayed:

> She hadna danced the floor once owre,
>   I'm sure she hadna thrice,
> Till she fell in a deadly swound,
>   And from it neer did rise.

Although bearing her child does not kill Janet at sea, as first presaged, the birth of this child sets in motion the train of events that ultimately kills her.[9]

Finally, "Johnie Scot" achieves suspense by exploiting the oppositional ambiguity of the commonplace "The first town he came to." The commonplace usually occurs at the end of a ballad, with one of two functions. It may be the build-up to the happy wedding, as in Andersen's example:

> The first town that they came till
>   They made the mass be sung,
> And the next town that they came till
>   They made the bells be rung.
>
> And the next town that they came till
>   He bought her gay claithing,
> And the next town that they came till
>   They held a fair wedding.
>   (Child 110F 40–41)

Or it may build up to the discovery that the loved one (whether sweetheart or sister) is dead. "The formula family embraces the two fundamental concepts of love and death that we have seen walking hand in hand throughout this study."[10] In the "Johnie Scot" tradition, however, the formula occurs early in the story, at a point where it is difficult to tell which supra-narrative function is being served. The oppositional ambiguity heightens the suspense by emphasizing the only two possible outcomes of Johnie's journey: he will win his bride, or he will find her dead. Displaced as it is, however, the formula does not give away the outcome. Once again, in the realm of possibilities, love and death are conjoined.

Renwick, Rogers, and Andersen take different approaches in their quest to discover how the concrete visible elements of the ballad world, the characters, props, and actions, function to articulate a single value system. They discover that these symbolic elements, however manipulated by the analyst, still polarize around the opposite values of love and death.

In some ten of Agnes Lyle's ballads, however, the love-death symbolism goes farther, and the opposites are identified. Weddings are funerals. Marriage kills. In some cases this annuling of oppositions may take place on the linguistic and symbolic level, as in "Mary Hamilton," already discussed: Mary is going to an execution that has been called a wedding, and she dresses accordingly. But sometimes it may take place on the level of plot, as well. Fair Janet, for instance, is going to a wedding that she knows is her funeral, and she too dresses accordingly. Similarly, the outlyer bold in "Babylon" seeks a wife and finds death. The fair bride in "Eastmure King" wakes to find her wedding bed awash with the blood of her slain husband. Earl Richard's decision to marry causes his death. The younger of the "Twa Sisters" dies because she is to marry. Barbara Livingston and the hero of Yarrow die because they have married. Hind Horn, as appeared above, has to undergo symbolic death to win his bride. In the pieces from the fragments too, insofar as they can be reconstructed, the opposition is regularly annulled. Fair Margaret blames her death on an unwise marriage; the heroine of the "Broken Token" marries one who has practically come back from the dead; and the hero of "The Week Before Easter" finds a wedding occasion to contemplate suicide. Even in the happy full-length ballad of "Lord William" the heroine tells her father:

> "I must marry that Southland Lord,
>   Father, an it be your will;
> But I rather it were my burial-day,
>   My grave for to fill."

The marriage-funeral motif has a foundation in tradition, but in this repertoire it undergoes particularly emphatic reiteration. It is probably impossible to determine the exact significance of this reiteration, beyond suggesting that in these ballads the love-death opposition deconstructs itself. Nevertheless, the wedding-funeral identification is pervasive enough to be designated a mark of the repertoire, distinguishing it from Scottish balladry as a whole, and characterizing it as the work of a single singer. The following chapter will consider such another distinguishing mark of the repertoire, pervasive distrust of the gentry.

Politics and Perfidy

Any given performance of a traditional ballad is the product of converging forces, including the tradition of the ballad as received by the performer, the oral technique of the performer, and the personality of the performer. The personality in turn includes more than the innate traits that determine the basic orientation of the personality, whether light-hearted or serious, easygoing or high-strung. It also incorporates the life experiences, preferences, prejudices, and tastes involved in the formation of the personality, and the entire cultural context as assimilated by the personality.

Because ballads express so much of the singer's personality and background, analysis and comparison of ballads can reveal the singer's personal contribution to a variant. G. Malcolm Laws has written:

> Variation can reveal much more than the basic fact of traditional existence. From the ways in which ballads vary we can learn something about the mental process of the singers, their taste in subject matter, and even their attitudes toward the songs they sing. (1957, 94)

The first way in which singers reveal themselves is in the very choice of songs to sing. Lucille Burdine's study of Julie Hefley and Susie Campbell, from remote Newton County, Arkansas, reveals that although the sisters learned songs from the same sources—their father and their schoolteacher— they remember and perform strikingly different repertoires of songs from their childhood:

> Driving home, I think of these two wonderful ladies. Julie, the romantic one, who thirty-five years ago liked to picnic with her teenage sons and other youngsters, including myself, remembered all the children's songs, the nonsensical songs, and the song entitled "Oh Robin Redbreast." Susie, the more conservative of the two, and Pentecostal, remembered "The Great Titanic," "The Miner's Child," and "Pretty Polly." How much like each one of them! (1985, 4)

Like Julie and Susie, Agnes Lyle exercises striking choices in her selection of songs. The preceding chapter has indicated the preference for pieces which identify marriage with death. More generally, in full-length ballads and in broadside fragments, tragedy dominates the repertoire. This domination too is a matter of choice, of preference, not of chance or inevitability. For despite the fact that love and death seem to be the favorite ballad subjects, tragic ballads do not dominate the ballad repertoire as a whole. Warren Roberts points out that "although tragic ballads form a large and important group, the majority of the English and Scottish traditional ballads is non-tragic. Several examples indicate that the non-tragic ballads are fully as ancient and as characteristic as those containing tragic action" (1951, 78). In Roberts's count only 115 of the 305 ballads are uniformly serious in tone and tragic in outcome. But in the Lyle repertoire 16 out of the 22 long texts, and even 3 out of the 7 broadside pieces indicated in the Memorandum are tragic. This proportion is quite high in view of the Roberts statistics.[1]

This repertoire, not excluding the "happy" ones, is a study in human perfidy. All of the full-length pieces except for "The Wee Wee Man," assign a prominent place to human treachery, malice, or faithlessness. The corpus is thus the obverse of Mrs. Brown's corpus, in which true and faithful love is the uniting leitmotif. The human perfidy in Agnes Lyle's versions of these ballads takes many forms, but in almost every case some kind of betrayal is involved. Those the hero or heroine should be able to trust—family, lover, king—prove false. In "Fair Janet," "Johnie Scot," "Lord William," "Jamie Douglas," and "Braes o Yarrow" the woman's family opposes her love, whereas in "Sheath and Knife" the man's family seems to be in opposition. "Twa Sisters," "Babylon," and "The Cruel Mother" center on murders by a sister, a brother, and a mother respectively. "Hind Horn," "Earl Richard," "Little Musgrave," and "Mary Hamilton" present faithless lovers, and "Little Musgrave" again, "The Eastmure King," "Gypsy Laddie," and "Jamie Douglas" present traitorous spouses. In "Sweet Trinity" the betrayer is an employer, and in "Sir Patrick Spens," "Johnie Scot," and "Lord Derwentwater," he is the king himself.

Two examples will make clear the way in which the treachery is underlined in Lyle texts. "The Twa Sisters" is a classic tale of perfidy and misplaced trust. The Lyle text, characteristically, dwells on the cruelty of the older sister. And indeed the sister is cruel. Two Child texts, for example, equip her with a long pole to push the drowning girl back, should she come too close to land. But only Agnes Lyle provides the following grisly detail:

> She clasped her hands about a brume rute,
> But her cruel sister she lowsed them out.

Treachery can go no further.

"The Eastmure King" is another such tale of perfidy and misplaced trust. The Lyle text has an elemental, almost primitive quality. The passions of the principal characters are simple and strong, and lead to violent acts. The beginning of the ballad (stanzas 1–8), with three kings vying for one girl's heart, is by turns romantic and dramatic. The heroine proves herself an unusually strong person. Marrying for love, she chooses from among her suitors the one who values her "womanheid / and beautie." But when she awakens to murder, her first thought is not romantic or tragic, it is practical:

How is she to avoid implication in this crime. The Eastmure king appears out of the darkness. Whether or not she realizes that he is the murderer, she is in need of a savior and she entrusts herself to him. The central part of the ballad shows great mastery of ballad resources, considerably more subtle, for instance, than the parallel treatment in Mrs. Brown's version. In that version the conversation about the child takes place in the murder chamber. The woman knows what the murderer has done and what he intends to do before she goes off with him. In the Lyle version, however, the woman entrusts herself to the Eastmure king first. At this point in the ballad the king has not revealed his true colors either to the lady or to the listener. He is guilty of a crime, true enough, but it seems to be a crime of passion, a terrible but powerful expression of his love. Here the singer exploits the formula "He mounted her upon a steed," with its understated final lines:

> She turned her back against the court,
> And weeping rode away.

The polarized supra-narrative significance of the commonplace, elopement or abduction, heightens the suspense by its ambiguity. As they ride through the night the murderous king brings up the subject of the child to be born. If the child is a girl, he promises to provide as many as five nurses. Perhaps his love is real after all. But at the end of stanza 11 he vows that if the baby is a boy, he will not let it live; he has finally revealed himself for the villain he really is, and the heroine is wholly in his power. Or so it seems. But a simple switch with a village woman provides the heroine with a daughter and the village woman with a son.

Treachery is emphasized in yet another way in the last act of the ballad. The finale, in which the nearly grown son avenges his father's death, is framed by references to a garden. In stanza 15,

> This boy . . . is to the garden gone,
> To slay that Eastmure king.

Stanza 18 concludes the ballad with the lines:

> So then he slew that Eastmure king,
> Beneath the garden tree.

In this case the annular structure is carried to such lengths that the references to the garden frame the references to the slaying. This killing in a garden, underneath a tree, is a relic of an ancient motif more common perhaps in Scandinavian than in Anglo-Scottish folklore. The motif seems to connote treachery, whether treachery committed, as in the *Hamlet* tradition, or treachery avenged, as in the present ballad. Thus the garden, both as scene of action and as framing device, sets the son's vengeance in an ageless context, lends to it an archetypal sanction, and highlights the treachery of the crime that it avenges.

One narrative element connecting this tale of treachery and treachery avenged with the wedding-funeral ballads was mentioned in the preceding chapter. When the heroine, on her wedding night, wakes from "a drowsy dream," she finds "her bride's-bed swim with blood." This image of the blood-soaked wedding bed also occurs in the A text of "Fair Margaret and Sweet William" (Child 74). In that ballad, however, the bloodied bed is only a dream, a nightmare. In the present ballad, nightmare has become literal reality, though the phrase, however appropriate, still reflects an association with the word "dream," which occurs in the preceding line. This wedding bed in which the blood is that of the groom and not of the bride constitutes one of the most striking wedding-funeral images in the repertoire.

Treachery is the subject of the longest recurrent "theme" (in the oral theory sense) in the repertoire. In three of the ballads, "Johnie Scot," "Sir Patrick Spens," and "Lord Derwentwater," a king writes a long letter to a noble-minded Scots youth. In each case perfidy is afoot, once on the part of the king ("Johnie Scot"), once on the part of a single courtier ("Sir Patrick Spens"), and once on the part of a strong coterie at court ("Lord Derwentwater"). "Johnie Armstrong," which Motherwell says Agnes Lyle also knew, customarily includes the same "theme." This "theme" is longer than a commonplace, but utilizes commonplaces in its construction. Like Andersen's commonplaces, it is not realized in identical wording each time Agnes Lyle uses it. But the affect, the supra-narrative function, remains constant. Lord defines the word "theme" as "[a group] of ideas regularly used in telling a tale in the formulaic style of traditional song. . . . The theme, even though verbal, is not a fixed set of words, but a grouping of ideas." The definition aptly describes the "King's Letter Theme." The ideas that are grouped together may be identified as follows:

1. Perfidy is planned against the hero.
2. King writes letter, seals it, and sends it to hero.
3. Hero receives letter and weeps.
4. Hero announces that he must obey summons.
5. A narrative agent or agents, or sometimes the hero himself, expresses a presentiment that hero will not return if he answers the summons.
6. Hero answers summons, but not alone; companions ride with him.

Agnes Lyle invariably expresses the second and third elements of the "theme" by the same two commonplaces, "The king did write a lang letter" (a commonplace omitted by Andersen), and "When Johnie looked the letter on" (admitted by Andersen), though the wording and rhyme scheme of the commonplaces vary from instance to instance. For the rest of the items, however, the differences in stanzas used, and in amount of narrative detail, are more substantial. Nevertheless, all elements appear, in unvarying sequence.

In this fixity of sequence the elements of the "theme" are somewhat like the "functions" in the Propp system.

A closely-related sequence should perhaps be mentioned. In "Geordie" and "Lord William" treachery is in the act of being carried out and a sequence much like the "King's Letter Theme" is invoked to bring rescue. This sequence has elements corresponding to elements 1–4, and 6 of that "theme." The principal difference is that the one summoned is different from the one betrayed. Although perfidy is part of the context, the summons itself is honest, coming as it does from the beloved rather than from the king. Since no trap is laid for the rescuer, who has surprise on his (her) side, element 5, presentiment, does not fit into the plot.[2]

Frequently in the Lyle repertoire the perfidy which threatens the hero or heroine is mindless, malicious, apparently unmotivated meddling. Thus, in "Sir Patrick Spens" the "auld rich knight" puts Young Patrick's name forward for the voyage. As Patrick reads his commission he breaks into tears of frustration and rage. He finds he has an enemy at court, but does not know who the enemy is or how to confront him. Nor can he escape the trap that the enemy has laid. In "Lord Derwentwater" the entire court turns against the good hero, again without any clear motive other than malice. In "Little Musgrave" the page can not resist creating trouble, and in "Jamie Douglas" the slandering Blacklywood plays Iago to Jamie's Othello. Even in the more happy ballad of "Geordie" a "bold bluidy wretch" at court, afflicted with jealousy and malice, tries to foil Mrs. Geordie's efforts.

As the preceding examples bring out, Agnes Lyle's assignment of perfidy often reflects a social bias. The one sure test of highborn station in her ballads is addiction to malice. The villains are jealous courtiers, treacherous kings, bored or murderous gentlewomen, and social-climbing fathers. The courtiers and pages prove their nobility by dropping a deadly word at the right moment. A brother of the Rose of Yarrow proves his nobility by stabbing her husband in the back. Earl Richard proves his nobility by betraying and mocking the woman he loves, and she responds in kind by killing him as she kisses him. The merchant class, moreover, shares in the perfidy of the gentry. The daughter of the merchant of Lurk kills her own babies, two fathers offer their daughters at the altar of upward mobility, and the shipmaster in "The Sweet Trinity" apparently lets his cabin boy die once the lad has done his job of sinking the enemy ship.

None of the sympathetic characters, however, with the exception of Lord Dunwaters and the two eloping princesses, is identified as titled, landed, or mercantile. In fact, the ballads reflect a surprisingly egalitarian view of humanity. The hero is the common man; the villain is anyone who sets himself up as gentry. In this respect, the ballads are of a piece with Scots literature as a whole, as described by Maurice Lindsay, who considers a "democratic element" to be one of the "most striking characteristics" of this literature, although:

"Democratic" is really not the correct word; it is rather a free manliness, a *saeva indignatio* against oppression, a violent freedom, sometimes an aggressive spirit of independence or egalitarianism. . . . It is sometimes explained as the result of the Celtic "polity" in which each, whatever his rank, is first and foremost a member of the clan, and also as a result of the pressure from England. . . . As a small country, Scotland may also have had a less exclusive separation of classes than, for example, France and England; that was certainly the impression formed by the French knights in Scotland in Barbour's time. The less rigid stratification of society in Scotland appears everywhere in Scottish literature. . . . In its negative form, this spirit becomes prideful arrogance and an envious dislike of anybody who is finer, more original, and more sensitive than others or seeks to rise above the common level. (95–96)

Negative or not, Lindsay's comments apply to the Lyle texts with astonishing aptness.

In accordance with the Lyle egalitarianism, even heroes who have titles in other versions become commoners in her versions. Sir Patrick Spens becomes Young Patrick Spens; Lord William becomes Sweet William. The father in "Sheath and Knife" has a house, not a hall or castle. Hind Horn is simply Young Hind Horn, no knight, and no lord of "many a town."[3] Johnie Scot must depend on a friendly Scottish prince to supply him with armed backing. And Geordie is plain Geordie Lukely, not the Laird of Gight. At times the social status is made quite explicit, as when the third sister in "Babylon" identifies her brothers as a minister, a ploughman, and an outlaw. In the fragments too the heroes are quite ordinary. The maid in the garden is but a maid, and her lover simply a young man. The hero walking out, "the week before Easter," is likewise simply a young man. Another text features two sailors. And the real heroes of "The Duke's Chase" are the dogs.

Agnes Lyle uses several ironic devices to bring out the contrast between honest folk and perfidious gentry. In "Eastmure King," for instance, the heroine's son is safer with the poor stranger woman than with the heroine's own kingly husband. Similarly, poor Mary Hamilton comes to the king's court "to learn some unco lair," but what she learns is "wantonness and play." A comparison of "Mary Hamilton" with "The Cruel Mother" raises an interesting question. Given that both women are child-murderers, why is there so much sympathy for one and none at all for the other? The explanation seems to lie in the different social positions of the two women: Mary Hamilton, a maid in the court, is a serving woman put upon by royalty.[4] But the lady from Lurk, coming from the wealthy merchant class, was hardly seduced by, and may well have forced her attentions upon the clerk. Whether or not she did, she is in a position of power, and those in positions of power receive no sympathy in the ballads of Agnes Lyle.

Recurrent repetition produces yet another king-commoner contrast already commented upon. When Johnie Scot, in stanza 15, cries out:

"If your old doughter be with child,
        As I trew weel she be,
    I'le make it heir of a' my land,
        And her my gay lady,"

he is throwing the king's own words from stanza 3 back in his teeth:

"If she be with bairn," her father says,
        "As oh forbid she be!
    We'll put her in a prison strong,
        And try the veritie."
                                    (Cf. stanza 2)

Unlike the king, Johnie is pleased about the coming birth, offering the
mother his hand and the child his land.

Given the repertoire's suspicion of the gentry, coupled with its emphasis
on marriage as instrument of death, it is not surprising that the paradigm of
treachery in the repertoire is a marriage or liaison between a lowborn person
and a member of the gentry. In almost every case in which this union is
consummated, the upper-class person then betrays the common person in
some way. The Laird of Linlyon, for instance, steals plain Barbara Livingston
from her young man of Dundee, and the girl is so miserable she dies of grief.
Jamie Douglas believes rumors rather than his innocent wife and lets his
jealousy destroy her. Lady Barnabas persuades her young lover to ignore the
warning given him. And the king lets Mary Hamilton go to the gallows.
Fortunate are the women who elude such a fate: the fair maid who baffles
the Baffled Knight and the Bailie's daughter who ends up with her Sweet
William. Even Fair Janet preferred death to marriage with the Southland
Lord.

Agnes Lyle's version of "Little Musgrave" and her version of "The
Gypsy Laddie" (see chapter 4) each tell such a story of a liaison between a
gentlewoman and a lowborn man. Because the ballads have been so popular, both in later tradition and in the Renfrewshire of Agnes Lyle's own day,
there is a wealth of material for comparison, and one can speak with assurance of the choices which the singer has exercised in forming her version.
"Little Musgrave," in particular, has retained its grip on the imaginations of
singers in the twentieth century, in both Scotland and the United States.
Agnes Lyle's version, on first reading, seems to be telling the same story as
these later versions. But a closer study reveals that the essence of the Lyle
story, its emotional core, is particular to this singer. The passions involved,
the sympathies aroused, and the sensibilities expressed are all unique and of
a piece with sensibilities, sympathies, and passions throughout the repertoire. Twentieth century singers have shown great sympathy for the il-
licit lovers in this ballad, as for the lovers in "Gypsy Laddie." A group of
Ohio singers, mother and daughters, has the husband in "Little Musgrave"
cry out:

> "I've killed as fair a lady
>   As ever the sun shone on,
> Likewise as brave a man
>   As ever Scotland bore."
> (Bronson 1959–1972, no. 81: 40, stanza 25)

In another American version the lady declares to her husband, who is standing over her with a loaded pistol:

> "Much better I liked his little finger
> Than you and all your kin."
> (Bronson 1959–1972, no. 81: 21, stanza 21)

The lady who runs off with the gypsy in American versions of "Gypsy Laddie" shows an equally amazing loyalty to her lover:

> "Yes, I've forsaken my house and land,
>   And I've forsaken my baby,
> I've forsaken my husband dear,
>   And gone with Black Jack Davy."
>   (Davis 1960, no. 33AA, stanza 9)

Such expressions of high-born loyalty are notably absent from the Lyle renditions of "Little Musgrave" and "The Gypsy Laddie." In "Little Musgrave" Lady Barnabas seems to be the second wife, married to a man considerably older than herself. She plays ball (stanza 1) and is of child-bearing age (stanza 11). Her husband, on the other hand, has a daughter of marriageable age (stanza 13). She seems to be an idle and discontented woman, with nothing constructive to do. She is the one who makes the first move. When Mossgrey refuses rather strongly, she insists. Her discontent with her husband is obvious:

> "But he's awa to the king's court,
>   And I hope he'll neer come hame."

Further, she keeps an old sword in the bed and threatens to kill the page with it; there is no reason to think she would hesitate to carry out her threat, given the opportunity. When Mossgrey, alarmed, wishes to leave, she tells him the horn belongs to her father's sheep-herd and petulantly pesters him to lie down: she's getting cold.

There is no hint of love between the two. Mossgrey even curses the woman when caught in bed with her, but there is nothing he can do. With two swift strokes Lord Barnabas dispatches the guilty pair. His order for the burial of the two lovers is, in the context, bitterly ironic:

> "And lay her head on his right hand,
> She's come o the highest kin.

She has demonstrated her high breeding by getting Mossgrey killed.

The parallels between the Lyle "Little Mossgrey" and the Lyle "Gypsy Laddie" are many. In that ballad too a woman of high degree, tired of her elegant life, seeks thrills among the common folk. In that ballad too the result is death for the man she becomes involved with (and for his fifteen brothers as well). Neither the gypsies nor Mossgrey can be called guiltless, but their punishments far exceed their crimes because they have allowed themselves to become entangled in a web from which they can never free themselves. The final stanza of "The Gypsy Laddie" expresses bitter irony:

> "We are sixteen clever men,
>   One woman was a' our mother;
> We are a' to be hanged on ae day,
>   For the stealing of a wanton lady."

Mossgrey too has died because of a wanton lady. The moral seems clear: Getting mixed up with the gentry can only get a person into trouble, for the gentry love to use a person for thrills but won't stand by him.

These two ballads—and most of the others in the repertoire as well—seem to be expressing genuine anger. It might seem risky to speak of anger in a traditional text. And yet anger is precisely the affect that distinguishes this text from the comparable material, whether contemporaneous or more recent. As has appeared above, more recent texts emphasize the poignancy of the death of the two young lovers, in the one case, and the charm of the gypsy and the pluck of the lady, in the other. Of earlier texts of "The Gypsy Laddie," only the Child 200B version is close to Agnes Lyle's in both time and geography, but several versions are more or less contemporaneous. In these versions the earl does not always win out in the end. The lady, instead, may assert determination, as the B text has it, to drink the beer she has brewed. And the gypsies themselves sometimes go scot-free. Of texts of "Little Musgrave," eight Scottish versions in Child are contemporaneous with Agnes Lyle's (D–I, K–L). At least four of these come from Southwest Scotland (E, G, H, and I), and the John Smith version, which Emily Lyle prints from the Crawfurd manuscript (Lyle 1975, 178–181), makes a total of five Southwestern versions, nine altogether, contemporaneous with the Lyle version. A comparison between these other Scottish versions and the Lyle version suggests strongly that the angry tone of the Lyle version must be attributed to the choice of the singer, not to the tradition of the region. The text which Andrew Crawfurd collected from John Smith, for instance, takes a very different tone. In Smith's version the focus is on Mosgrove, as the hero is called, rather than on the lady. Mosgrove seems to be a totally irresistible person. His charm and beauty are radiant. When Lady Bangwell has "fixt her eyes on Little Mosgrove / As bright as the morning Sun" (the diction is not unlike Agnes Lyle's here, by the way), she is so swept off her feet that she offers him anything for one hour of his company. Lord Bangwell too finds Mosgrove attractive and charming, and seems to understand the irresistible power of his personality. When the footpage tries to force the issue, Lord Bangwell blows his horn twice, hoping that Mosgrove will hear it and be gone. The boy, however, sleeps through the warning and does not awaken until Lord Bangwell enters the bedchamber. Waking up, Mosgrove does not curse the lady but expresses regret for her ill fortune:

> "Wo be to your wedded Lady
> That in of my arms do sleep."

Bangwell kills only Mosgrove, and even that he regrets instantly:

> "Wo be too my merrey man all
> That did not hold my hand
> For I hea kill'd one of the fairest creaturs
> That ever the sun shin'd on."

Though all the distinctive elements of this version—the beauty of Mosgrove, the attempt to bribe the page, the warning sounded by the husband himself, and the regret over the death—are found in other variants of "Little Musgrave," both in and out of Child, Smith achieves a unique blend in this very fine text. Like the later American versions this contemporary Renfrewshire version displays a deep sympathy for all the parties of the drama. The final impression is one of tenderness and grief, not of bitterness and anger. In this respect Smith's version is very different from that of Agnes Lyle.

The angry tone of the plot conflicts is reflected in the narrative structure of the Lyle ballads. In particular, eighteen of the twenty-two ballads build to a closing stanza (or more) giving a principal character the proverbial last word. For characters in four of the ballads this "last word" is really more of an action: Willie rings the bells of Linkum to vindicate Janet's virtue; Johnie Scot blows a blast on his horn to vindicate Scotland's honor; Geordie's wife rides off with her rescued husband "all for the pride o Geordie"; and:

> The bridegroom had her first to wed
> But Young Hyn Horn had her first to bed.

But in the remaining fourteen cases, the characters find words of rebuke, accusation, or irony with which to close their stories. This chapter has already commented on the bitterness of the gypsies' final accusation and the irony of Lord Barnabas's final order. Mary Hamilton provides another example when she bids the king:

> "Hold your tongue, my sovereign leige,
> And let your folly be."

The children of the cruel mother, when she begs them to pray for her, reply that "there is pardon for us, but none for thee." After revealing the crime of the cruel sister, the fiddle strung with the fair sister's hair adds, "God neer let her rest till she shall die." When the lusty laird of Linlyon, who could have found dozens of willing women, steals Barbara Livingston from the man who loves her and whom she loves, her Dundee lover sums up the complaint of all who have been oppressed by the powerful:

> "Woe be to thee, Linlyon,
> An ill death may thou die!
> Thou micht hae taen anither woman,
> And let my ladye be."

And so the catalog of reproaches continues.

But what evidence is there that Agnes Lyle chose these endings for her ballads? Might one not argue that all these perfidious elements are traditional, and it is only coincidence that so many appear in this repertoire? Unfortunately for that argument Agnes Lyle herself has provided evidence of the element of choice in the formation of her versions. The pertinent ballad is "Geordie." In her "Geordie" the hero's wife is completely self-reliant, though a "bold bluidy wretch" at court tries to discourage and obstruct her petition to the king. In the Child A, C, and H texts, however, an aged lord at court *helps* Geordie's wife by persuading the king to let her ransom her husband. Agnes Lyle, as she herself testified, knew that line of development for the story. Motherwell, at the end of his transcription of her text, appended the following note:

> Of the preceding ballad Agnes Lile says she has heard her father sing a different set all of which she forgets except that there was nothing said of "a bold bluidy wretch" and in place of what is given to him [*sic:* the bluidy wretch?] in this version there were the two following stanzas:
>
> > "I have eleven babes into the north,
> > And the twelfth is in my body, O
> > And the youngest o them's in the nurse's arms,
> > He neer yet saw his daddy." O
> >
> > Some gied her ducks, some gied her drakes,
> > And some gied her crowns monie,
> > And she's paid him down five thousand pound,
> > And she's gotten hame her Geordie.
> >
> > > (Motherwell 1825–1826, 370;
> > > Child 1882–1898, 4: 140, 137)

In other words, she grew up hearing the ballad sung with the world on Mrs. Geordie's side and no element of perfidy intruding.

It would be fascinating to discover the turn of thought which led Agnes Lyle from her father's version, in which the generosity and goodness of people is so touchingly brought out, to her own, in which the lady relies only on herself, and from her father's version, in which there is no wanton malice, to her own, with its "bold bluidy wretch." Certainly she has chosen the bitter part, and it shall not be taken from her.

Indeed, faced with such bitterness in ballad after ballad, one feels compelled to attribute anger to the singer herself. Probably unmarried, was she disappointed in love, perhaps through interference of her own family? Involved in a depressed cottage industry in a village culture, was she disillusioned with the weaving fraternity of Kilbarchan, having found that hardship breeds distrust, even among old friends?

Such speculations about Agnes Lyle's personal experiences or about her experiences with fellow villagers can be no more than that: speculations. When, however, query approaches politics on the regional and national levels, it finds itself on surer footing. There was much in the economic and social life of Scotland in 1825 to embitter the daughter of a Kilbarchan weaver.

By 1825 radical ideas—socialist, republican, and democratic—had been rife for almost a hundred years in Scotland. The American revolution, for example, had been fought for principles hammered out in part by Edinburg lawyers. Paine's *Rights of Man*, in Gaelic as well as English, circulated to all parts of the land. And in the next county an Owenite community of mill workers was seeking Utopia in Lanarkshire. Weavers were prominent in all of these movements. The ballads of Agnes Lyle show a political and social consciousness reflective of the times.

TABLE 1
Political Oppositions in the Ballads of Agnes Lyle

	Tory	Radical
Nationality	English	Scots
Class	Gentle	Common

In terms of polity, the ballads depict the Scotland of the period, not some mythical or historical reconstruction. There are, for instance, no Jacobite songs in the group. Even the originally Jacobite piece "Lord Derwentwater" has lost its Jacobite slant. The controlling oppositions in the songs likewise correspond to political realities, or at least to political perceptions, in the region and era (See Table 1). The king in the repertoire is the king of England, hates Scots, and can't be trusted—not a bad summary of the way radical subjects north of the border viewed the Hanoverians. The pervasive opposition of commoner to gentry in the repertoire reflects the upper class embrace of Toryism within Scotland itself (and so, from the radical point of view, its abandonment of Scottishness), in reaction to the various forms of radicalism embraced by the working class. These oppositions are resolved only once in the repertoire, ironically, by marriage, when Johnie Scot's faithful English princess, abandoning her dowry, assumes the nationality and status of her commoner husband in the clan system of Scotland. In short, Agnes Lyle, in her ballads, offers a biting assessment of social and political realities.

If, then, one considers the declining fortunes of the working man in Scotland in the ten years preceding 1825, the unique political position of the weaving fraternity within which the singer grew up, the treatment that fraternity met at the hands of the government and of the landed and mercantile classes in the so-called radical War of 1820, and the state of the monarchy which was demanding the working Scot's loyalty, surely one does not need to look any further for a plausible explanation of the bitter anger which pervades this body of ballads.

And so we come to the end of our examination of a test case, that of Agnes Lyle of Kilbarchan. Part I indicated the historical footing on which we stand when we speak of the singer and her times. It then went on to indicate the textual footing on which we stand when we speak of her songs. Part II described a repertoire suffused with formulicity and wholly traditional in technique, poetic and aesthetic. The technique in particular is consistent in its dependence on a meter, the meter of the standard ballad quatrain, as we might expect of a metrical art. Part III revealed that this repertoire is impressed by the stamp of a distinctive personality that reveals itself in its competence and artistry in handling traditional techniques and expressing traditional values. But, as so often happens, this personality also betrays itself in its obsessions and angers—especially in its annulment of the traditional love-death opposition of balladry in a marriage-funeral identification—and in its constant rearrangement of traditional elements of plot, character, and diction to present a picture of the honest Scots working class betrayed by the perfidious gentry.

The songs have been responsibly collected from dictation or singing. They exhibit the pervasive formulicity, along with many other compositional elements, which we have come to identify with orally recreated verse narratives. And taken as a whole they exhibit a consistent style in utilizing these elements, reinforced by consistent and even idiosyncratic deployment of traditional and repertoire-particular ballad leitmotifs, indicating that they are the ballad renditions of a single singer. It seems appropriate, then, to call this group of ballads an oral repertoire in the Parry-Lord sense of that term, and to turn to it for a better understanding of the ballad matrix, that network of personalities, forces, and conditions which gave birth to the great ballads of the classic period.

Conclusion

The Ballad and Oral Theory

Oral theory is just that—a theory, a coherent model which seeks to account for more of the phenomena, and for more facets of the phenomena, than any previous model could. If it is to be judged, it must be judged as a theory. The evaluative question, then, is not "Has it been proved?" (for it can't be proved), but, "Does it account for the phenomena?"

The preceding chapters have been concerned with "accounting for the phenomena" in a single repertoire, that of Agnes Lyle of Kilbarchan. It is now time to extrapolate from one case to the field as a whole and present at least a preliminary model of oral composition in Anglo-Scottish balladry of the classic period.

1. THE FORMULA

By the time of Agnes Lyle, ballad language had lost its pristine purity, if indeed it ever possessed such. In particular, the language of this singer is sometimes "infected" with broadside diction, especially in "Geordie," "Jamie Douglas," and lines like the following from "The Eastmure King":

> For I do swear and do declare
> Thy botcher I will be.

But such use of broadside diction does not necessarily require that a broadside text be posited in the immediate ancestry of a particular ballad. Singers of the late classical period use broadside diction as one of the resources they draw upon to form a ballad and treat broadside-based couplets and stanzas in the same free way they treat other older formulas. Their ballads are, paradoxically, no less oral for an occasional echo of the broadside press. "The Eastmure King," for instance, one of the most "infected" Lyle texts, is fully oral in its architectonics. Even the diction is full of the singer's favorite phrases: "Milk-white steed," "Hold your tongue," "Out and spoke," "When bells were rung and psalms were sung," and so on. The entire text, in fact, is typical of the singer at her most controlled and most formulaic.

Whatever the feelings about broadside diction, however, no critic seriously quarrels with the judgment that ballad language in general is formulaic in some sense. The problem hitherto has been that theorists tried to devise and use a single univocal definition of the words *formula* and *formulaic*. This attempt has been especially troublesome for oral studies (see especially Andersen 1985, passim; Foley 1988, 63, 69–70, 100–102). *Formula* is an analogical term.[1] Because it is an analogical term, a definition such as Andersen's, developed to describe phenomena on the level of commonplace, will fail when applied to phenomena on other levels. Andersen concludes from this failure that formulas are found only on the commonplace level. Such a conclusion and such a use of the word seems too restrictive. Corresponding phenomena on other levels are also formulas, each in an analogous though somewhat different sense, with distinctive morphology and distinctive modes of operation.

Many of these formulaic levels have been identified and discussed in the work of Buchan and Andersen, in preceding chapters of this study, and elsewhere. The work of Anders, in particular, provides a convenient catalog of many hundreds of formulaic expressions culled from Child and other significant collections. It is now possible to draw up a fairly complete typlogy of formulaic usage in the Anglo-Scottish ballad. The surest basis for such a classification of formulas is linguistic level, for characteristic formulaic elements can be identified on all linguistic levels from phoneme to total ballad text. But because the formula is usually a metrical as well as a linguistic unit it will sometimes be more convenient to denominate categories with metrical terms (e.g., half-line formulas).

Of course formulaic language is all interconnected. It is seldom possible to isolate formulas, except conceptually. And what is one kind of formula on one level may well function as part of a larger formula on another level, as in the case of the formulaic *l* alliterations in the letter commonplace, to be discussed below. Still, when independent free-floating formulas can be singled out in the following discussion, they will.

The simplest linguistic level is that of phoneme. Whether or not purely phonemic phenomena should be called formulas, they are certainly formulaic at times. Alliteration is one of these formulaic phenomena; it is often what makes a phrase spring immediately to the lips, a phrase such as "daughter dear," "busk the bride," "large and lang," "cheer and charcoal clear," "fair and full," "gien me the geeks," and hundreds more. In some cases the alliteration itself seems to be the formula, the matrix into which the expression must be fitted. A notable example occurs in the familiar commonplace describing the reading of a letter. The first line of this commonplace seems to have an *l* alliteration formula embedded in it. In "Johnie Scot" Agnes Lyle realizes this line thus:

> When Johnie read this letter long.

The corresponding line in "Sir Patrick Spens" is similar. But in "Lord Derwentwater" she sings:

> The very first line that my lord did read.

There is still an *l* alliteration, even without mention of the letter. The *l* alliteration is preserved, sometimes with and sometimes without mention of the letter, in the following examples from other Motherwell texts:

> The first line of the letter he read (99C, 6);
> When Johnie looked the letter upon (99D, 9);
> The first line that Johnie looked on (99E, 6);
> The first lang line that he looked to (99F, 6).

The alliteration frequently carries over into the second line, with mention of loud laughter. Of course there are realizations of the commonplace which do not include the alliteration. It is not a universal invariant in the commonplace but rather a formulaic element of the commonplace in the repertoires of some singers, and perhaps of some regions.

Rhymes, both internal and final, constitute another form of phonemic formula. The relatively limited selection of rhymes to serve a wide variety of purposes within a repertoire is an interesting example of formulaic economy. Singers seem to think in terms of their set of habitual rhymes when fitting their expression to the demands of rhymed strophes. Buchan (1972, 155–158) provides dramatic evidence of how a stanza can change in characters or action within the matrix of a common rhyme. In some ballads, such as the Yarrow ballads and "Barbara Allen," a particular set of rhymes common to the tradition is a dominant formulaic element.

One step up, on the level of morpheme, particular rhymes sometimes form a mold into which the expression of lines and even stanzas is fitted. One of the most common ways this happens is with word pairs analogous to the word pairs in Hebrew parallelism. The following example from "Earl Richard" will help clarify the concept. Stanza 13 runs:

> "Come down, come down, my wee pyet;
>   An thou'll come to my knee;
> I have a cage of beaten gold,
>   And I'll bestow't on thee."

Stanza 15 is an iterative repetition of this stanza:

> "Come down, come down, my wee pyet;
>   An thou'll come to my hand,
> I have a cage of beaten gold,
>   And thou's be put therein."

In these correlated stanzas the words *knee* and *hand* function as a word pair. Substitution of one word for the other in a word pair permits iterative repetition in parallel ballad stanzas in a way analogous to the way word-pair substitution permits repetition in parallel verses of Hebrew poetry. A similar word pair, *sleeve/gore*, occurs in versions of "Johnie Scot," including Mrs. Brown's:

> "O here's a sark o silk, lady,
>   Your ain hand sewd the sleeve . . .
>
> Ha, take this sark o silk, lady,
>   Your ain hand sewd the gare."
>   (99A, 12–13)

    Seam and *son* in stanzas 15 and 16 of the Lyle "Sir Patrick Spens" constitute another such word pair. Other singers use other word pairs at this point in the narrative. The Child B and O texts, for instance, use the word pair *hand/knee* (*ee*, that is, *eyes*, in the B text) already seen in connection with "Earl Richard," while other texts structure stanzas around rhymes on *hand* and *hair*.

    The next highest level of linguistic organization on which formulas can occur is that of the phrase.[2] Formulas on this level include ballad clichés such as "cheer and charcoal," "wee pen knife," "beaten gold," "milk-white steed," "silver slippers," "houkit a grave," "wide and deep," and so on. These phrases are often unvarying, but not always. The grave can be "dug" as well as "houkit," and it may be "long and narrow" instead of "wide and deep." Likewise, the lady may wear "silver shoon" instead of "slippers," or offer "coal and candle light" instead of "cheer and charcoal."

    While many formulaic phrases are a half-line long, the true half-line formula seems to be a distinct type that includes many formula families. The most noticeable of these families is very simple: two one-syllable words are repeated once to make a half line, usually at the front rather than the back of the line: "Rise up, rise up," "Come down, come down," "Oh no, Oh no," "A priest, a priest," "A boon, a boon," "Ye lie, ye lie," and so on. A half-line formula of this family is usually followed by another half-line formula, either an epithet, a name, or an inquit: "My bonny boy," "Little Mossgrey," "Lord Barnabas said."[3] In expanded form the formula frequently spills over into the next line:

> "Licht down, licht down, Earl Richard," she says,
>   "O licht down and come in."

A related type of terracing occurs when a two-beat half-line formula is repeated to fill a whole line or even two lines:

> "I winna licht, I canna licht,
>   I winna licht at all."

    As the foregoing examples make clear, the essential characteristic separating half-line formulas from formulaic phrases is utilization of the half-line as a distinct narrative unit.

    Whole-line formulas may be four-beat formulas, three-beat formulas, or variable. Linguistically they are either phrases or clauses but not really full periods. Many free-floating four-beat formulas function as incipits or narrative connectors; e.g.,:

> There were ladies, they lived in a bower;
> As they came into Edinburgh town;
> Ben and cam then Sweet Willie;
> She called upon her waiting maid.

Free-floating formulas which exist only in a three-beat form are rare. The Lyle repertoire includes variations of "She sealed it with a ring" and "To her love in Dundee" ("To Will ayont the sea"). But the three-beat lines are also the place for formulas built around grammatical forms. Here occur longer prepositional phrases, such as "Beneath the garden tree," "Since Saturday at morn," "Upon the road so high," "Instead o beaten gold," and "For wantonness and play." Here occur many participles: "The tears came trinkling down," "But I am coming home," "Rocking her eldest son," "Thinking to be slain," "Sits gabbing on the tree," and "Coming marching in their sicht." Here occur the relatively rare frequentatives, futures, and compound verbs, such as "About its neck did hing," "Did him a traitor call," "Shall ring for her the morn," and "O busk and mak you braw." And here abound infinitive phrases such as "To see men doing the same," "To learn some unco lair," "And for to kiss her sweet," "To fight for King Jamie," "My grave for to fill," "The city for to see," and "Torches for to burn." Some "grammatical" formulas fall into easily identifiable patterns. In the last three infinitive examples just given, for example, there is an underlying structure which might be diagrammed thus:

(direct object) + for + *(infinitive)*

But in some cases there does not seem to be any underlying use of a widespread pattern: the formulaic idea seems to extend no further than filling out the short line by using an infinitive, participle, compound form, or preposition.

Three-beat formulas can be expanded to fill a longer line by the addition of a name, inquit, or epithet:

> "How likes thou the bed, *Mossgrey?*"
>
> . . . .
> "Weel I love the bed," *he says.*
>
> . . . .
> Says, "Tell no tidings of me, *my boy.*"

And four-beat formulas can be shrunk to fit the shorter line by dropping these optional elements, as well as in various other ways, as the following examples of repetition show:

> "For as thou did wi Earl Richard,
> So would thou do wi me."

. . . .
"Come saddle to me my horse," he said,
Come saddle to me with speed."

. . . .
When they came into fair London town,
Into the courtiers' hall.

Four-beat and three-beat formulaic phrases combine to form larger patterns. Thus, in the Lyle repertoire, the four-beat formula "Out and spak her ain bridegroom (. . . an auld rich knight," etc.) is followed by the formula "And an angry man was he (. . . a sorry man," etc). Even when the phraseology of the second line disappears, the *ee* rhyme remains, as in "An ill death may he die" ("Sir Patrick Spens," 2), or "And a blithe blink from his ee" ("Lord William," 18). Many other kinds of half-stanza formulaic expressions dot the repertoire. Some of these are fairly redundant, formed by various kinds of expansions and repetitions, as the discussion of smaller units has indicated. But some full-scale, two-line formulas convey fresh information in the second line. Compare, for instance, the following Lyle realizations of a single formula:

Sweet William's gone over the seas
Some unco lair to learn.

. . . .
The youngest o them is to the king's court
To learn some unco lair.

The first realization is a fairly straightforward description of William's matriculation at a foreign university. The second is an ironic comment on Mary's loss of innocence at what should have been a school of gentility. In each case the second line adds to the information contained in the first line.

The next level of linguistic organization, after phrase and clause, is full period or sentence. In the ballad a sentence usually fills out a stanza (cf. Lord 1985, 403). And as sentences are formed of phrases and clauses, so full-stanza formulas are invariably formed, at least in part, of smaller formulaic elements. One of Agnes Lyle's favorite formulas is the "Come saddle to me" commonplace. Her four realizations, in "The Gypsy Laddie," "Geordie," "Lord William," and "Lord Derwentwater," are all multiforms of the same basic structure and idea, both over all and line for line:

Line 1: Call for a horse; e.g.,: "Come saddle to me my horse, he said."
Line 2: Emphatic repetition; e.g.,: "Come saddle to me with speed."
Line 3: Statement of length of journey; e.g.,: "For I must away to fair London town."
Line 4: Statement of reason for journey; e.g.,: "For me was neer more need."

As a unit this commonplace is found widely in Anglo-Scottish tradition and is one of the thirty or so commonplaces with distinct supra-narrative function to which Andersen assigns a privileged position in the tradition. But the first line, in three of the four Lyle realizations, also belongs to its own linear formula family. Mary Hamilton's plea, " 'But bring to me a cup,' she said," belongs to the same family and like the realization in the "Come saddle to me" commonplace, is followed by a restatement of the line.

Some full-stanza formula families are quite diverse, including both commonplaces and nonce stanzas. The third stanza of "Fair Janet" is the commonplace:

> They had not sailed one league, one league,
>   One league but only three,
> Till sharp, sharp showers fair Janet took,
>   She grew sick and like to die.

This formula is related to the commonplace stanza 2 of "Mary Hamilton":

> She hadna been in the king's court
>   A twelve month and a day,
> Till of her they could get na wark,
>   For wantonness and play.

Each of these commonplaces has multiform variants. Andersen considers them separate formulas, but on a deeper level they are united not only in structure and diction, but also in narrative idea. This essential narrative idea is that life has scarcely progressed a certain distance in time or space when ("Till") something bad happens. The commonplace "She hadna pu'd a flower, a flower" is a close parallel on this deeper level. It may be assigned to the same larger family, as may the following context-bound formulations from the "Fair Janet" tradition:

> Fair Janet was nae weel lichter,
>   Nor weel doun on her side,
> Till ben and cam her father dear,
>   Saying, Wha will busk our bride?
> . . . .
> She hadna danced the floor once owre,
>   I'm sure she hadna thrice,
> Till she fell in a deadly swound,
>   And from it neer did rise.

The essential narrative idea in all these expressions of the formula is that life has scarcely progressed a certain distance in time or space when ("Till") something bad happens.

Stanzaic formulas regularly form stanzaic pairs. The many ways these double formulas occur have already been indicated in the discussion of pairing techniques in Chapter 3 and in the discussion of word pairs, above. It is probably well, however, to distinguish pairs united only by some form of repetition from pairs united by the necessity of more than one stanza to convey the full narrative idea. The latter group includes some common ballad incipits and explicits. The "Rose and briar" commonplace, for instance, makes full narrative use of its two stanzas to describe the graves first and then the intertwining plants that grow from the graves. The "Hold your tongue" commonplace that ends a number of the ballads likewise takes two stanzas to express its complete idea:

> Out and spak her father dear,
>   Says, What needs a' this sorrow?
> For I'll get you a far better lord
>   Than ever died on Yarrow.

> "O hold your tongue, father," she said,
>   For ye've bred a' my sorrow;
> For that rose'll neer spring sae sweet in May
>   As that rose I lost on Yarrow.

Just as stanzaic formulas include lines and couplets which exist as formulas on their own level, so the two-stanza "Hold your tongue" commonplace includes a stanza with a life of its own as a one-stanza commonplace. Apart from the "Yarrow" rhymes—which come from the formulaic tradition of the "Yarrow" ballads, not of the "Hold your tongue" commonplace—the two stanzas are independent of each other in diction and sentence structure, and each conveys its own information. In addition to its occurrence in "The Braes o Yarrow," this true two-stanza formula is found at the end of the Lyle "Jamie Douglas" and (arguably) "Mary Hamilton," as well as (much modified) "Sheath and Knife," and in many texts outside the repertoire.

After the stanzaic pair, the next highest level of formulaic organization is the cluster or run. A run always consists of a series of commonplaces. It can be lengthened or shortened by including or omitting commonplaces. But a given run does not really provide choice among commonplaces to be used or permit inclusion of other non-commonplace formulaic lines and stanzas. One common run includes the commonplaces "Where can I find a bonny boy," "Here am I a bonny boy," "When he came to the broken bridge," and "What news, what news." Other "Bonny boy" runs utilize other combinations of commonplaces. The "Long letter" commonplace, sometimes inaugurates a run that includes "The first line he read," "Come saddle to me my horse," and "Out and spoke."

Runs sometimes function as "themes" in balladry, but the two can be distinguished. A run is a sequence of commonplaces, but a "theme" is a sequence of narrative elements; the formulas and commonplaces used to express that "thematic" sequence can vary from ballad to ballad and text to text. When Lord says, "The theme, even though it be verbal, is not a fixed

set of words, but a grouping of ideas," the student of ballads wants to add,
"Not a fixed set of commonplaces either." Another way to express the distinction is to say that a run is a surface structure, but a "theme" is a deep
structure.[4] Thus, while Agnes Lyle's "King's Letter Theme" invariably includes the "Long letter" commonplace, the development from there is different in each of the realizations of the "theme." In "Johnie Scot" the king
writes the letter in stanza 4, and the mother speaks out two stanzas later. In
"Lord Derwentwater" the king writes the letter in stanza 1, and the lady gay
does not speak out until four stanzas later. In "Lord Derwentwater" the hero
responds to the letter by calling for his horse in the words of the appropriate
commonplace, even though this commonplace does not occur in the other
realizations of this "theme." Nor do the nuncupative will and the "He has
sent it not with a boy, a boy" commonplace. But let the last stanza of each
"theme" stand for all the differences in realization among the Lyle variants,
despite identity of basic narrative elements.

> Aye they sat, and aye they drank,
>   They drank of the beer and wine,
> And gin Wednesday gin ten o'clock
>   Their hair was wat abune.
>   ("Sir Patrick Spens")

> Away they gade, awa they rade,
>   Away they rade so slie'
> There was not a married man that day
>   In Johnie's companie.
>   ("Johnie Scot")

> They had not rode a mile but one,
>   Till his horse fell owre a stane:
> "It's warning gude eneuch," my lord Dunwaters said,
>   "Alive I'll neer come hame."
>   ("Lord Derwentwater")

On the level of the whole ballad two types of formulas can be identified.
The first is called by Andersen a formula ballad (1985, 78). His example is the
song "Come Mother, Come Mother" (cf. MacColl and Seeger 1977, 112–115).
Made up entirely of a stable series of well-known commonplaces, the song is
like a run gone amok, a run so extended that it constitutes the whole song.
The second type might be called the formulaic ballad, by analogy with the
formulaic tale. Members of this type are one-formula pieces which do not
vary greatly from performance to performance, though anyone who understands the basic formula can expand or compress the ballad at will. "The
Maid Freed from the Gallows" is a prime example, remarkably stable across
a wide linguistic and geographic range. The wit-combat songs and "Our
Goodman" would also seem to belong to this category. Communalists were
fond of citing ballads such as these in their expositions; it was easy to imag-

ine a singing, dancing throng joining in, once the basic pattern set. But the single-formula character of these ballads is just the reason why they are not good fodder for discussions about ballad creation and transmission.

The above attempt at classification has demonstrated that many other schemes are possible. One might wish to distinguish grammatical formulas, incipits and inquits, formula families, free-floating formulas, or any of a dozen other categories. Formulas associated in one classification might well be separated in another. For instance, in Andersen's category of "true ballad formulas" characterized by stable supra-narrative function, linear, half-stanza, stanza, and stanza-pair formulas associate quite happily.

One particularly necessary alternative to classification by linguistic level needs to be developed here. Formulas originate neither from the same impulse nor from the same mental process. This diversity has led to seemingly contradictory descriptions of the formulaic process. Lord, in *The Singer of Tales*, describes formulas as substitutionary. Opponents of the formulaic approach tend to see formulas as memorial. And Edwards (1983) and Andersen see them as generated on the deep level. But all three modes of formulating seem to occur in tradition, providing set or memorial formulas, substitutionary formulas, and generative formulas.

There are, first of all, set formulas, which do not vary in wording, even over a wide geographical and temporal range. These are usually short epithets and phrases such as "wee pen knife," "beaten gold," "milk-white steed," and so on. These ballad "clichés" have been noted and commented upon many times. There is no need for a complex model of formulation to deal with them. They are simply remembered.

On the next level of complexity, balladry is full of expressions such as "Rise up, rise up, _____," "Out and spoke _____," "It fell upon _____," "Fair _____," "Sweet _____," and "Merry _____." One may fill in the blank with any appropriate and metrical expression. A simple substitutionary model seems sufficient to deal with these inquits, epithet-phrases, and other expressions, once they have acquired a relatively fixed surface structure.

More complex formulaic expressions call for a generative model with a unifying idea on the deep level and multiformity on the surface level.[5] In some cases, in fact, it is possible to identify several levels of deep structure. In the "They had not" formula family discussed above, the commonplace idea is able to generate Agnes Lyle's "They had not sailed a league, a league" stanza and many related realizations. But on a deeper level this formula family is able to generate this commonplace, the commonplace which Agnes Lyle renders "She had not been in the king's court / A twelvemonth and a day," and the commonplace "She hadna pu'd a flower, a flower," as well as the several context-bound formulations in "Fair Janet," all of which are related in narrative idea and structure. Once realized, such commonplaces can then set, on the surface level, at least in a particular region or in the practice of a particular performer, and become subject to substitutionary variation ("She had not . . . he had not"). Finally, they can be parodied on the surface level, without respect to the ideas and affects which are part of the deep (or the supra-narrative) structure. In "Lord Derwentwater" Agnes Lyle sings:

> He has not sent it with a boy, with a boy,
>   Nor with anie Scotch lord;
> But he's sent it with the noblest knight
>   Eer Scotland could afford.

In "The Eastmure King" she sings:

> This boy was sixteen years of age,
>   But he was nae seventeen,
> When he is to the garden gone
>   To slay that Eastmure king.

Each of these stanzas seems to be modelled upon stanzas belonging to the formula family under question. And yet neither realizes the basic relationship of events characteristic of the formula family. One substitutes hierarchical progression for temporal or spatial progression. The other introduces an act that, though violent, is desirable. The stanzas, accordingly, are not realizations of the deepest structure of the formula but parodies on the surface level.

One may speak then of three modes of production for formulas. They may spring full blown from the memory. They may be created by substitution or parody on the surface level. Or they may be generated from a deep structure. Furthermore, a formulation which has been generated from a deep structure may subsequently be manipulated on the surface and even set in memory. The opposite process is also possible: A singer who intuits the deep structure latent in a remembered phrase may generate new expressions of the formulaic idea.

2. AGNES LYLE AND ANNA GORDON BROWN

Prior to this study, the only classic oral ballad repertoire to receive extensive study had been that of Anna Gordon, Mrs. Brown of Falkland.[6] Comparison of Agnes Lyle's repertoire with that of Mrs. Brown can provide deeper understanding of oral ballad making.

Mrs. Brown tended to sing romantic and magical ballads, all but one of which, "Sir Hugh" (Child 155A), concerned the course of true and sometimes false love. Even the two "historical" ballads in her repertoire, "Bonny Baby Livingston" (Child 222A) and "The Baron of Brackley" (Child 203C), include distinctly romantic elements. Though the Lyle ballads include only one revenant piece, they likewise represent the more romantic branch of the

Anglo-Scottish tradition. But the realizations of these ballads are completely different in tone and emphasis from Mrs. Brown's realizations. Agnes Lyle, like some of her Kilbarchan neighbors, gives her ballads a nationalistic emphasis (Andersen 1985, 327). And she seasons this nationalism with a bitter cynicism unique to herself.

One of the most remarkable things about Mrs. Brown's ballads is their uniformity. David Buchan's careful and extended analysis shows that the most diverse stories, from the most diverse sources, have all been fitted into a common narrative mold, developed according to a single system of composition. This system, which seems to have been learned when Mrs. Brown was a child, produced ballads which may be described thus: stanzaic narrative poems involving three principal characters, a hero, a heroine, and a villain, in an amatory story—except in the case of "Sir Hugh"—told through stanzas of dialogue alternating with stanzas of narrative in a three-act structure, all elements arranged symmetrically in harmonic and contrapuntal annular, binary, and trinary patterns.

The most remarkable evidence of the consistency of this narrative technique is that these thirty-three or more ballads admit of classification into three types solely on the basis of the role played by the villain! In the largest class, ballads of family opposition, the villain is a member of the family. In the second class, ballads of other love, the villain is a rival. In the third class, murder ballads, the villain is the murderer. In this third class, as well, the villain may overshadow one of the other characters in importance. In "Sir Hugh," for instance, the Jew's daughter is more important than Sir Hugh's mother, the "good" female character. This procrustean uniformity seems to have been imposed upon the ballads by Mrs. Brown. Variants of these ballads by other singers often have different deep character structures or a different number of acts, to name but two of the more obvious differences. Mrs. Brown was asked for songs of a particular type. She looked on the songs of her childhood as belonging to that type. Apparently she reconstructed those all-but-forgotten songs not in all their diversity but according to a single system, a system likewise learned in her childhood. In all probability she was the first and last singer ever to sing "The Twa Sisters," for instance, in that elaborate form produced by her system.[7]

The circumstances under which Agnes Lyle sang for William Motherwell were rather different from the circumstances under which Mrs. Brown dictated her ballads. And there is nothing like the same uniformity of technique in the pieces she sang. Presumably Agnes Lyle's texts were still a part of her daily life. For the most part she did not have to reach into her past to revive a long-dormant skill. Nor did she have to reconstruct her favorite songs "the way they must have been." Nor, again, did she distinguish among the songs she sang in the same way Mrs. Brown obviously distinguished ballads of her childhood from other songs. Mrs. Brown was consciously singing one particular type of song. While it would be a mistake to exaggerate her level of education, her concept of ballad was rather sophisticated, and she knew her

Percy. Consequently, even without stepping outside the traditional technique or system that she had mastered in childhood, she could impose that sophisticated concept upon the ballads she sang. Agnes Lyle, on the other hand, simply knew songs. She knew all kinds of songs. The evidence suggests that she did not consciously reflect on the differences between the various types of songs she knew. On 24 August 1825, for instance, she produced "The Cruel Mother" and "Hind Horn," rather different sorts of couplet ballads; "Johnie Scot," an orally recreated standard-quatrain ballad with political overtones; "The Wee Wee Man," a song; "The Baffled Knight," a slightly bawdy broadside piece; and the ill-remembered "The Sweet Trinity." The ballads of Mrs. Brown represent a conscious selection from songs of childhood by a sophisticated informant, whereas the ballads and other songs of Agnes Lyle represent a cross section of the current repertoire, active and passive, of a singer for whom ballads are a vital part of the singing experience of daily life and contemporary politics.

Agnes Lyle knew the technique of the orally recreative ballad singer, but she did not draw on that technique every time she sang. She was equally capable of remembering a fixed text such as "The Wee Wee Man," or loosely recreating a half-remembered piece such as "The Twa Sisters." When she did produce a full oral recreation her technique was in many ways like that of Mrs. Brown. It involved the same binary, trinary, and annular patterns, the same stanzaic, character, narrative, and sometimes even tonal structures. It was an expressive system into which an individual ballad might be assimilated and in terms of which it might be uttered. It was, however, a more limited and less monolithic system than that of Mrs. Brown, whose every ballad was totally assimilated into the system and expressed totally in terms of that system.

Mrs. Brown's technique somehow transcended metrical considerations. Of her technique Buchan says (1972, p. 142), "As the one corpus contains both couplet and quatrain texts demonstrably structured by the same methods, the traditional maker must have been able to move with relative ease between the two forms." Agnes Lyle's technique depended on the standard ballad quatrain, and in that meter she was more than competent. But she did not experience "relative ease" when she moved into singing couplet ballads. The nearest to success she came in this regard was with "Hind Horn." For "Babylon" and "The Cruel Mother" she went outside the system to discover a completely separate principle of structure. The four ballads in non-standard quatrains provided other difficulties in addition to the uncongenial meter. In one case, "The Braes o Yarrow," she achieved an outstanding success, difficulties notwithstanding; in the other three cases her success was only moderate. In general, the ballads in couplets or non-standard quatrains suffered most stress in the stanzaic structure, while retaining most control in narrative structure, confirming that the difficulty was not with the story but with the stanza in which the singer had to tell the story.

With regard to diction, both singers had favorite phrases which they used again and again. Agnes Lyle, however, was more free in her realization of formulas. She seldom used the same wording from stanza to stanza, except in the case of close emphatic or incremental repetition. In particular, her realizations of commonplaces were amazingly multiform, as a comparison of the four versions of the "Come saddle to me" stanza will demonstrate. Andersen's research confirms that such freedom in the realization of commonplaces is characteristic of the oral poet (passim, but especially chs. 3 and 5).

The rhyming practice which Agnes Lyle shares with Mrs. Brown provides further evidence of the orality of the repertoire (see Buchan 1972, 151–155). The rhyme *ee* occurs exactly the same percentage of times in the standard quatrain Lyle ballads as it does in the Brown ballads, twenty-eight percent. As in the Brown repertoire, the largest group of consonantal rhymes involves *n* sounds (*and, an, in,* etc.). *D* and *t* rhymes are also common in both repertoires, though the *r* rhymes, so common in the Brown repertoire, are rare in the Lyle. Like Mrs. Brown, Agnes Lyle draws on more than one dialect for rhymes, rhyming *away* with *day,* for instance, and *awa* with *braw.* The principal difference in rhyming practice between the two women is that Agnes Lyle is considerably more liberal in what she admits as rhyme, rhyming *head* with *sleep,* for instance, *green* with *down* and *gone,* and *slain* with *within, dream,* and *on.* Mrs. Brown's more conservative rhyming practice probably reflects her literate education and her experience reading and composing literary verse, which would lead her to avoid slant rhymes.[8]

In Agnes Lyle's ballads, as in those of Mrs. Brown, alliteration is wholly traditional. Though a principle decorative element in the verse, it is never used in purely decorative fashion. It regularly functions to relate words and ideas, as in "grass-green growing," "lay the saddle saft," and "come to Mary's Kirk." In those ancient phrases, such as "busk the bride," "lang letter," and "hunting horn," that have become part of the standard language of the ballad singer, the alliteration also functions to make the phrase memorable and easily recalled in moments of need.

Consideration of the similarities and differences in the oral styles of these two singers can lead to a deeper understanding of the process of oral creativity itself. The principles at work in the practice of each singer are the same. The techniques for developing these principles and the degree to which songs are assimilated to technique vary considerably. It is dangerous, therefore, to speak of *the* way oral performers recreate ballads.

3. THE WAY ORAL PERFORMERS RECREATE BALLADS

One of the great triumphs of the Parry-Lord school has been the demonstration that for epic the moment of creation, the moment of performance, and the moment of transmission coincide; all three of these processes go on at the same time, in fact, are in some sense a single epic process. Aspects of a single process or not, however, the three can be distinguished conceptually and, at least in the case of some genres, separated as well. To discuss how oral performers recreate ballads, the processes involved must be distinguished. Generally speaking the processes are the acquisition of oral recreative technique, the learning of a traditional ballad story, the development of that story within the limits and according to the structures of the technique, and the performance of that ballad, often for an audience which includes a future singer of the ballad. During the time when the singer is becoming competent the first three processes often coincide. During this apprenticeship period the singer, like Lord's apprentice epic singer (1960, 20–29), probably practices repeatedly prior to performance. Even competent singers will practice or sing for themselves more than for an audience. In a genre as short as the ballad, such private practice will tend to stabilize (not "fix") the text.[9]

About such stable texts several observations are in order. First, they will betray their origins in their overall oral architectonic and in their pervasive formulicity. Second, not being "fixed," they will always be open to improvisation and innovation. The inspiration of the moment, a better idea, or the influence of another version can at any performance induce changes, minor or major. Third, a person exposed to frequent repetitions of such a stable text, such as the child of a ballad singer, might learn the particular version more or less word for word, in a more or less memorized way, and so pass on a now-fixed text. Fourth, even if this child or other person is habitually an orally recreative singer, nothing is to stop the singer from learning that particular piece in a memorial way, the same way the hymns or psalms are learned in church, for instance;[10] nor, on the contrary, is there anything to stop the singer from learning it freely and orally, the way other ballad stories are learned, and fashioning therefrom a new rendition.

Once singers become proficient it is quite possible for a singing session involving two or more such singers to include a performance that is simultaneously composition and transmission as well. Even during the learning period, processes can not always be separated, for the singer learns the technique by listening, as well as by singing, and there can be no singing without at least one or two ballads to sing.

Like the story, the tune is learned as an idea, rather than a fixed series of sounds. The Bronson anthology demonstrates the tremendous variation that tune ideas can undergo, variation in range, in scale, in mode, in tempo, and in harmonic structure. Learning the basic tune idea, each singer realizes it according to personal ability and taste, one singer producing something rich and subtle, another producing something simple and effective, a third producing something crude and monotonous. Moreover, though text and tune are integrated, not all great ballad storytellers are great ballad musicians. The two surviving tunes from Agnes Lyle suggest that she belongs to the "simple and effective" school. Mrs. Brown's tunes are more troubling, though it is hard to know if the trouble originates with the singer or with the transcriber.

The fewer mentors chosen or attended to, the more singer will sing like mentor. For a time. But great singers will eventually develop their own style and approach, as Agnes Lyle did. This style may be conservative or innovative, monolithic or adaptive, stable or improvisatory. These variations are not the significant thing. What is important is that the ballad has been forged in the oral crucible, and embodies an oral aesthetic. It tells the traditional story in formulaic language on all levels from phoneme up, structures its elements according to the binary, trinary, and annular principles of an oral architectonic, and expresses its unique cultural and thematic insights in terms of the binary oppositions of the traditional worldview. As such, it is never fixed for the orally recreative singer, but at any point, even after the hundredth performance, it can change to accommodate a new insight or a new view of the material.

The difference between singing fixed and singing stable songs is in some ways like the difference between going somewhere in a strange city by following memorized or written directions and going somewhere routine in a familiar city. The driver in the strange city must look for just the landmarks and make just the turns prescribed in the directions or risk never getting to the destination. The driver taking a routine trip in a familiar city probably goes the same way regularly, out of habit. But this driver, at any time, can go some other way because of traffic, desire for change, curiosity to see if it's faster, or mere whim. The first driver drives by rote. The second driver knows the way, and can vary that way at will. And, just as the driver, once that driver knows where something is in a familiar city, can go there without needing directions, so the ballad singer, once that singer knows where a song goes, can go there too. The singer may go the same way every time, or may vary. What Lord says of the epic singer seems to apply here as well: "In a truly oral tradition of song there is no guarantee that even the apparently most stable 'runs' will always be word-for-word the same in performance" (1960, 125). The oral tradition is always open to change.

It is usually easy to distinguish ballads forged in an oral crucible from broadside texts, ballad imitations, and other types of folk or popular songs. But the immediate singer is not always the original creator of the version. Sometimes, as has been noted, a stable text in one generation becomes a fixed text in the next. Such fixed texts then take on an existence of their own. They may even become the dominant tradition, as may have happened in North America. In such a tradition stabilized ballads texts will live, grow, and die according to a law of their own. That law deserves a book of its own, many books, but the law of transmission of fixed texts must not be confused with the law of oral recreation that has been the subject of this study.

I began this study by proposing to survey the field of contention in the new "ballad wars." What this survey has shown is that the debate between the proponents and opponents of the oral approach becomes almost a debate about vocabulary, not about actuality. When the oral model is applied carefully, with due regard to what happens in the case of short sequences of formulas, the description of balladry that emerges is remarkably like the description of balladry that emerges from moderate and sensible contemporary applications of a text memory model, such, for instance, as that of Eleanor Long. The oral model has the advantage, however, of accounting for the generation of the text and the oral architechtonics and aesthetics therein embodied.

In balladry, and probably in other short oral genres as well, the issues of generation and transmission seem separable in ways that they are not in longer genres, such as epic, wayang kulit, or Navajo sing. In the case of a fairly stable ballad the performance or performances at which a second singer learns the ballad probably do not coincide with the series of practices and performances during which the first singer stabilizes her version. And the second singer, once she learns the ballad, may sing it much as she has heard it, or she may generate something quite different in structure, in diction, in emotional content, and even in melody. So, on the issue of transmission the memorial and the oral approaches, unlike the high road and the low road, arrive at Loch Lomond together. But on the issue of generation of the text the oral formulaic approach goes beyond the text memory approach to suggest how the text is generated in the first place, and what are the uniquely oral qualities of that text, both structurally and aesthetically.

Appendix

Tunes of the Ballads in the Agnes Lyle Repertoire

Here follows a full list of the ballads and what can be ascertained about the tune of each:

10—"Twa Sisters"
No clear analogues in Bronson; closest analogues in C and D groups ("Hey Edinboro"→"Hey with a gay, with a grinding O").

14—"Babylon"
Motherwell tune 26 fits Lyle text. Could discrepancy in words be explained by unconscious conflating with J. Goldie's text, caused by quoting from memory?

15/16—"Sheath and Knife"
Only one tune extant, from Charles Kirkpatrick Sharpe. Motherwell did send Sharpe the Lyle text. Did he also send him this tune? Refrain very like hers, as Bronson notes.

17—"Hind Horn"
Motherwell tune has different words. The ballad has a single tune tradition, unrelated to other ballad tune traditions, though not to other Scottish folksongs.

20—"Cruel Mother"
Most tunes are related, and also related to "Geordie" and "Yarrow" tunes. Impossible to determine a tune family on basis of text family.

38—"The Wee Wee Man"
No clear tune tradition

58—"Sir Patrick Spens"
Tune has a single, Scottish tradition.

64—"Fair Janet"
Only two extant tunes, closely related, and both Scottish.

68—"Earl Richard"
Motherwell gives two tunes, and identifies the appropriate text for the first but not for the second. The Manuscript has only two full texts of "Earl Richard," the one identified with the first tune in the appendix, and the one from Agnes Lyle. The second *Minstrelsy* tune, then, could be from Agnes Lyle. (Note that Emily Lyle identifies the first tune with Mary McQueen's text. 1975, xxii.)

81—"Little Musgrave"
Motherwell tune is the earliest recorded for the ballad, but Lyle text does not fit. Quite possible that this tune is similar to Agnes Lyle's tune. Her incipit, however, suggests that her tune may come from another tradition, the "Drumdelgie" tune family, (Bronson group B), not generally associated with Scottish texts—but the association had to come from somewhere!

89—"The Eastmure King"
"This is sung to the tune of Johnie Scot" (Motherwell 1825–1826, 341). Motherwell
gives one "Johnie Scot" tune, but the fit to the Lyle text of "The Eastmure King" is
not perfect. Bronson includes a tune for this ballad from the Blaikie manuscript, but
that tune shows no close relationship to "Johnie Scot" and so is probably not AL's
tune.

99—"Johnie Scot"
Motherwell gives a tune for "Johnie Scot," but not from this singer. The Lyle text is
related textually to the "Mary Hamilton" tradition. For tune relations see 89 and 222.

112—"The Baffled Knight"
The Chappell and Durfey tunes (Bronson B and C) are set to texts close to Agnes
Lyle's. But it is impossible to know what tune was used with this broadside text in
Southwest Scotland in the 1820s.

173—"Mary Hamilton"
Blaikie Ms has three tunes. One of them could easily be from this singer. The first
two are nearly identical, and of a musical structure (ABAB) that lends itself easily to
expansion into 6 lines.

200—"Gypsy Laddie"
Bronson's B group includes several Scottish versions with a final stanza similar to
Agnes Lyle's, suggesting that her version belongs to this text-tune tradition.

204—"Jamie Douglas"
This ballad is usually sung to the tune of "Waly Waly," and the Lyle version includes
"Waly Waly" stanzas, so it seems safe to posit a variant of that tune for this ballad.
Motherwell does give a maverick tune in the *Minstrelsy*, but the accompanying words
suggest that it is not the Lyle tune.

208—"Lord Derwentwater"
Tunes are rare. Bronson includes 4, one indisputably from Agnes Lyle. Of this tune
he says, "Motherwell's tune is an excellent example of folk music. Its feeling is major,
but it ends on the second, so as to make a graceful return to the beginning. Techni-
cally, therefore, it may be classed as Dorian. It has many relatives in tradition, one of
the best known, possibly, being Cecil Sharp's 'Outlandish Knight' [Child 4]" (3: 264).

209—"Geordie"
"Sung to a tune something similar to 'My Nannie O' " (Motherwell 1825–1826, 367).
Simpson gives a tune under this name (1966, no. 319, p. 507), which seems related to
the tune now associated with the Irish songs "The Bantairo" and "B for Barney."
Some of the Bronson group A tunes and texts sound like what Motherwell may have
been talking about.

214—"Yarrow"
Bronson identifies 5 groups. The Lyle text is most like that of the Scott 1833 text, set
uniquely to the tune "Leader Haughs and Yarrow."

222—"Bonny Baby Livingston"
Bronson gives only two tunes, a late one from Aberdeen and a Charles Kirkpatrick
Sharpe one. The Sharpe tune has a text very like that of Agnes Lyle, though longer,
and ends on the second, like her "Lord Derwentwater." Agnes Lyle's incipit is like

that of "Little Musgrave." Motherwell implies that the tune is that of "Johnie Scot" (1824–1827, 162).

254—"Lord William"
"The only tune preserved for this clumsy piece is that printed by Motherwell, a plagal major which Andrew Blaikie of Paisley secured for him [from Agnes Lyle]. If it suggests any relatives, they lie among Sharp's variations of 'The Unquiet Grave' (No. 78); but it is chiefly in the third phrase that the resemblances are found" (Bronson 1959–1972, 4: 62).

286—"The Golden Vanity"
Bronson gives a Blaikie tune (no. 58) that may be the one about which Motherwell wrote Sharp (see Child 5:142). This tune is 4-phrase, not 5-phrase, and set to different words from the Lyle text. But in general the Bronson Ad tunes, to which group Bronson assigns this tune, are distinctive in being Scottish tunes set to texts in which the second line is a refrain line. The text in Bronson closest to Agnes Lyle's text is that from Allie Long Parker of Hog Scald Holler, Arkansas, collected in 1958 (No. 103). The Parker version includes the tool for use, nine holes, and hats and caps, calls the ship the *Turkish Ugarlee*, and even interjects the "Lowlands low" refrain after the first line, as the Lyle version also does. Sending the Lyle text to Charles Kirkpatrick Sharpe, Motherwell commented that the tune was different from two other tunes he had heard (Child 1882–1898, 5: 142). Was that tune, like the text, closer to what Allie Long Parker was later to sing?

Fragment 1: "But sixteen years of age she was" No information available about possible tunes.

Fragment 2: "The week before Easter" Tunes given in Sharp may represent the tradition.

Fragment 3: "A fair maid walking in a garden" No early tunes; tradition fairly constant today.

Fragment 4: "There were two sailors were lonely walking" All records are recent for "Basket of Eggs."

Fragment 5: "It was in the middle of fair July" Probably sung to tune called "Two Rigs of Rye."

Fragment 6: "As I went out on a May morning" Musical tradition quite recent, and quite jolly.

Notes

INTRODUCTION

1. His first article on the subject (*Journal of American Folklore* 1961, 113–115) was entitled "The Formulaic Improvisation Theory of Ballad Tradition—*A Counterstatement*" (Italics added).

2. For a careful survey of oral theory and of the response by scholars to the work of Parry and Lord, and especially to *The Singer of Tales*, see Foley 1988.

3. Emily Lyle (1975) has edited part of the Crawfurd manuscript, one of the most important early collections to come to light since Child.

4. For a complete discussion of these theories, not always positive, see Andersen 1985, 17–40.

5. Carol Edwards indicates that the Parry definition of a formula has generative implications. Edwards 1983, 161.

6. Indeed, it has been argued, e.g., by Gerould (1932, 125), that the ballad quatrain is in fact "a couplet with seven stresses to the line." Certainly, at fourteen stresses, the ballad stanza is not significantly longer than the ten-stress South Slav epic couplet of which Lord spoke.

7. The word "theme" has a meaning in oral-formulaic criticism distinct from its set of meanings in general criticism. To keep the two domains of usage clear I will retain quotation marks whenever I take the term in the oral-formulaic sense first expounded by Lord.

8. Such stability also occurs in other, shorter genres of South-Slavic oral-formulaic poetry, such as laments and the brief Christian epics, though Lord does not discuss these examples in detail. See Foley 1983; 1988, 75–76.

9. The terminological distinction is only implicit in Lord, who uses the terms *stable* and *fixed* interchangeably but subdivides fixity into more and less, or into fixity and apparent fixity. Lord 1981 returns to this question.

10. The Andersen-Pettit essay also criticizes briefly Anders's *Balladensänger und mündliche Komposition*. In this criticism stability is again a sticking point (see especially p. 6). The present writer finds Anders's book valuable for its demonstration of the scope of the formulaic system in Anglo-Scottish balladry.

11. See especially his discussion, 271, of the commonplace "The first step/first town."

12. The recently published repertoire of Mary McQueen confirms that singers knew a variety of songs. See Lyle 1975.

13. The concept was first expounded by Whitman with reference to the *Iliad* (1958, Chapter 11). Niles (1973) discusses the "Chanson de geste," and Lord (1986, 53–64) applies the concept to Avdo's epic *The Wedding of Smailagić Meho*. Buchan's application to the ballad is especially detailed (1972).

14. Actually, he is not entirely alone in stanza 8. The word *they* indicates that he has some retainers with him. But these retainers do not enter into the plot.

1. THE RADICAL AND THE TORY

1. Shaw (1980) provides a good description of the Scottish textile industry before 1830 as well as a helpful guide to sources.

2. The New Statistical Account credits Kilbarchan with seven parochial schools in addition to several private ones (380).

3. Information from *Statistical Account* and *New Statistical Account.*

4. Details concerning the Radical War of 1820 are derived, unless otherwise noted, from Ellis and Mac a' Ghobhainn.

5. Goldie's poems are given in Ellis and Mac a' Ghobhain, 344–346. The ballads are Child 10H and 14C.

6. Two other important Scots singers, Mrs. Brown of Falkland and Mrs. Storie, are also referred to frequently by their maiden names, Anna Gordon and Mary Mcqueen, respectively.

7. For a fuller account of the editorial history of *Minstrelsy Ancient and Modern* see McCarthy 1987, 310–313.

2. THE MANUSCRIPTS AND THE SONGS

1. E.g., David Buchan, Bronson, present study. The information in the preceding paragraph comes from examination of the autograph Manuscript and of the Harvard copies of the Manuscript and the Notebook. The present author has not succeeded in examining the autograph Notebook.

2. The unascribed texts are "Lady Maisry" (Child 65C), Ms. p. 472, and "The Elfin Knight" (Child 2E), Ms. p. 492. The errors, discussed below, involve a confusion of names between Agnes Lyle and Agnes Laird.

3. E.g., Child 1882–1898, 5: 398; Bronson 1959–1972, 4: 523.

4. It is not the purpose of the present study to do a new edition of the ballads of Agnes Lyle to replace Child's work. On the contrary, one of its purposes is to provide an entree into *The English and Scottish Popular Ballads.* To that end, texts are given as edited by Child. In referring to individual ballads the titles from Child are used whenever appropriate. When the Child title seems especially inappropriate for a particular text (e.g., 89: "Fause Foodrage") an alternative title is used. In one case Child assigns a text to two different places in the canon. In that case (Child 15b-16f) the title which seems to fit Agnes Lyle's text better has been used. In referring to characters within the ballads, names are spelled as in the text: the hero of Agnes Lyle's text of "Little Musgrave," for example, is Mossgrey. The ballad fragments are given in the unedited form in which they appear in the Notebook, sans punctuation, *sans* consistent spelling. Quotations from Motherwell's notations, where reference is made to Child, are given in the edited form in which they appear in Child. Otherwise they are given in the form in which they appear in the Notebook or Manuscript.

5. Child 20H and 99F.

6. "The Gay Goshawk" is the fifth item in a memorandum of songs in the repertoire of Agnes Laird, running pages 26 to 30 in the Notebook. The first four items on the list consist each of a stanza or a half stanza and a brief plot summary. The fifth item consists of this whole text. The memo is dated 18 August, but the Manuscript states that the song was collected on 24 August. Probably Motherwell included only the first stanza when he compiled the list on 18 August, and added the remaining stanzas when he returned to the singer on 24 August.

7. Christie 1876–1881, 2: 224–225; Ord 1930, 31–32; Gardner and Chickering 1939, 163; MacColl 1965, 67; *Bulletin of the Folksong Society of the Northeast* [Greig 1963], I: 8.

8. See below, chapter 7.

9. For a complete discussion of tune relationships, see appendix.

10. The fragments also include pieces composed in four-beat quatrains, rhyming either *a b c b* or *a a a b*. But one piece, "The Fox Chase," exhibits a considerably more complex metrical scheme. One could describe it as a quatrain of feminine rhyme, *a b c b*, the first line a tetrameter, the second and fourth trimeters, and the third a hexame-

ter with internal rhyme. Or one could quibble with Motherwell's transcription and describe it as a five-line stanza rhyming *a b c c b.*

3. THE WEAVER'S DAUGHTER SINGS

1. Emphasis on individual scenes, with little narrative transition between scenes, seems characteristic of oral tradition in general. One thinks, for example, of Homer, *The Song of Roland,* and even the Märchen.

2. This "Talliant" puzzled Motherwell, and puzzles the present writer too. Comparison with other texts suggests that the word is a corruption of *Italian,* but *Italian* could as easily be a rationalization of *Talliant,* and the meaning of the term may indeed be lost. Johnie with sword in hand, walking across the plain, seems to represent a reconstruction of a scene in which Johnie stroked his sword on the grass. The sword in the straw in this singer's "Little Musgrave" may be a similar reconstruction. The last two lines of stanza 18 likewise appear to be a reconstruction, but the original meaning is unclear. Child suggests that the king's champion actually leaps over Johnie's head, and Johnie spits him with his sword while he is thus overhead (1882–1898, 2: 378).

3. Andersen identifies three commonplaces structured more or less according to this pattern: "She hadna pu'd a flower, a flower," "He hadna been in fair England, a month but barely ane," and "He hadna ridden a mile, a mile/They hadna sailed a league, a league." The flower commonplace is built on progress through a task, gathering flowers, rather than through time or space. See fuller discussion of this formula family in Conclusion.

4. Confronted with such alliterative richness the reader is bound to think of Anglo-Saxon verse or verse of the Alliterative Revival. There does not seem, however, to be any direct connection beyond the most general aptness to alliterate in the genius of the English language, Old, Middle, and Modern. In ballad English the alliteration commonly falls on adjacent stresses within a half line. When the alliteration ties a whole line together, as in:

> And when we come to Mary's Kirk,

or

> Ben and cam the bride's brethren,

alliteration almost invariably falls on the last stress of the line, a rare place for alliteration in Anglo-Saxon and not common in alliterative Middle English.

5. Important discussions of acoustic patterns in oral tradition include Lord on South Slavic (1965, 55–57), Peabody on Greek (1975, chapter 5), Creed on Anglo-Saxon (1981), and Buchan on Scots (1972, Chapter 12).

4. THE WEAVER'S DAUGHTER NODS

1. Long applies the terms to types of singers or makers rather than to stances. The point of using the word *stance* is to suggest that a given singer at different times or with regard to different songs may take different stances, that is, may belong to different types.

2. Similarly, it would not be too surprising if Mrs. Brown sang "The Lass of Roch Royal" more from memory than from oral recreation (See introduction). The presence of one or two memorized pieces in her repertoire would not disqualify her for status as an oral-formulaic singer, since her repertoire as a whole is closely unified in oral

style, theme, and sensibility. The presence of such a piece would only indicate that she too, probably unconsciously, could take more than one stance toward ballads.

The word *memorize* is used here for lack of a better. This learning of a heard text, albeit a fixed text, should not be identified with that learning of a read text which is usually referred to by the word *memorize*. Cf. Lord 1961, 5, 36; 1981, *passim*.

3. I.e., 1–9, 10–21; or 1–9, 10–16, 17–21. Other logical divisions are also possible.

4. Possibly "Eastmure King" ought to be included, though the imagery is not nearly so dense in this ballad.

5. "The Wee Wee Man," collected the same day, likewise belongs with these fragments: it is a "walking out" piece like the last five fragments, and the text is more or less fixed.

5. THE WEAVER'S DAUGHTER SOARS

1. On "Edward," see Taylor 1931; and Bronson 1969, 1–17. On "The Maid Freed from the Gallows," see Long 1971. On the riddle or wit-combat ballads, see Toelken 1966; Coffin, 1983; and Buchan 1985. "Our Goodman" has not inspired scholarship of similar stature.

2. North American ballad collections reflect this dual aspect of the "Babylon" tradition: The first sub-tradition, in which the anagnorisis hinges upon a name, is found, though rarely, in the Appalachian region, while the second, though usually with two, not three brothers, is found in New England and north to Newfoundland. In the Scandinavian tradition the anagnorisis occurs when the killer (or more usually, killers, who are usually but not always brothers) shows up at the father's house and tries to bribe someone with the silk clothing of the daughters. The Bergman film *The Virgin Spring* follows this tradition of the story.

3. Or, according to which he has envisioned his vision.

4. Cf. p. 103, where she explicitly discusses combing in a different version of "Braes o' Yarrow". Andersen says of Rogers's ideas on combing (which he had read in an earlier version): "Some of her observations are very much in line with the general interpretation suggested here" (Andersen 1985, 115).

6. LOVE AND DEATH

1. In a note (3, p. 244) Renwick adds a fourth category, the "idiomatic" or obscene, but excuses himself from discussing it because early collectors neglected such material and there is not any sizeable selection from pre-twentieth-century sources. Would that Motherwell had not put off printing the *Paisley Garland*.

2. Of course the tradition from which these songs come *is*, by contemporary standards sexist. Recognition of that sexism seems to be part of Renwick's point in using the terms *masculine* and *feminine*. The signifying traits, whether masculine or feminine, are exhibited by male as well as female characters, both in the Renwick sample and in the Lyle repertoire.

3. Social disparity: "Cruel Mother," "Fair Janet," "Earl Richard"(?), "Little Musgrave," "Eastmure King," "Johnie Scot," "Baffled Knight"(?), "Mary Hamilton," "Gypsy Laddie," "Lord William," and "Bonny Baby Livingston." Love for intrinsic reasons: "Twa Sisters," "Sheath and Knife," "Hind Horn," "Fair Janet," "Eastmure King," "Johnie Scot," "Jamie Douglas," "Braes o' Yarrow," "Bonny Baby Livingston," and "Lord William." In some sense, context figures in all the pieces, but this seems to be because it is impossible to tell a story in which characters have no context.

4. Rogers (48–50) points out yet another function of games: they serve to bring out the great qualities of a hero and to win him the heroine. The joust in "Johnie Scot" serves this function, though it is more serious than most games.

5. Thus, like Fair Annet, Mary Hamilton puts the rightful wife to shame by the splendor of her dress, a parallel emphasized in Child's G and I texts, which include variants of the following stanza:

> The queen was drest in scarlet fine
> Her maidens all in green;
> An every town that they cam thro
> Took Marie for the queen.
>
> (Child 173G)

Cf. Andersen 1985, 252. Rogers's description of Tove (DgF 121), "a combination of the wronged sweetheart who outshines the bride, and the royal favorite who, by flaunting the tangible proof of her advantage, arouses the ire of the legitimate wife" (78), seems equally apt for Mary Hamilton.

6. But see stanzas from Child 64A and E, below, in which Janet dresses much like Mary.

7. A more conventional use of the magic music motif occurs at the beginning of "Gypsy Laddie," when the gypsies sing so sweetly to the Lady of Cassilis that "they coost their glamourye owre her."

8. See, for example, Andersen's discussion of "Playin at the ba" (119 ff.); "Sat drinking at the wine" (124 ff.); "When he came to fair Ellen's gates" (221 ff.); "He hadna ridden/sailed" (259 ff.); as well as the discussion later in the present chapter, of "The first town he came to" in "Johnie Scot."

9. This formula is discussed more fully in the conclusion.

10. In "The Gay Goshawk" (Child 96) she only appears dead. Andersen discusses an alternate formula, "The first step she stepped." This formula "typically is associated with progression step by step into the water" (266) and has a fairly distinct supra-narrative function of signalling imminent danger or death, usually for the one stepping.

7. POLITICS AND PERFIDY

1. The non-tragic ballads in the repertoire include four melodramas with happy endings: "Hind Horn," "Johnie Scot," "Geordie," and "Lord William." The two fixed-text pieces, the farcical "The Baffled Knight" and the plotless "The Wee Wee Man" should probably be classed with the four comic broadside pieces: "The Broken Token," "The Basket of Eggs," "The Beggar Laddie," and "The Duke's Hunt."

2. A final example of summons by letter, that in "Bonnie Baby Livingston," uses none of the elements or associated commonplaces of the "King's Letter Theme."

3. See especially the B, D, and F texts; but cf. the Peter Buchan text (Child 17H), stanza 2:

> 'In gude greenwood, there I was born,
> And all my forebears me beforn.'

4. The ballads reflect 19th c. Scottish society, in which a maid was a servant, not 16th c. Franco-Scottish society, in which a maid-in-waiting was a gentlewoman.

CONCLUSION

1. The classic example of an analogical term is *healthy*. The ancients point out that one may say a man is healthy, and likewise say that his urine is healthy, to which the

moderns would add that his diet too is healthy. The word does not mean exactly the same thing in each case, but there is relationship between the health of the man, the health of his diet, and the health of his urine which is reflected in the use of the same word in analogous senses for all three phenomena. (Use of the word *analogical* here must not be confused with uses of the word *analogy* elsewhere in oral studies. See Foley 1986, 25, 30.)

2. The next level after phoneme would seem to be morpheme. But, formulas always involve more than one element; the level which regularly involves two or more morphemes is the level of phrase. The figure on the morphemic level which corresponds to alliteration on the phonemic level is anaphora, a very common figure in the ballad: "Rise up, rise up," "What news, what news?" etc.

3. Sometimes these may really be quarter-line formulas, as in the first line of the next example ("Licht down, licht down, Earl Richard," she says). The vocative "Earl Richard" ("Earl Marshall," etc.) and the inquit "she says" ("he says," "they said," etc.) occur independently in tradition, and must be considered, on some level, as representing separate formula families. But such quarter-line formulas are a bit like split hairs: though they exist, they merit no more than a footnote in the over-all scheme of things.

4. For a fuller discussion of this much-vexed term "theme" and the varying, often tradition-specific ways in which scholars have sought to define it, see Foley 1988, 37–38, 42, 49, 53, 68–69, 72–74, 100–102, 105.

5. In addition to the examples below, see also Anders (1974), who provides literally hundreds of examples of lines and stanzas with complex formulaic interrelationships.

6. See introduction.

7. Even in Mrs. Brown's repertoire, however, there is some difference in structural complexity between the couplet and the quatrain ballads. "Some of the couplet texts, then, have a less sophisticated integration of units in the stanzaic structure and have a weaker overall concentration on the three interacting characters, but in general the couplet ballads exhibit the same architectonic characteristics as the quatrain ballads" (Buchan, 1972, 142).

8. It is also possible that the Northeast is more exact in rhyming than the Southwest.

9. Lord 1981 provides a detailed discussion of this issue with reference to the short epic, to "themes," and to lyric.

10. Mrs. Brown's "The Lass of Roch Royal" may be an example.

References

Abrahams, Roger D. 1970a. "Creativity, Individuality, and the Traditional Singer." *Studies in the Literary Imagination* 3:5–34.
_____, ed. 1970b. *A Singer and Her Songs: Almeida Riddle's Book of Ballads.* Baton Rouge: Louisiana State University Press.
Anders, Wolfhart H. 1974. *Balladensänger und mündliche Komposition: Untersuchungen zur englishen Traditionsballade. Bochumer Arbeiten zur Sprach- und Literaturwissenschaft.* Munich: Wilhelm Fink.
Andersen, Flemming G. 1985. *Commonplace and Creativity: The Role of Formulaic Diction in Anglo-Scottish Traditional Balladry.* Odense: Odense University Press.
Andersen, Flemming G., and Thomas Pettitt. 1979. "Mrs. Brown of Falkland: A Singer of Tales?" *Journal of American Folklore* 92:1–24.
Andersen, Flemming G., Otto Holzapfel, and Thomas Pettitt, eds. 1982. *The Ballad as Narrative: Studies in the Ballad Traditions of England, Scotland, Germany, and Denmark.* Odense: Odense University Press, 1982.
Baring-Gould, Sabine, and H. Fleetwood Sheppard. 1895. *Songs and Ballads of the West.* London: Methuen.
Barry, Phillips, et al. 1929. *British Ballads from Maine.* New Haven: Yale University Press.
Brock, William R. 1982. *Scotus Americanus.* Edinburgh: Edinburgh University Press.
Bronson, Bertrand H. 1959–1972. *The Traditional Tunes of the Child Ballads.* 4 vols. Princeton: Princeton University Press.
_____. 1969. *The Ballad as Song.* Berkeley: University of California Press.
Brown, Frank C. 1952–1964. *The Frank C. Brown Collection of North Carolina Folklore.* 7 vols. Durham: Duke University Press.
Buchan, David. 1972. *The Ballad and the Folk.* London: Routledge and Kegan Paul.
_____. 1983. "Ballad Tradition and Hugh Spencer." In Porter 1983, 173–191.
_____. 1985. "The Wit-Combat Ballads." In Edwards and Manley 1985, 382–400.
Buchan, Peter. 1891. *Gleanings of Scotch, English, and Irish Scarce Old Ballads.* Aberdeen: D. Wylie and Son.
Burdine, Betty Lucille. 1985. "It's Paydirt." Paper presented as part of the Symposium "After Randolph: Current Research in Ozark Folksong," at the Annual Meeting of the American Folklore Society, Cincinnati, Ohio, October 1985.
Chappell, W., ed. See *Roxburgh Ballads.*
Child, Francis James. 1882–1898. *The English and Scottish Popular Ballads.* 5 vols. Boston: Houghton, Mifflin.
Christie, W. 1876–1881. *Traditional Ballad Airs.* 2 vol. Edinburgh: Edmonston and Douglas.
Cockburn, Henry. 1974. *Memorials of His Time.* Ed. Karl F. C. Miller. Chicago: The University of Chicago Press.
Coffin, Tristram Potter. 1961. "Mary Hamilton and the Anglo-American Ballad as an Art Form." In Leach and Coffin 1961, 245–256.
_____. 1977. *The British Traditional Ballad in North America.* Rev. ed. with special supplement by Roger deV. Renwick. American Folklore Society Bibliographical and Special Series. Austin: University of Texas Press.
_____. 1983. "Four Black Sheep Among the 305." In Porter 1983, 30–38.
Coffin, Tristram Potter, and MacEdward Leach, eds. 1961. See Leach, MacEdward, and Tristram Potter Coffin.
Conroy, Patricia, ed. 1978. *Ballads and Ballad Research: Selected Papers of the International Conference on Nordic and Anglo-American Ballad Research, University of Washington, Seattle, May 2–6, 1977.* Seattle: University of Washington.

Crawfurd, Andrew. See Lyle, 1975.

Creed, Robert P. 1981. "The Beowulf Poet: Master of Sound Patterning. In Foley 1981, 194–216.

Davis, Arthur Kyle, Jr. 1929. *Traditional Ballads of Virginia*. Cambridge: Harvard University Press.

———. 1960. *More Traditional Ballads of Virginia*. Chapel Hill: University of North Carolina Press.

Edwards, Carol L. 1983. "The Parry-Lord Theory Meets Operational Structuralism." *The Journal of American Folklore* 96: 151–169.

Edwards, Carol L., and Kathleen E. B. Manley. 1985. *Narrative Folksong: New Directions; Essays in Appreciation of W. Edson Richmond*. Boulder, Colorado: Privately Printed.

Ellis, Peter Berresford, and Seumas Mac a' Ghobhainn. 1970. *The Scottish Insurrection of 1820*. London: Victor Gollancz.

Euing Collection of English Broadside Ballads, The. 1971. Ed. John Holloway. Glasgow: University of Glasgow Publications.

Flanders, Helen Hartness. 1960–1965. *Ancient Ballads Traditionally Sung in New England*, 4 vols. Philadelphia: University of Pennsylvania Press.

Foley, John Miles. 1983. "Literary Art and Oral Tradition in Old English and Serbian Poetry." *Anglo-Saxon England* 12:183–214.

———. 1985. *Oral-Formulaic Theory and Research: An Introduction and Annotated Bibliography*. Garland Folklore Bibliographies. New York: Garland Publishing, Inc.

———. 1988. *The Theory of Oral Composition: History and Methodology*. Bloomington: Indiana University Press.

———, ed. 1981. *Oral Traditional Literature: A Festschrift for Albert Bates Lord*. Columbus, Ohio: Slaviaca.

———, ed. 1986. *Oral Tradition in Literature: Interpretation in Context*. Columbia: University of Missouri Press.

Fraser, Antonia. 1970. *Mary Queen of Scots*. New York: Delacorte Press.

Friedman, Albert B. 1961. "The Formulaic Improvisation Theory of Ballad Tradition—A Counterstatement." *Journal of American Folklore* 74:113–115.

———. 1983. "The Oral-Formulaic Theory of Balladry—A Re-Rebuttal." In Porter 1983, 215–240.

Gardner, Emelyn Elizabeth, and Geraldine Jencks Chickering. 1939. *Ballads and Songs of Southern Michigan*. Ann Arbor: University of Michigan Press.

Gaskin, Brenda A. 1955. *The Decline of the Hand-Loom Weaving Industry in Scotland During the Years 1815–1845*. Ph. D. diss., University of Edinburgh.

Gerould, Gordon Hall. 1932. *The Ballad of Tradition*. Oxford: Clarendon Press.

Gilmour, David. 1879. *Reminiscences of the Pen' Folk, Paisley Weavers of Other Days, etc*. 2d ed. Paisley: Alexander Gardner.

Goldstein, Kenneth. 1971. "On the Application of the Concepts of Active and Inactive Traditions to the Study of Repertory." *Journal of American Folklore* 84:62–67.

Greig, Gavin. 1963. "Folk-Song in Buchan." *Transactions of the Buchan Field Club* 9 (1906–1907): 2–76. *Folk-Song of the North-East* (1909, 1914). Reprinted together as *Folk-Song in Buchan and the North-East by Gavin Greig*. Foreword by Kenneth S. Goldstein and Arthur Argo. Hatboro: Folklore Associates.

Greig, Gavin, and Alexander Keith. 1925. *Last Leaves of Traditional Ballads and Ballad Airs*. University of Aberdeen University Studies No. 100. Aberdeen: University of Aberdeen.

Harker, Dave. 1985. *Fakesong*. Milton Keynes: Open University Press.

Henderson, Hamish, and Francis Collinson. 1965. "New Child Ballad Variants from Oral Tradition." *Scottish Studies* 9:1–33.

Henry, Mellinger. 1938. *Folk-Songs from the Southern Highlands*. New York: J. J. Augustin.

Holloway, John, ed. See *Euing Ballads*.

Hustvedt, Sigurd Bernhard. 1930. *Ballad Books and Ballad Men*. Cambridge: Harvard University Press.

James, Thelma G. 1933. "The English and Scottish Popular Ballads of Francis J. Child." *Journal of American Folklore* 46:51–68. Condensed in Leach and Coffin 1961, 12–19.

Jones, James H. 1961. "Commonplace and Memorization in the Oral Tradition of the English and Scottish Popular Ballads." *Journal of American Folklore*, 74:97–112.

Karpeles, Maud. 1970. *Folk Songs from Newfoundland*. Hamden, Connecticut: Archon Books.

————, ed. See Sharp, Cecil, 1974.

Kennedy, Peter, ed. 1975. *Folksongs of Britain and Ireland*. New York: Schirmer.

Laws, G. Malcolm, 1957. *American Balladry from British Broadsides*. American Folklore Society Bibliographical and Special Series, No. 8. Philadelphia: American Folklore Society.

————. 1964. *Native American Balladry*. Rev. ed. American Folklore Society Bibliographical and Special Series, No. 1. Philadelphia: American Folklore Society.

Leach, MacEdward, and Tristram P. Coffin, eds. 1961. *The Critics and the Ballad*. Carbondale: Southern Illinois University Press.

Lindsay, Maurice. 1977. *History of Scottish Literature*. London: Hale.

Long, Eleanor. 1971. *"The Maid" and "The Hangman": Myth and Tradition in a Popular Ballad*. Folklore Studies, No. 21. Berkeley: University of California Press.

————. 1973. "Ballad Singers, Ballad Makers and Ballad Etiology." *Western Folklore* 32:225–236.

————. 1986. "Ballad Classification and the 'Narrative Theme' Concept Together with A Thematic Index to Anglo-Irish-American Balladry." In Shields 1986, 197–213.

Long, Eleanor, and D. K. Wilgus. See Wilgus, D. K., and Eleanor R. Long.

Lord, Albert B. 1960. *The Singer of Tales*. Cambridge: Harvard University Press.

————. 1974. "Perspectives on Recent Work in Oral Literature." In *Oral Literature: Seven Essays*, ed. Joseph J. Duggan. New York: Barnes and Noble, 1–24.

————. 1981. "Memory, Fixity, and Genre in Oral Traditional Poetries." In Foley 1981, 451–461.

————. 1985. "Bela Bartok and Text Stanzas in Yugoslav Folk Music." In *Music and Context: Essays for John M. Ward*. Ed. Anne D. Shapiro. Cambridge: Harvard University Department of Music, 385–403.

————. 1986a. "The Merging of Two Worlds: Oral and Written Poetry as Carriers of Ancient Values." In Foley 1986, 19–64.

————. 1986b. "Perspectives on Recent Work on the Oral Traditional Formula." *Oral Tradition* 1:467–503.

Lyle, Emily B. 1972. "The Matching of Andrew Blaikie's Ballad Tunes with Their Texts." *Scottish Studies* 16:175–180.

————, ed. 1975. *Andrew Crawfurd's Collection of Ballads and Songs*. Vol. 1. Publications of the Scottish Text Society, Fourth Series, No. 9. Edinburgh: The Scottish Text Society.

M'Alpie, James. See Motherwell, William, ed. 1828.

M'Conechy, James. 1865. See Motherwell, William. 1865.

MacColl, Ewan. 1965. *Folk Songs and Ballads of Scotland*. New York: Oak Publications.

MacColl, Ewan, and Peggy Seeger, eds. 1977. *Travellers' Songs from England and Scotland*. Knoxville: University of Tennessee Press.

MacKenzie, W. Roy. 1928. *Ballads and Sea Songs from Nova Scotia*. Cambridge: Harvard University Press.

McCarthy, William B. 1987. "William Motherwell as Field Collector." *Folk Music Journal* 5:295–316.

Montgomerie, William. 1958. "William Motherwell and Robert Smith." *Review of English Studies* 9:152–159.

———. 1966. "A Bibliography of the Scottish Ballad Manuscripts 1730–1825." Part 1. *Studies in Scottish Literature* 4:3–28.

Morris, Alton C. 1950. *Folksongs of Florida*. Gainesville: University of Florida Press.

Motherwell, William. [1824–1827]. *A Ballad Notebook*. Library, Pollock House, Glasgow (?). Child Copy: Harvard University Library Manuscript 25242.16, Houghton Library, Harvard University.

———. 1825. Letter from William Motherwell to Charles Kirkpatrick Sharpe, 8 October 1825. Harvard University Library, Manuscript 25241.56F, Houghton Library, Harvard University.

———. [1825–1826]. *The Motherwell Manuscript*. Manuscript Murray 501, Glasgow University Library. Child Copy: Harvard University Library Manuscript 25241.20, Houghton Library, Harvard University.

———. 1827. *Minstrelsy: Ancient and Modern*. Glasgow: John Wylie.

———. 1865. *The Poetical Works of William Motherwell*. With a Memoir. Ed. 3. Glasgow: Forrester.

———, ed. 1828. *Certain Curious Poems Written at the Close of the XVIIth and Beginning of the XVIIIth Century . . . Principally from the Pen of Mr. James M'Alpie*. Paisley: J. Neilson.

New Statistical Account, The. 1845. Vol. 7. Edinburgh: Wm. Blackwood and Sons.

Niles, John D. 1973. "Ring Composition in *La Chanson de Roland* and *La Chançun de Willame*." *Olifant* 1, ii:4–12.

Nygard, Holger Olof. 1978. "Mrs. Brown's Recollected Ballads." In Conroy 1978, 66–87.

Ord, John. 1930. *The Bothy Songs and Ballads*. Paisley: Alexander Gardner.

Paredes, Amerigo. 1958. *With His Pistol in His Hand: A Border Ballad and Its Hero*. Austin: University of Texas Press.

Parry, Milman. 1971. *The Making of Homeric Verse: The Collected Papers of Milman Parry*. Ed. Adam Parry. Oxford: Clarendon Press.

Peabody, Berkeley. 1975. *The Winged World: A Study in the Technique of Ancient Greek Oral Composition as seen Principally through Hesiod's* Works and Days. Albany: State University of New York Press.

Peacock, Kenneth. 1965. *Songs of the Newfoundland Outposts*. National Museum of Canada Anthropological Series, No. 65. Ottawa: National Museum of Canada.

Pepys Ballads, The. 1929–1932. Hyder Edward Rollins, ed. 8 vols. Cambridge, Mass.: Harvard University Press.

Percy, Thomas. 1775. *Reliques of Ancient English Poetry*. Ed. 3. London: J. Dodsley.

Porter, James. 1976. "Jeannie Robertson's 'My Son David': A Conceptual Performance Model." *Journal of American Folklore* 89:7–26.

———, ed. 1983. *The Ballad Image: Essays Presented to Bertrand Harris Bronson*. Los Angeles: Center for the Study of Comparative Folklore and Mythology, University of California, Los Angeles.

Propp, Vladimir. 1968. *Morphology of the Folktale* (1928). Ed. 2, rev. Austin: University of Texas Press.

Randolph, Vance. 1946–1950. *Ozark Folk Songs*. 4 vols. Columbia: The State Historical Society of Missouri.

Renwick, Roger deVan. 1980. *English Folk Poetry: Structure and Meaning*. Philadelphia: University of Pennsylvania Press.

Richmond, W. Edson. 1963. " 'Den utrue egtemann': A Norwegian Ballad and Formulaic Composition." *Norveg* 10:59–88.

Riddle, Almeida. See Abrahams 1970b.

Roberts, Leonard. 1974. *Sang Branch Settlers: Folksongs and Tales of a Kentucky*

Mountain Family. Publications of the American Folklore Society, Memoir Series, vol. 61. Austin: University of Texas Press, 1974.

Roberts, Warren. 1951. "Comic Elements in the English Traditional Ballad." *Journal of the International Folk Music Council* 3:76–81.

Rogers, Edith Randam. 1980. *The Perilous Hunt: Symbols in Hispanic and European Balladry*. Lexington: University Press of Kentucky.

Rollins, Hyder Edward, ed. See *Pepys Ballads*.

Roxburgh Ballads. 1966. Ed. W. Chappell (vol. 1–3) and J. Woodfall Ebsworth (vol. 4–8). London: Ballad Society, 1871–1899; reprint, New York: AMS Press.

Sharp, Cecil. 1974. *Cecil Sharp's Collection of English Folk Songs*. 2 vols. Ed. Maud Karpeles. London: Oxford University Press.

———, with Olive Dame Campbell. *English Folksongs from the Southern Appalachians*. Ed. Maud Karpeles. 2 vol. London: Oxford University Press, 1932.

Sharpe, Charles Kirkpatrick. 1823, 1976. *A Ballad Book* (privately printed). In *Four Books of Choice Old Scottish Ballads*. Ed. Thomas George Stevenson. Edinburgh: Privately printed, 1868. Reprinted as *Choice Old Scottish Ballads*, Wakefield: E. P. Publishing.

Shaw, John P. 1980. "The New Rural Industries." Chapter 13 of *The Making of the Scottish Countryside*, ed. Martin L. Parry and Terence R. Slater. London: Croom Helm.

Shields, Hugh. [1986]. *Ballad Research: The Stranger in Ballad Narrataive and Other Topics*. Dublin: Folk Music Society of Ireland/Cumann Cheol Tire Eireann.

Simpson, Claude M. 1966. *The British Broadside and Its Music*. New Brunswick: Rutgers University Press.

Sinclair, Sir John. See *Statistical Account*.

Statistical Account, The New. See *New Statistical Account, The*.

Statistical Account of Scotland, The. 1791–1799. Sir John Sinclair, ed. 21 vol. Edinburgh: W. Creech, etc.

Taylor, Archer. 1931. *"Edward" and "Sven I Rosengård": A Study in the Dissemination of a Ballad*. Chicago: The University of Chicago Press.

Thigpen, Kenneth A., Jr. 1972. "An Index to the Known Oral Sources of the Child Collection." *Folklore Forum* 5:55–69.

———. 1973. "A Reconsideration of the Commonplace Phrase and Commonplace Theme in the Child Ballads. *Southern Folklore Quarterly* 37:385–408.

Thom, William. 1844. *Rhymes and Recollections of a Handloom Weaver*. London: Smith, Elder, etc.

Toelken, J. Barre. 1986. "Riddles Wisely Expounded." Western Folklore 45:1–16.

Whitman, Cedric H. 1958. *Homer and the Heroic Tradition*. Cambridge: Harvard University Press.

Wilgus, D. K. 1959. *Anglo-American Folksong Scholarship Since 1898*. New Brunswick: Rutgers University Press.

———. 1986. "The Catalog of Irish Traditional Ballads in English." In Shields 1986, 215–227.

Wilgus, D. K., and Eleanor R. Long. 1985. "The *Blues Ballad* and the Genesis of Style in Traditional Narrative Song." In Edwards and Manley, 435–482.

Wimberly, Lowry C. 1928. *Folklore in the English and Scottish Ballads*. Chicago: University of Chicago Press.

Wordsworth, Dorothy. 1874. *Recollections of a Tour Made in Scotland, A.D. 1803*. Ed. J. C. Shairp. New York: G. P. Putnam's Sons.

Index

B. PEOPLE, PLACES, MOVEMENTS AND EVENTS

C. TOPICS

WILLIAM BERNARD McCARTHY is an associate professor of English at the Pennsylvania State University.